MATCH FIT

MATCH FIT

An Exploration of Mental Health in Football

Johnnie Lowery

pitch

First published by Pitch Publishing, 2023

Pitch Publishing
9 Donnington Park,
85 Birdham Road,
Chichester,
West Sussex,
PO20 7AJ
www.pitchpublishing.co.uk
info@pitchpublishing.co.uk

A CIP catalogue record is available for this book from the British Library.

ISBN 978 1 80150 468 3

Typesetting and origination by Pitch Publishing

Printed and bound in India by Thomson Press

Contents

Acknowledgements

MATCH FIT would not have been possible if it were not for the 60 – plus people who have given up their time to speak candidly to me about their own personal mental health stories. Such generosity allows others to learn from their experiences, thus improving mental health awareness in society, as this book sets out to do. I won't list them all here, as you will come across them in due course, but I am incredibly grateful to each and every one of them.

I must thank my parents for supporting me on this writing journey since I first decided to put pen to paper and start on *Six Added Minutes* whilst still a teenager. They have kept me grounded whilst never trimming my ambition. Mum in particular has supported me the whole way through this writing process, using her expertise and background in proofreading to painstakingly go through my first drafts, giving me helpful feedback along the way. I wouldn't have been able to complete this project without them.

I should also thank my mates, who haven't seen much of me over the last couple of years as I've worked on researching and writing the book. Perhaps they've been secretly delighted at that!

Thanks also to Jane at Pitch Publishing, who has helped turn my dream of getting this book published into reality. Jane has been a joy to work with and has made everything very easy for me.

Introduction

I WAS depressed in my school years, but I didn't know it. The jump from primary school to secondary school is tough for everyone, I told myself, and I was sure that there were other people in my class who would cry themselves to sleep on a Sunday and take an age to get out of bed on a Monday morning, as they just couldn't find the energy to drag themselves up. It was natural, I felt, that having got through such a long week I was happy to stay in the house and keep myself to myself on a Friday evening, even if my mates were out together having fun. My refuge was football every Saturday afternoon – a trip to Gander Green Lane, home of Sutton United, or an exciting away trip to a town I'd probably never been to before. There, I could feel part of something separate to my everyday life. It was an escape, for sure, something that kept me going through the next week, and then the next week after that. It allowed me to survive. No more, no less.

It wasn't until I went to university in 2017 that I began to understand what mental health was. I don't think I'd ever even heard the term until then, and if I had then it hadn't registered with me. There was nothing wrong with my mental health, I thought. I could survive, I was fine.

But as time went on with me living away from home for the first time, things began to make sense. It wasn't normal to cry yourself to sleep. It wasn't normal to not want to wake up in the morning. Eventually, I sought counselling and took my first steps towards managing my mental health. My life isn't perfect, I still have bad days, but I can cope now. I know all the tricks in the book to stop my mind before it spirals further down towards the ground. I live a fulfilling, enjoyable life in which I can flourish, which certainly isn't something I would have said about my school years. It's all come through simply understanding what mental health is.

Certainly, I wasn't alone in my experience. In 2017, the year I went to university, one in nine children aged five to 16 were identified as having a probable mental health problem. This shot up to one in six by July 2021. I wonder if more children are suffering with their mental health, or if we're just getting better at spotting it. After all, conversation around mental health is becoming more common. You regularly see documentaries, often featuring celebrities, explicitly talking about mental health. Mental health podcasts have sprung up like dandelions since the pandemic, helping to normalise any challenges someone might be facing, taking away the element of shame that can pervade if you don't understand what it is you're going through. The football world has its part to play in this great push to improve the world's knowledge on mental health.

In all honesty, football was hardly a source of mental health enlightenment for me whilst I was at my lowest ebb. If anything, the sport has probably been guilty of being even less accepting of mental health struggles than society as a whole, until recently. With the game promoting extreme masculinity as the only way, not only would players be expected to put their emotions to one side but this attitude spread to the terraces as well. I met many of my best mates through watching Sutton United, but before 2017 I never spoke to any of them about my mental health. I simply didn't think that it was the environment for that conversation and I was worried about how they might react. Things have changed now, and Danny Rose speaking about his struggles with depression, for example, will no doubt have been a massive help to thousands of young boys and girls with mental health challenges. It's this positive effect that I'm trying to capture with *Match Fit*.

I wouldn't have bought a book about mental health when I was struggling. When you don't understand a problem, you don't really want to acknowledge it – it's an alien concept and you don't have the time or inclination to change that. However, I did buy plenty of books about football. Football is a great conversation starter. How many times have you been down the pub with your mates, started off by chatting about last night's game and ended up talking about whether crabs think humans walk sideways six hours later? Perhaps, just maybe, you might even talk about your feelings at some point.

For *Match Fit*, I've spoken to around 60 wonderful people from the football world – players, managers, referees, supporters, academics … the list goes on. All of them have been incredibly generous with their time and opened up bravely and honestly about their own experiences with mental health. I am so very grateful to them all. The result, I hope, is that somebody picks up this book and learns something about mental health which can help them down the line

Essentially, this book is for the teenage me, for those struggling with their mental health who perhaps might not even know it. If it helps just one person then the hundreds of hours I've put into the project over the last three years will all have been worth it.

Chapter 1

The Player

IN MANY ways, Gary Speed appeared to have the world at his feet. Having won the final edition of the old First Division in 1992, the Welshman went on to play 535 games in the Premier League for Leeds United, Everton, Newcastle United and Bolton Wanderers. Always viewed as the model professional, Speed was a likely candidate to go into management once he eventually retired and so it proved. After a brief spell in charge of Sheffield United, he was appointed manager of his country in December 2010. Such was Speed's initial success, it surprised nobody when Wales were awarded FIFA's Best Movers title the following year, having gained more ranking points than any other nation. Away from football, Speed was married to his childhood sweetheart Louise and had two loving children. His own parents later reflected that to someone looking in, it appeared that Speed had everything going for him.

When Gary Speed took his own life in November 2011, the football world was shocked and saddened. Nobody saw it coming. A terrible tragedy, Speed's untimely passing forced football in the UK to open up to its relationship with mental health. The default position was one of ignorance – footballers can't suffer with their mental health; their lives are perfect. Who wouldn't give their right arm to get paid hundreds of thousands of pounds a week to live their dream?

The reality isn't always so straightforward. In John Richardson's book, *Unspoken: Gary Speed: The Family's Untold Story*, former Wales team-mate Neville Southall describes Speed as a 'perfectionist' who would always be frustrated after defeats and perhaps may have found it mentally tough to uphold the incredibly high standards he set himself throughout his career. Matt Hockin, Speed's good friend at Bolton, mentions that he felt as though Speed used his football career to define his whole life and was particularly worried as he looked ahead to the end of his playing days. Tellingly, Louise Speed explains that her husband himself couldn't understand that people who seemed to have everything could experience depression, and so never associated himself with it. The recent rise of mental health awareness in football sadly came too late to save him.

Though mental health was effectively an afterthought within football ten years ago, Speed's death wasn't an isolated case. German football had its own tragic awakening in 2009 when one of the leading contenders for the number one jersey at the 2010 World Cup, Robert Enke, died by suicide. Throughout his career, Enke had struggled with the pressure of the spotlight, with a diary entry published in Ronald Reng's biography, *A Life too Short: The Tragedy of Robert Enke,* showing how the goalkeeper was 'paralysed by fear' during his time at Barcelona. The death of Enke's young daughter added further pressures to his mental state, but Enke felt unable to open up to anyone within the football world about his depression, feeling it was incompatible with playing at the top level. As things spiralled, the Hannover 96 captain felt ashamed of taking time out and missing games, thinking of himself as a failure. Seeing no way out, he stepped in front of a train. Prior to Enke's death, the only notable player in Germany to have spoken about their mental health was former prodigy Sebastian Deisler, tipped as the saviour of German football as a teenager in the late 1990s. However, Deisler had retired from the game by 2007, perhaps amplifying Enke's fears that his depression would not be compatible with playing top-level professional football.

How many more people will have suffered in silence, feeling they couldn't open up and seek help within football's ultra-competitive and hyper-masculine environment? In February 2012, only a few months after Gary Speed's untimely passing, the career of a footballer once the subject of a documentary entitled *The Man Who Will Be Worth Billions* was coming to an end. Rather than wrapping up with Champions Leagues and World Cups under his belt, though, Vincent Pericard played the last of his club football at Havant & Waterlooville in the Conference South. Having made his Juventus debut in the Champions League ten years earlier, aged 19, against an Arsenal side containing the likes of Patrick Vieira and Thierry Henry, Pericard was unable to progress into the elite of the game and spent the majority of his career in the second and third tiers of English football. Reflecting on what might have been, Pericard's lightbulb moment came when he realised it was his mental health, rather than the injuries that had plagued him throughout his playing days, that had caused the greatest damage to his career. But it wasn't until after his retirement that he realised he was struggling with depression.

'I think for me it all really started when I had a series of repeated injuries at Portsmouth. I didn't realise that it was taking a toll on my mental health because I wasn't aware of that or educated around it. I didn't really pay attention to it. I put it into the back of my head in an unconscious state and just pushed forwards. But unfortunately, what I was doing was just accumulating that feeling of frustration, feelings of "why me", and that feeling of "there's nothing I can do about it". It was dragging me into that dark space. That's what I remember now – going home and feeling the frustration, feeling like I had low value, having low energy, not having any motivation. Those were the early symptoms. If I knew that at the time, I could have started taking mitigating measures for it not to escalate.

'It was quite scary, because I woke up in the morning and I would put on a mask. I would put on a brave face, saying, "you know what, I'm going to training" and I only needed to wear this mask for two to three hours, then go home and remove it. It was really about psyching myself up, driving to the training ground and putting on a smile in order to hide my inner suffering, my pain, my frustrations, so that people didn't realise it, especially my manager. That's not a way of living. It created frustrations between what you feel and how you portray yourself to others. When you're in that state, this is when a desperate area of mental health and depression arises.'

By no means was Vincent Pericard the only footballer at the time suffering in silence without necessarily even understanding what they were going through. In the 2019 *A Royal Team Talk* documentary on mental health, Thierry Henry is asked if he ever struggled with depression in his career. His answer was that he simply didn't know. He was never educated on it, never allowed to even contemplate it, the football world almost instinctively blocking any route into what might have been seen as a weakness. Craig Bellamy was one of many players shocked into introspection by the death of Gary Speed, seeing similarities between his former Wales and Newcastle team-mate and himself. Bellamy had previously refused to see a mental health professional, admitting he saw it as a sign of weakness, but was forced to recognise his obsession with football was a significant risk factor for him when things weren't going well on the pitch. During a loan spell at Cardiff, for example, big things were expected of the former Liverpool and Manchester City man dropping down a league to his hometown club, but injuries took their toll and Cardiff were ultimately defeated in the play-offs. During this time, Bellamy was so down he rarely left the house other than for training, and his marriage broke up as a result, even though it was the first time in years he had been living with his wife and children, who had settled in Cardiff whilst he travelled the country to optimise his football career.

When Speed passed away, Bellamy saw some of the traits he thought might have been contributory factors in himself. Described as a glass-half-empty man by his wife, Gary Speed would have spells where he would effectively shut himself off from conversation at the training ground if he was feeling down, according to Bellamy. Throughout his own career, Bellamy concedes his team-mates would know to avoid him on days he was feeling down – days which would almost always be brought about by injury troubles or even just a spell out of the side. It's clear that the pacy frontman saw football as his life and identity. This single-mindedness may have brought Bellamy a degree of success on the pitch but clearly ravaged his mental state, and it took the death of a close friend in Gary Speed for him to even realise the scale of the damage.

The consequences of Vincent Pericard's struggles were almost disastrous too. The Cameroonian-born striker reached his low point during a spell at Stoke City. Stuck in a vicious cycle of needing to prove himself and trying to come back too soon from injury only to make things worse again, Pericard started to feel worthless. On a night in which Pericard knew he wouldn't sleep due to the anxieties building up inside him, he took a sleeping pill. Something in his head snapped, however, and rather than stopping at one pill he took the rest of the packet, feeling that nobody would miss him if he didn't wake up. Thankfully, Pericard survived and finally understood he needed to seek help. He credits being referred to a performance coach, to work on the mental side of his game whilst at Stoke City, as the first step on a journey that ultimately saved his life, as it opened up his mind to counselling further down the line. As crucial as this was for Pericard, he looked to keep it a secret, with the dressing room at any of his clubs not the sort of place to disclose anything about mental health or even the general field of psychology at the time.

'Football is meant to be a team sport but really it is very individualistic. When you've got a squad of 21 players, every player is looking after themselves because they are working within a limited contract which basically depends on their performance on the pitch. My team-mates had their own challenges to go through. They didn't have the space, the capacity, the skill or knowledge to sympathise and have compassion for what I was going through and to help.

'It's very easy to feel isolated, because it's you in the centre of it with your team-mates with their own problems. You might have your family, but they don't really see behind the scenes, they see you as a star celebrity and that's it. They wouldn't understand why you would suffer from your mental health. So for me, after going home, this is when you feel very lonely. I'm sure you've heard the example of singers, who've been on stage being applauded by 60,000 people – as soon as the show is finished, they go back to their hotel room and feel very, very lonely, because there's no intimate relationship with anyone. Football is exactly the same.'

* * *

Until perhaps the last five to ten years, a dressing room of acquaintances rather than friends has been the accepted norm in football. I spoke to John Salako, most notably of Crystal Palace and England, to understand what the footballing environment was like in the 1980s and 1990s. Sitting in an office in south London in his new life in business, Salako admits the culture was 'cut-throat' right from the early days as an apprentice, when the senior pros would see you as a threat to their livelihoods. Fights in training would be commonplace, and Salako recalls that Mark Dennis in particular would threaten to break his legs if he went past him. He might laugh about it now, but it didn't take much for a sense of bitterness to pervade and make the dressing room a very unpleasant place. The first time Salako was relegated, for example, in the 1992/93 season, he suffered a serious knee injury early on in the campaign and spent several weekends working for Sky. When it came to the end-of-season gathering, one of the senior players launched into a rant at Salako, seemingly furious at the fact he had appeared on TV whilst injured, thereby supposedly contributing to the club's fate. Salako was only trying to look after himself, worried he might need a financial backup if he couldn't get back to the level he had been at before. Yet the buck had been passed on to him for a relegation in which he played a minimal part. Though furious, he had to grit his teeth and get on with it.

Stories of what is now seen as a toxic dressing-room atmosphere were commonplace in the 1980s and 1990s, but it's clear football's bullying culture has never truly gone away. Luke Chadwick made his senior debut for Manchester United at the age of 18 in 1999, but this exposure brought him an unwanted form of attention aside from any on-pitch fame. He was relentlessly mocked on the TV show *They Think It's All Over* for his appearance, to the point where it became what he was best known for. Chadwick has recently spoken about the impact this had on his anxiety, with the embarrassment it caused him meaning he felt unable to open up about it at the time. More recently, the story of the academically keen Nedum Onuoha having his A-Level schoolbooks burnt whilst coming through at Manchester City came to light, told by Stephen Ireland as just one anecdote of what he described as a 'really mentally challenging' environment where the only advice he received was 'just toughen up and get on with it, stop being a baby'. As recently as 2022, Crawley Town manager John Yems was suspended and later left his role, due to bullying behaviour, including racial discrimination against his players.

Salako highlights a young Stan Collymore in particular as someone who was 'eaten up and spat out' of the dressing room at Crystal Palace, the striker having to leave the club for Southend in 1992/93 as he found it so tough. As Collymore notes himself in his autobiography, he flourished at clubs where he was cared for but often struggled at places where his wellbeing was further down the agenda. Take Aston Villa, for example, where Collymore's manager, John Gregory, publicly derided him for taking time away from football due to his depression. Perhaps unsurprisingly then, having been prolific at Nottingham Forest and Liverpool, Collymore struggled at Aston Villa and was allowed to leave just a few years after signing for his boyhood club. The sport's reluctance to acknowledge the significance of the mental side of the game for so long was not only damaging to individuals but also to clubs themselves, with Villa having paid at the time a club record £7 million for Collymore's services in 1997.

Conceding that he comes very much from football's old school, Salako admits he would have scoffed at the concept of mental health during his playing days, seeing any admission that you were struggling as a sign of weakness in an environment where strength was paramount. He wouldn't have been the only one. It was expected that players would leave any problems they had at the door, be it bereavement, divorce, or even just mental struggles with no obvious cause. The sport was, and to an extent still is, a results business, and anyone not performing would be unceremoniously cut and cast onto the scrapheap. Counselling is part of the game now, which is undoubtedly a positive thing. However, it was life after professional football rather than the macho culture of the sport itself that eventually opened up Salako's eyes to the realities of mental health.

'Certainly for me, it's only been later on in life that I've discovered what it feels like to have depression and anxiety. That's been hard for me to comprehend because I've spent so long going "no, no, no, this doesn't happen, I've got to just deal with this". I'm a classic throwback and I still struggle to go and speak to someone and say, "I need help". I don't think we thought like that back then. I wouldn't think players would admit to it. We were a lot more insular. But there must have been a lot of people who felt like that and that's when you realise – there must have been people at some stage that were dealing with stuff and just couldn't talk about it. You couldn't bring that into that environment.

'Life can become depressing really quickly after you stop playing. You miss the lads, you miss the games, you miss that buzz. You had somewhere to go and someone to be with, something to look forward to. When that stops, I think that's quite hard to deal with. Often, lads have to deal with divorce, alcohol, substance abuse, bankruptcy, financial hardship. It can just become chaotic. You were always aware that you were one bad tackle away from ending your career. Your career is short-lived as a footballer. I always hate actors and musicians and other sportsmen and sportswomen like golfers. They can play until they're about 60 and keel over, so it's always a shame with footballers that you have a shelf life.'

The fear of what life after football might look like can be a significant issue for players. This was brought home in devastating fashion in March 2021 when Yeovil Town captain Lee Collins took his own life. Collins's widow, Rachel Gibbon, explained at the inquest that her husband, aged 32 at the time of his death, had been struggling with the thought of what to do next when he had to retire from playing. Coaching and management didn't seem like a good fit with all the pressures involved, but the man who had been a professional footballer since February 2007 couldn't see himself transitioning into an office job. Feeling that as captain he couldn't show any signs of weakness, Collins instead turned to alcohol and recreational drugs to self-medicate, causing his mental state to further spiral until his death. Gibbon has called for more proactive mental health support for lower-league footballers in particular, and Salako agrees that more support to help footballers transition out of the game is essential. There was little in the way of transition advice and support in the early 2000s when Salako retired, and even after finding his new career in business, he admits a lot of clients will want to talk more about football than how he can help them financially. It has been hard to shake off that footballing identity.

It was this identity conundrum that played a large part in Marvin Sordell choosing to get out of professional football early and on his own terms. Sordell is a former professional footballer but would be more likely to introduce himself to you as a businessman, a producer, or even a poet. These certainly aren't pursuits that were encouraged during Sordell's time in professional football – in fact, quite the opposite. During his time at Bolton, the striker's mother received a phone call from the club chairman, declaring in no uncertain terms that Sordell needed to concentrate more on his football and less on other hobbies, including cooking and playing the piano as well as the regular therapy sessions he was having at the Priory site in Altrincham. With this resistance to developing any other side of his personality, football became all-encompassing for Sordell, who struggled as the game established a stranglehold on him, suffocating him into submission, particularly during spells out of the first team.

'My whole identity was wrapped up in a game and performance which at times you don't even get the opportunity to participate in. Being a footballer and not being able to play football is one of the hardest things. Every single moment I did have on a football pitch was a reflection of what my mood was going to be.' He likens it to an office worker's emotions plummeting every time they made a typo or sent a bad email. 'It's very unhealthy for your emotions to go from high to low a lot in such a small space of time. And for me, it got to a point where I began to stop feeling the highs and started to only feel the lows, and as they became lower and lower, the highs became lower too, so as opposed to living in this whole spectrum I was only living in the lower parts of it.

'I think it's difficult really to describe because there are so many things … that come across your mind around that period of time if you're feeling low. Anyone who suffers from depression will say the same thing: they can't necessarily point to a single thing or a single moment and describe it in great detail. It's just they understand that they don't feel good at all and that's the best way I can describe it. That led to me attempting to take my own life because I was at a point where I didn't see a future, I didn't see how life could go on beyond where I was at the time. I felt like I was in such a dark place that the respite and the light and the freedom and the release would come from just not being here and not existing anymore.'

Sordell's suicide attempt came just seven months after he had been told to concentrate on his football by Bolton Wanderers. By this point, he had been moved out on loan against his wishes to Charlton Athletic, struggling to cope with the pressure his £3 million price tag brought. Sordell admits he struggled to cope with these external pressures, with nobody to support him at the club and his family living away from him. I ask Sordell if he ever received any support for his mental health in his football career. He thinks about it for a while and comes back with a bleak answer. All the way from his time at Fulham's academy to an injury-fraught spell at Northampton immediately before he retired, nothing was ever provided.

The honesty with which Sordell speaks about the depths of his depression is crucial in opening up the conversation for those currently still playing professional football. In something of a vicious circle, Sordell struggled to rationalise his mental health issues, feeling guilt at the fact he knew he was in a privileged position, not understanding why he could feel down when there were so many people in the world in far worse positions but seemingly happy. This in turn made him feel lower still, until he eventually came to understand that mental health can negatively affect anyone, regardless of who they are and what they do. Sordell's openness means this learning process will hopefully be swifter for anyone suffering with those feelings now. It is an openness that is still rare in football. Tellingly, one of the most honest accounts of a mental health battle in football comes from 'The Secret Footballer'.

The Secret Footballer is a now retired former Premier League player who has anonymously written a series of books and newspaper columns about his life in the game. It's the threat of being sued that prevents him from revealing his identity, but there's no doubt anonymity would have made opening up on severe depression and suicidal thoughts easier whilst he was still playing at the top level. Amongst other things, the Secret Footballer talks of automatically defaulting to measuring his life based on his on-pitch performances as opposed to 'real terms'. He feels that any enjoyment gleaned from playing football is negated by the pressure and expectation of the game at the top level, with this pressure acting as a 'poisoned chalice' and a major factor in his depression. His work-life balance was so skewed that the Secret Footballer missed important weddings and funerals throughout his career, probably losing friends as a result. Some of the most powerful comments come from his wife, who says there were days where she went to bed not expecting to see her husband again, such were the depths of his low points. She reflects, 'The most impressive thing is that he got out alive.' Her husband feels he wasted his life as a footballer, she muses, and feels he should have quit after reaching the Premier League, as he couldn't top that achievement. The general experiences talked about are so similar to Sordell's that you might think my interviewee was the Secret Footballer, had the dates of their careers aligned. The reality is that many footballers will surely have felt the same way, but very few feel able to admit it.

Despite his dislike of large parts of the game, the Secret Footballer has admitted more than once to returning to play after having previously decided to retire, being drawn back in by a simple love of the sport that stems from childhood. Marvin Sordell too has always loved football itself, but even this was not enough to keep him playing professionally beyond the age of 28. Lessons in the cut-throat nature of the sport were delivered to Sordell from as early as seven years of age, when his mother was told he would not be signed for a Sunday League team he trialled for, as he was 'shit'. Though dedicated to making it professionally in his teenage years and training hard accordingly, Sordell admits he questioned this desire when playing at under-16 level for Fulham, as he found the culture whereby authority was never to be questioned restrictive. This feeling only ballooned further as Sordell progressed to the top of the professional game until it became overbearing. Football stopped being enjoyable for the kid who had spent his entire childhood with a ball at his feet.

'It's just part of being a football player now, unfortunately, that because you're paid a decent wage people just assume that's licence to do and say anything they want to you, which is sad really because at the end of the day football players are still human beings who are doing their job. But this is the case and it definitely had an impact on me. There were things in the media which obviously came out as well whilst I was playing, talking about my use of social media and things like that. I didn't have it much actually, because I knew when to just keep myself to myself and stay away from all that, because you can add fuel to the fire purely by being in the presence of people. Sometimes, you just stay away from everything and it allows the media to sort of ease off.

'I remember coming up through the academy and speaking to senior players and they would say, "You need to do what you need to do just to survive." Not many people come into the football industry as players and thrive. People might read that and go, "well, they earn so much money". But only some do, the majority don't. So, mostly, you get to a point where you realise that it's not about trying to have everything perfect, it's just about trying to keep your head down and just survive. At the end of the day, it does become a job and it does become about setting yourself up for your future and looking after your family. I learnt as I got older how to fit in. Something that everyone always says in football is just "play the game" with your team-mates, with your coaches, laugh at the jokes and get involved when you need to get involved, dip your toe in, but you can still keep yourself to yourself. It's what you have to do to survive in the game because at the end of the day everything is based on how people perceive you.'

After ten years in the professional game, Sordell eventually decided he'd had enough of just surviving. Being treated poorly by his club Burton Albion was the final straw for the man who had represented Great Britain at the 2012 Olympics, and the 28-year-old announced his retirement in July 2019. The story made headlines due to the unusual nature of a professional footballer actively choosing to quit the game at what might be considered their typical peak age, but Sordell isn't the only one to have made that decision. World Cup winner André Schürrle retired aged 29, stating that he no longer wanted to face the loneliness that came with top-level football's inherent competition. Dutch midfielder Davy Pröpper followed suit in January 2022, frustrated with an overly crowded schedule of matches to please sponsors and TV cameras, exacerbated by a lack of contact with his family due to the COVID-19 pandemic.

Now free from the shackles of regimentation that come as part and parcel of professional football, Sordell's creative side has been able to flourish. He runs a couple of businesses and is the co-founder of production company ONEIGHTY, whose work includes feature films with the likes of John Stones and Raheem Sterling. Sordell maintains a keen interest in the football industry, sitting on the newly established PFA Players' Board with a view to bringing about greater awareness and support for mental health issues in the game. He talks of having many goals in life, with one of these being to bring about a change in the culture of professional football. Nobody is better placed to understand the problems that currently exist, and Sordell has no shortage of ideas and enthusiasm.

'One of my biggest goals is to change football for the better and make it a more positive working environment. That comes down to wellbeing first and foremost, changing the culture of football, the relationship between football and clubs, players and fans. A lot of the relationships are not necessarily healthy.

'I'm dedicated to changing [it] because at the end of the day a lot of these people are just human beings, normal human beings, and this is an industry that is very, very unique in that you have a high level of emotion and a high level of money. So you've got big business and big emotion. There is no other industry I can think of that is like it – it's either one or the other. It's about understanding how to manage that, how to navigate that, how to really get people on board with the fact that it's very different.

'The first thing is to unlearn. You have to get people to understand that the way we see things in football isn't right, the way football is isn't right, the culture of bullying isn't right. We have to do that first and foremost, because if you don't, people will just think, it's fine because it's always been like this, why is it a problem? But you have to understand that it has always been a problem. Then you can re-educate people in understanding what it is really like and why it's wrong, and then you begin to put things in place to make things better.'

There is hope. As we bring our discussion to a close, Sordell admits he was afraid that the reaction from the public and his team-mates would be overwhelmingly negative when he first spoke about his mental health struggles. This didn't turn out to be the case: far from it. The conversation that sprung from his tentative first steps helped Sordell, and surely many others still keeping their mental health struggles secret, realise they weren't alone. It was the medium of writing that allowed Sordell to feel comfortable in expressing his feelings. Sordell's poem *Denis Prose* (which I have included here with his kind permission) is particularly powerful in explaining the emotional conflict Sordell was going through. It describes him at his lowest, going into training with both himself and passenger Denis Prose (an anagram of depression) in the car, representing two sides of his consciousness. As the passenger takes charge, the poem ends in suicide – so nearly the fate that befell Sordell himself, before he spoke up about his mental health and sought help. Sordell's message is urgent but assertive – Denis Prose could be the passenger in any footballer's car.

Along the road I start to drive,
With Denis Prose right by my side.
He's only small, but I notice him,
As I gaze and watch the sun come in.

The birds are singing,
The flowers bloom.
It's all so beautiful,
Until you give him room.

As the sky clouds over, he starts to grow,
But the car is still in my control.
Swerving anxiously from lane to lane,
Whilst the glorious sunshine, turns to grey.

This drive's becoming ever so tough,
And Denis Prose has had enough.
Big enough now to master the wheel,
Says, 'I'm in control, just trust me, deal?'

A passenger on my very own journey,
Reduced to watching raindrops so large it's unearthly.
I have no power but no longer afraid,
Since Denis Prose took over, I've just obeyed.

He tells me, close your eyes until I say,
On this journey, you cannot stay.
I'll take you to where there is peace,
And above all, a place to sleep.

. . .

Now you can open.
But he's gone, as my eyes have just awoken.

I look into the distance,
See pearly white doves,
And the youngest to oldest,
Of all my loves.

This place is so peaceful,
But the silence is deafening.
Don't weep for me though,
I'm free! I'm in heaven.

Michael Bennett had a football career that will be relatable to many in the game. Showing plenty of promise in his childhood, he was fast-tracked through to Charlton Athletic's first team at the age of just 17, being involved in the England youth set-up as he began to feel as though the world was at his feet. However, as is the case with so many promising young players, a serious injury stopped Bennett's progress in its tracks and he never truly recovered. Left to mourn what might have been, the winger from Camberwell spent the rest of his career flitting between sides in all four divisions of the Football League before finishing up at part-time Canvey Island whilst he planned for life after football. After initially planning to stay in the game as a coach or agent, Bennett's head was turned by his careers officer at college who told him his strong active listening skills would make him a good counsellor. Becoming a qualified therapist in 2004, Bennett has gone on to obtain a master's degree in counselling from the University of East Anglia and in July 2021 qualified as a Doctor of Education.

Throughout this learning curve, Bennett has applied his skill set to the world of football. His playing days were in the same era as John Salako's, and the former Crystal Palace and England man's comments on the toughness of the dressing room and stigma around mental health at the time are reiterated by Bennett as we chat over Zoom. He emphasises that whilst he experienced mental health challenges throughout his career, he never had any form of support. Keen to change that, Bennett set up a company called Unique Sports Counselling in 2005 to provide anonymous support to footballers who felt they might need help.

When approaching clubs to offer his services, though, the vast majority said there was no issue with mental health in football and their players did not require Bennett's support. The idea was evidently ahead of its time and in 2007 Bennett was forced to pursue an alternative path as education adviser at the Professional Footballers'

Association (PFA). Initially, his role was focused on delivering practical options to players who were about to retire from professional football so they could move seamlessly out of the game and minimise the mental impact of that transition. It wasn't long before the role became significantly wider-ranging.

Reflecting on events that led to the formation of the dedicated PFA Wellbeing Department in February 2012, Bennett pinpoints two key catalysts: the release of a mental health handbook the PFA distributed to its members in 2011; then, just as this started to normalise conversation around mental health in football, the tragic news of Gary Speed's suicide. The shock that reverberated around football prompted many to contemplate their own mental state instead of pushing it to the side. So many more players started to ask for help that it necessitated the foundation of an entire new department to cater for that demand. That department has gone from strength to strength in the years that followed and continues to provide a vital service for professional footballers in England.

Dr Michael Bennett has been head of the PFA Wellbeing Department since its inception. The department's remit is wide-ranging, with no two days being the same. Bennett and his team will regularly help professional footballers with issues from addiction to loneliness, from financial hardship to low mood with no obvious cause. Whatever the issue, and there is no single theme that dominates, Bennett holds one key principle front and centre to his work. It stems from his own experiences as a player and closely relates to some of Marvin Sordell's most prominent comments.

'In my own experience, I felt we were treated as footballers rather than a person who played football. You're labelled as a professional footballer. Your identity, your self-worth is all around being a professional footballer. When that's gone, who are you? And so when I go and do my talks at clubs and I speak at seminars or do interviews, the first thing I say is, I don't deal with footballers. I deal with a person that plays football. It's the person I'm interested in, not the footballer, and that's key. Without the person there is no footballer. This person at this precise moment in time is going through a difficult time, whatever that is, and requires emotional support and empathy. My work is to put football aside. What I'm trying to do is get clubs and organisations to understand that you are dealing with a person that plays football for your football club.'

Everyone who has played professional football in the English league system is eligible for PFA membership. There are currently around 55,000 members, with 4,000 of them active players and the rest retired. The mental health support available to these members takes two key forms, the first being one-to-one help provided on an ad-hoc basis. A 24/7 wellbeing helpline is available for any player to access immediate support. From this, players can be referred to a nationwide network of counsellors for 12 free sessions or could enter a residential rehab facility run by Sporting Chance. The number of players accessing this support has been on an upward trend, albeit briefly reversed during the pandemic as players struggled with finding somewhere quiet for a confidential conversation. Bennett stresses that there's no overestimating just how important that confidentiality is to the success of the PFA's wellbeing provision. Though attitudes are changing across the board, many players still fear being seen as 'weak' or 'a liability' by their managers if they openly discuss their mental health, and so are keen for anything they say to be kept secret from their clubs. This may or may not be the case and will of course differ from club to club, but the peace of mind offered by the PFA being independent and confidential is vital in ensuring players feel comfortable in coming forward.

The second pillar of the PFA Wellbeing Department's work looks at ensuring that players are educated on the topic of mental health and can pick up early signs they are struggling. Bennett's colleague Jeff Whitley delivers mental health workshops to clubs, with ex-players such as Whitley (who suffered from addiction throughout his career) sharing their own stories of mental health for the current crop of professional footballers to relate to. The aim, as Bennett explains, is to outline football's 'industry hazards' to players so they are prepared for what they might face throughout their careers.

'When I ask players the question, "how do you look after yourself emotionally before a game on Saturday?" they look at me in disbelief. They've never been asked that question before and don't know what the answer is. So I say to them, it's important for you to understand what your mental health and wellbeing is like and how you can address it and make it work for you so it's beneficial from a holistic standpoint. And so our workshops are around looking at what we call the industry hazards. These industry hazards are the challenges that individual players are going to come into contact with on their footballing journey.' Bennett says the Wellbeing Department's work is prompted by research and players' answers to surveys and covers issues like the pressures of the game, isolation, having no voice, injuries, short-term contracts, new managers making changes, gender and religion. 'These are all things that impact individuals' wellbeing. It's happening every day and they're not even aware it's happening to them.

'When you make them aware that these are some of the things players have said that have impacted their wellbeing, players can identify with it straight away. So, the key for us is making these players aware of the industry hazards they may come into contact with … [and] how to access support.'

As part of his studies with the University of East Anglia, Bennett produced a 242-page research paper that examined and described some of the industry hazards endemic in professional football. Elements of his research's four overarching themes are visible in each of my conversations with Vincent Pericard, John Salako and Marvin Sordell. One theme is 'The Mask', reflecting the defence strategies developed by players to hide their vulnerable selves, with Pericard using this exact terminology to describe his experience of depression at a time where he felt unable to ask for help. Sordell's description of his identity being wrapped up in his on-pitch performances fits into Bennett's theme on 'Snowballing Self', exploring a fragile self-perception for players, whilst Salako relates his experience with injuries to Bennett's 'Rollercoaster' theme which represents the ups and downs with extreme highs and lows that come naturally in professional football.

Being attuned to these industry hazards and the signs players might be affected by them is a key aspect of Bennett's role. It's a topic that would have been skirted over even five or ten years ago, but is starting to become more mainstream in the media. Take *Rooney*, for example, the 2022 documentary on one of England's greatest footballers. Wayne Rooney, now in his mid-30s and a lot more contemplative than his reputation from his playing days would suggest, reflects on struggling to deal with his propulsion into fame at the age of 16. Still a teenager, he carried the nation's hopes at Euro 2004, a tournament which ended in defeat to Portugal in a penalty shoot-out after Rooney went off injured. Though confident in his footballing ability at that time, he talks about experiencing more of a fear of losing than a desire to win. He concedes that as these pressures continued to build up throughout his career he developed a drinking problem, and at his lowest point worried he could have caused the death of himself or of others whilst drunk. Speaking on *BBC Breakfast* regarding the release of his documentary, Rooney states that despite all these issues he was going through, he could never have admitted them whilst playing. Bennett's job is to change that perception for players now.

The huge weight of expectation, as well as media intrusion into his private life from a young age, was the main industry hazard facing Rooney. Not everyone will be burdened by the messiah status a teenage Rooney was appointed by the English game, but there are plenty of other industry hazards out there that have recently hit the headlines. In the wake of *Rooney* being released, Chris Sutton admitted to struggling with his mental health after his £10 million move to Chelsea in 1999. With the price tag demanding goals, Sutton netted just once in the league and became a laughing stock for the English media. At the time, Sutton felt too ashamed to speak to anyone and internalised his concerns, a move which created a vicious cycle which was only broken when he left the club to join Celtic. Only now has Sutton felt able to openly speak about the effect on his mental health, but it isn't as though English football has been oblivious to the pressures transfer fees might bring. Indeed, Tottenham famously signed Jimmy Greaves for £99,999 in 1961, as Bill Nicholson didn't want him to have the extra burden of being the first £100,000 player in British football. It might not have been the language used at the time, but this all links back to the concept of mental health.

Of the 55,000 PFA members, however, only a select few are bought and sold for large transfer fees. For the majority, the most common move is a free transfer as players are told they won't be retained at the end of the season. Michael Bennett was predominantly in this boat himself and knows the stresses and strains it can bring. Since the COVID-19 pandemic, club finances have become more stretched and so Bennett has amplified concerns over the number of players being left in the limbo of one-year contracts, worrying for half of that season over whether another contract would be forthcoming at its conclusion. He explains to me that the provision from the PFA is identical for all its members, whether they play for Manchester United or Accrington Stanley, and that one of the key aims at present is to move towards a more proactive needs-led approach. Similar to the research

Bennett carried out for his studies, this involves asking players what they need and using this feedback to optimise the services provided. In general, the idea that mental health provision needs to be proactive, rather than reactive, is becoming more and more central to the playbook. It's a concept that is at the forefront of the work the Chris Mitchell Foundation does in Scotland.

The Chris Mitchell Foundation is reactive only in the way it came about, sadly born out of tragedy after the suicide of the Scottish footballer whose name it bears. Mitchell was an intelligent child but always dreamt of being a professional footballer, leaving school at 16 to pursue this ambition. Everything seemed to be going to plan when he made his debut for Falkirk in the Scottish Premier League whilst still in his teens as well as being called up to Scotland U21. Unfortunately, injuries stunted his progression and by his mid-20s Mitchell had dropped out of the professional game altogether, playing for Clyde whilst working in a factory. His talent was always evident despite his injury struggles. His father, Philip, proudly describes to me how Mitchell won Queen of the South's player of the season award in 2013 from right-back even though the club's centre-forward had netted more than 40 goals that season.

Mitchell's persistent foul luck with injuries finally became too much for his career when he experienced complications after spinal surgery in 2015. His spell playing part-time at Clyde did not last long and by February 2016 he had quit football altogether to focus on a job as a salesman. However, Mitchell struggled to deal with the career change and his mental health began to deteriorate. Tragically, despite having seen a doctor for his depression and having been prescribed anti-depressants, Mitchell took his own life in May 2016. It appeared that the support he had sought towards the end of his life came too late to save him.

For Philip and the rest of the Mitchell family, mixed in amongst the grief was frustration at the failings of football as a whole to spot and address the signs of Chris's mental distress in what was his workplace for the majority of his life.

'The rehabs [for Mitchell's injuries] weren't great. Teams weren't great at looking after players under rehab. If you're not playing in the first team, you're not an asset for them at that time. Everybody who was in the dressing room turned right onto the training pitch and those who were injured turned left and did their own thing. So you were sort of marginalised and Christopher didn't like that. So when these things were happening, which were quite regular, he used to get down a wee bit.

'For the next fortnight or so [after Mitchell's death] people were coming to the house, ex-team-mates and managers. We were saying, "How has Christopher got himself into this situation? Is there any support in football for when you're needing help in relation to your wellbeing?" And they couldn't say that there was anything. There was something in place but it was so poorly advertised that we didn't know about it. We could approach the SPFA, the players' union up here in Scotland, as a family but we never knew that. So, my daughter took it upon herself to do something about this. A short distance in the past there was no support whatsoever. Nothing. We don't know the majority of the stories going back ten or 20 or 30 years of footballers who were suffering at the time.'

Set up as a family-run charity propelled by Philip and his daughter Laura, the Chris Mitchell Foundation set itself the not insignificant task of filling the gaps in Scottish football's mental health provision. It is the belief of both Philip and Laura that better mental health awareness at the clubs he played for and across the world of football as a whole might have helped spot the warning signs in Chris long before he reached crisis point, even though that came after his retirement from the game. Someone proactively noticing something wasn't quite right with Chris and reaching out to him might have stopped it. Even on the day of Chris's suicide, Philip points to opportunities to save his life, likening the bus journey a clearly distressed Chris took on the way to the level crossing at which he took his life to a World War II plane from a film, spiralling towards the ground. Even something as simple as someone asking Chris if he was OK might have snapped him out of that spiral, a parachute to save his life and bring him back to his senses. Sadly, nobody on that bus had the education or confidence to do so.

The way the Chris Mitchell Foundation has gone about addressing this shortcoming in football is simple but remarkably effective. Working with the Scottish Professional Football League (SPFL) Trust, the Foundation delivers mental health awareness training courses to staff at all 42 professional clubs in Scotland. The two-day accredited course is delivered by director of Positive Mental Health Scotland Mark Fleming and covers all aspects of mental health and how to deal with them, with the main outcome being teaching people to spot signs of anxiety, depression and psychosis before signposting the sufferer towards professional help. With the capability to deliver it either in person or online, over 800 people have been upskilled courtesy of the Chris Mitchell Foundation. With five people on average from each Scottish professional side having already completed the course, the hope is that this increase in knowledge and awareness will take the onus off the player to come forward. It is this switching of responsibilities which is key for Philip, as he explains.

'There's a negative stigma with mental health. It's seen as a weakness within you if you've got mental health issues. And that's why people don't put their hands up and ask for help, because they feel ashamed, they think they'll be the butt of the jokes. They possibly think that Scottish football is a small pond with a lot of fish in it, and everybody knows everybody else's business. If you are brave enough to put your hand up, there's still people in football that disregard mental health, and these people could define that as baggage for years to come. When that player comes up for a new contract or a new club or whatever, they'll remember, "Well, he had mental health issues – I don't need that at my club. I've got other things to deal with."

'That's why we've got these people in clubs that can approach people in confidence, ask the question, get a conversation going and see where that takes them. We've turned it around 180 degrees. They've got all this training and knowledge; if they see a change in somebody's demeanour or whatever, they can approach them and ask the right questions. That might just be enough to help them. If they really need professional help, these people can't fix them but they can help put them on … the road to professional help. It's been a huge, huge success.'

It is hard not to wonder how different attitudes towards mental health in football, and the outcomes associated with these attitudes, might be had this sort of training been the norm ten or 20 years ago. Perhaps, when Gary Speed was reaching the end of his playing career and wondering what was next, somebody could have put their arm around him and reassured him help was there if he needed it. Perhaps someone at one of Robert Enke's clubs could have spotted when he withdrew himself after making a mistake and made sure he found psychological support to help him through, rather than seeing him as someone who couldn't handle the big stage. It might even have helped several talented young footballers reach their true potential. Michael Johnson, for example, was seen as a prodigy when he broke through to the Manchester City first team at the age of 19. Struggling with issues of self-esteem, however, he fell away from the top of the professional game, often trying to cope and give himself a temporary high by drinking too much and frequently visiting nightclubs. Instead of this being seen as a sign that Johnson needed help, he was accused of being 'big-time' and retired from football at the age of 24, saying he wanted to be 'left alone to live the rest of my life'. One of England's great hopes for the future never made it beyond a handful of games for Manchester City.

The purpose of this postulating isn't to point fingers at any individuals at the clubs mentioned. The system as a whole ten to 15 years ago didn't do enough to recognise the importance of mental health, and each individual was merely a part of this system, a product of the inertia rather than a cause. Steps to remediate this have only been recently introduced and there is still a long way to go. The English Premier League, for example, created new rules in 2019 that mandated clubs to have their players partake in one session annually to learn about mental health and the wellbeing support available. It's hardly game-changing, but is certainly a start. The work of the Chris Mitchell Foundation is clearly a key part in advancing the dialogue around mental health.

It hasn't all been straightforward for Philip and Laura in running the Chris Mitchell Foundation, however. Philip describes how the SPFA, in stark contrast to their English counterparts, have done little to support their campaign. At a meeting in 2019 arranged through the Scottish government, SPFA chief executive Fraser Wishart declined to work with the Chris Mitchell Foundation on matters related to mental health, but said he would be in touch about working together in 'various other fields' within a week. At the time we speak three years down the line, Philip still hasn't received any further correspondence. His biggest challenge, though, is the extreme commitment involved in keeping the Foundation going. It is family run, after all, effectively from the kitchen table. It can be exhausting for the Mitchell family to continually revisit and relive the toughest period of their lives, and Philip admits there will soon come a point where the family must move on.

At the time we speak, though, Philip and Laura aren't done just yet. Philip has called for mental health awareness training to be mandatory and to be incorporated into UEFA training licences for coaches, to make it more ingrained in the sport. The mental side of the game has always been crucial, after all. Sir Stanley Matthews in his autobiography talks of breaking down in tears of despair after hearing fans at a train station criticising him after an appearance for England against Germany. His father, picking up on this, gave Matthews a vital lesson on the importance of mental resilience and the rest is, of course, history. Looking after your mental health is an essential part of mental strength and is an area football still has significant room for improvement in, almost 100 years on from Matthews's debut. Awareness is key, Philip Mitchell explains, and he envisages a world in which mental health and physical health are treated on a par in football clubs. Ultimately, the only way this can be achieved is to have knowledgeable people within clubs to change the culture from within.

Clive Cook, player care manager at Norwich City at the time we speak, is one of those knowledgeable people. An accredited sports psychologist, Cook has previously worked in roles related to education and welfare at both Liverpool and the English FA. Ever the scholar, he is just weeks away from moving on from Norwich City to further his studies as we chat over Zoom in January 2022. Cook explains to me that the area of player care has only started to become common in the last ten to 15 years – prior to this, professional footballers were more or less expected to just get on with things alone.

Nowadays, the job description of a player care manager varies significantly from club to club. Many top Premier League clubs have a Player Care department that primarily works to ensure expensive new signings are able to settle in and perform at their best on the pitch as a result. This isn't as simple as providing them with a new car or luxury purchase on demand, but rather involves a bespoke service that strategically and proactively looks to meet a player's every need. West Ham, for example, used to have a 30-page welcome pack for new signings, put together by their head of player care at the time, Hugo Scheckter. The information contained in the document was as varied as how the stadium's parking system operated to recommending a good company for children's birthday parties. Scheckter himself would ensure he was always available on speed dial if required so that the players he looked after felt constantly supported. The difference between happy and unhappy players is undoubtedly worth points to a side on the pitch across the season, not to mention to the asset value of professional footballers. Anyone looking to force a move, perhaps simply through being unhappy off the pitch, will most likely have to be sold for a cut-price fee and the club loses out as a result.

Clive Cook's role at Norwich did not involve producing player welcome documents or being available on a 24/7 speed dial. Instead, he was tasked with getting to know the players on a personal level with conversations about their lives and feelings away from football. The result was similar to the ideal scenario envisaged by the Chris Mitchell Foundation – should any player show signs of struggling with their mental health, Cook could approach them first and take the onus off them to seek help. All his years of experience provided Cook with the perfect toolbox with which to approach his task.

'You've got to be skilled in lots of areas. One of them would be body language. You might argue we do our best work in formal one-to-ones, but I pick up a lot of cues just seeing the players around the building. I remember a player walking through the restaurant one day towards the classroom with his hood up and his earphones in. Straight away, that's not something we encourage in the academy. One of the other players said, "He's been like that all day, he's not been in the right mood." So I went up and spoke to him – he was just having a tough day and wasn't feeling at his best. We've just got to get to know the players inside out. You build that trust and rapport and connection, and as soon as you've got that it's just easier.

'We use all sorts of different tactics to get the right support to the lads. A former colleague of mine just started at Chelsea and I said fundamentally the most important thing is to get your one-to-ones done with the players. One, because they will really value it, and two, we generally like talking about ourselves. I spoke to my colleague at Chelsea today and she said this one player opened up about things he'd never told anyone else before. That's the value of actually just sitting someone down, caring for them, and saying "You've got 30 minutes with me today, I want to know as much as I can about you in 30 minutes." Straight away, you're getting fantastic information and building that connection.'

For all his expertise, Cook's role at Norwich was predominantly limited to working with Professional Development Phase players, meaning the club's under-23 and under-18 players, as well as younger age groups. With his comprehensive knowledge of the benefits, Cook is surprised sports psychologists aren't used more commonly in senior football, particularly as there is no shortage of financial clout amongst Premier League clubs. Even Norwich – when managed by Daniel Farke – opted against bringing in a professional to deal with the mental side of the game for their first team. Given the challenges they faced on the pitch in the 2021/22 season, finishing bottom of the table with the worst goal difference since Derby County's disastrous 2007/08 season, it does seem like a costly oversight. Even looking at individual cases, young loan players Billy Gilmour and Brandon Williams faced abuse from their own supporters. Williams even alleged that he had been followed home by angry supporters after a 4-0 home defeat to West Ham. With both players barely out of their teens at the time, it can't have been an easy experience to deal with.

Cook explains a lot of top-level professionals pay out of their own pockets to see a psychologist, seeing the benefit in it even if their clubs don't. Cook's role in normalising discussion around mental health in Norwich's academy sides helps stand the game in good stead for five or ten years down the line. After all, these young players are the future of the game. Step by step, the culture is being changed to move mental health up the list of priorities and bring it in line with its physical equivalent.

'Something we do here which has worked really well is we have mental health ambassadors covering all age groups. The under-23s and under-18s are key age groups. We train them up in what we call mental health first aid. We say to them to look for signs in the dressing room or changes in behaviour and then they can deal with it and bring us that information, but it stays confidential. They might say, "So-and-so is struggling because of this." And then I'll speak to that player but they won't know the mental health ambassador has given me that information. It works really well.

'I've given players time off before due to psychological burnout, which normally occurs around October to November when the seasons change and there's less light. As you know, through evolution we're better with light than we are with dark, and some of them get affected by SAD [Seasonal Affective Disorder] syndrome. They need that break, so I give players time off and they come back after a couple of weeks and they're refreshed and a lot, lot better physically and mentally. They say, "I don't know why I feel a lot better" and I reply, "Because you've had two weeks off resting, you've not thought about football or your work, you've just gone back to being the person you are."'

The more young players that come through the system with mental health seen as normal in this way, the more players at the peak of their game will start talking about it too. To an extent, it's already starting to happen. Danny Rose made headlines in a pre-World Cup press conference in 2018 when he admitted to having depression brought on by the combined effects of injury sidelining him from action along with having to deal with a family tragedy. At the time it was unheard of, but several more international players have spoken about their mental health since Rose helped open up the floodgates for them. In October 2020, Ben Chilwell posted a message on Twitter in which he spoke about seeking mental health support to help him deal with 'everyday life' the previous year. Sticking with the

England theme, centre-forward Dominic Calvert-Lewin claimed that talking about his mental health had saved his life after a challenging 2021/22 season. The list goes on, from legends of the game such as Ashley Cole to renowned internationals still at their peak, like Paul Pogba, who confessed to going through a spell of depression during his time at Manchester United.

Nobody wants anyone to struggle, of course, but the openness that is becoming more and more common in the game is music to Michael Bennett's and the PFA's ears.

'I can definitely say the culture has changed. I can definitely say that it's a hundred times better than when I played. We've come a long way in a short space of time but there's still more work to do. I want it to be the case where people talk about mental health as if they have a physical injury. "I've pulled my hamstring, I'm going to see my physio." "I've got an emotional wellbeing issue, I'm going to see my physio or the PFA." I want it to be that same conversation.

'The idea about working with younger players is that if we can get the younger players to think that it's OK to talk about your mental health and normalise it as they come through, it will just be a normal conversation. So the key for me is educating our players, the younger players coming through and our players that are here already. Younger players look up to senior players, so if we can get the senior players talking more about their wellbeing, younger players will want to talk about it as well.

'In 2017, we did our first PFA mental wellbeing conference at St George's Park. We called it *Injured*, and the idea behind it being called *Injured* was that if you've got a physical injury, you're injured. If you've got an emotional injury, you're injured. They're both injuries. They should be treated the same way and we should be talking about it the same way. It has changed massively and I think the more we talk about it, the more we normalise it. It's normal. Everybody will go through and have mental health issues in some shape or form. People are on a different scale. Some are just lower, some are medium, some are high. But we're all on that spectrum.'

In a way, more players coming forward and seeking help with their mental health makes Bennett's job harder. After all, it gives his department more work to do, more demands to meet. But whilst this trend of openness continues to grow, so does the job satisfaction the head of the PFA's Wellbeing Department derives from his work. The more people who come forward, the more lives are improved. As is clear from my conversations with both Vincent Pericard and Marvin Sordell, some could even be saved.

Chapter 2

The Manager

FOR ALL the support that is available to professional footballers, it is invariably their manager with whom they spend the most time in a footballing context. Gone are the days of the autocrat, of the man bellowing at his players to get on with it, expecting them to perform almost as robots. Players are now seen as human, and managers generally understand they must treat them as such to get the best out of them. Take the success of Gareth Southgate as England manager, for example. Empathy and emotional intelligence have become his personal brand in the job, with several players including Ben White and Luke Shaw speaking publicly about the way Southgate's approach has benefitted their performances for their country. Southgate took charge of a side still in shock after defeat to Iceland in Euro 2016 and the subsequent Sam Allardyce scandal, and turned them into a team that played freely and seemed able to finally cast off the shackles of expectation so often burdened on England at major tournaments.

Though Southgate, as manager of England, is the most visible example of managerial empathy in the modern game, he is certainly not the only one. It's a skill that requires not just the ability to be a good listener but also to look out for other clues such as body language and facial expressions. Look around and you'll see a variety of different methods and styles but all with the same end goal – promoting the positive mental health of that manager's players to get the best out of them on the pitch as well as fulfilling the now commonly recognised duty of pastoral care. In what would have been an unusual move at the time, Carlo Ancelotti had reports made on all of his players at AC Milan, so he knew what communication styles they preferred. Allardyce attributes much of the success his Bolton side had in the early 2000s to his idea of appointing two player liaison officers, making Wanderers a more attractive proposition for potential new signings given their relative lack of budget. Something must have been working for Allardyce, as the notoriously difficult character El Hadji Diouf reportedly referred to his manager as 'Dad' during his time at the Reebok Stadium.

Now down in League One, Bolton Wanderers compete in the same division as Lancashire neighbours Accrington Stanley, who have a very different model to the delegation of duty that Bolton utilised during their time at the top. Manager John Coleman effectively doubles up as the player liaison officer, as well as the welfare officer and indeed a day-to-day counsellor of his players. He tells me that having all these responsibilities on his shoulders allows him to build a strong personal relationship with his players, which means they confide in him.

'I think you can split managers up into leaders, managers and coaches. I believe the best managers are leaders. I'm not saying I'm the best manager, but I like to class myself as a leader. I think in order to lead you've got to try and get a common goal; you've got to get a bond with your players. They've got to believe your cause is worth fighting for … Your dreams and your goals have got to become theirs. That's when you'll be more successful, or at least have a chance of being more successful.

'But likewise, they've got to feel your pain, and you've got to feel their pain. You've got to be able to understand them, so a lot of time is spent speaking to my players. This isn't necessarily about football, but just trying to get to know them better and getting a feel for what makes them tick. While it's not a popularity contest, I think in any walk of life if you enjoy what you do, you'll do it better. If you like the person you're doing it for, you're more likely to do it better, you'll more likely not want to let them down. I think one of the things that's made Accrington successful is that we do get every last drop out of our players. People are always commenting on that. That's not by luck, that's been down to a lot of hard work over the years.'

Accrington certainly have been successful in the time Coleman has been in charge. In fact, successful is probably an understatement. Under his management, they have risen from the Northern Premier League Division One to League One, winning four promotions to get there. Though a lot has of course changed in this time, the family feel to the club has remained a key pillar of its identity. Coleman talks of an open-door policy that has been in place since he first managed the club in 1999, whereby any player can come to him and get anything off their chest without the fear of it affecting their place in the side. To build a rapport, Coleman and his assistant Jimmy Bell often sit with the squad at breakfast and lunch and get amongst the conversation, engaging in whatever interests the players have, be it their children, pets, or even which horse they're tipping for the next race day. As he has gotten older, though, Coleman has stepped back from events such as players' nights out, keen to maintain a professional distance that allows his squad the right amount of freedom. After all, football managers must get results and cannot let sentiment and emotion cloud their judgement when picking the side, as Sir Alex Ferguson has often alluded to.

From the conversation that I have with Coleman, his managerial style appears to echo that of Brian Clough, who of course achieved phenomenal success at unfancied clubs in Derby County and Nottingham Forest. In his own autobiography, the man who won two European Cups attributes his success in management to caring about players and their families, creating a mutual respect that meant they wanted to work for him. He gives Kenny Burns as one prominent example – the Scotland international had a 'wild man' image in the late 1970s, but Clough, along with his assistant Peter Taylor, signed him anyway, prepared to take what they saw as a calculated gamble. Whilst being strict enough to keep his man on the straight and narrow, little touches such as spoiling Burns's wife when she came to the ground to watch a game kept him onside and contributed towards Burns twice winning Nottingham Forest's player of the year award. In recent interviews, Burns has described Clough as a 'father figure' to him, showing just how powerful a connection with his players Clough created.

Of course, it is far easier to keep your players happy when everything is going well. When I ask Coleman about his toughest challenges in football management, he highlights Accrington's period of financial trouble around 2011. The increasing cost of keeping a competitive side in the Football League combined with stagnating attendances saw Accrington issue a number of shares in 2011 in the hope of raising £1m. Though the buyers included the likes of Sir Alex Ferguson and a number of foreign investors, an early FA Cup exit at the hands of Notts County compounded financial worries further. With wages occasionally being paid late, Coleman employed humour to keep his players together.

'Rather than make it doom and gloom, I tried to make light of it. We'd be eating breakfast and I'd get the phone call and I'd just try singing to make a joke of it. I'd be singing "Paid in a fortnight, you're getting paid in a fortnight" or whatever. I got the message across, and they'd start laughing with me. I'd say, "Listen, come on, every time we don't get paid, we need to give our best performances. Let's show 'em." We had a bit of a reverse psychology with it, we used it to motivate ourselves and rally round and we did have some significant results when we went through that period. We got to the play-offs that year despite not being paid on a regular basis. But I'd be lying if I said it was easy, because it wasn't, and one of the reasons I chose to leave Accrington in the end was because I didn't believe what I was hearing. I'd never ever tell lies to the players, and I didn't believe we could sustain this.'

Ironically, Coleman's replacement at the struggling club was Paul Cook, who went on to manage Wigan

Athletic when they were plunged into administration in 2020. The 12-point deduction they were handed just weeks away from the end of the season moved them from seven points clear of the drop to five points inside it with a handful of games to go. Though they lost just one of their last six games, this run including an 8-0 win over Hull City, Wigan were relegated anyway. Cook described the week following administration as 'the worst, toughest week of my career by far' as he took personal responsibility to call many of his staff and try to reassure them as much as possible. After a 1-1 draw with Fulham on the final day of the season sealed Wigan's fate, a close-to-tears Cook then remarked that he felt 'physically sick'. There's no doubt managing a side in the mire financially is one of the toughest experiences a manager can face, challenging their own mental health as well as that of their staff and players.

Coleman returned to manage Accrington for a second spell in September 2014, just two and a half years after leaving for Rochdale. By this point, new owner Andy Holt had taken over and cleared the club's £1.2m debt, paving the way for a more stable future. One of Coleman's best signings in putting together a side that eventually won League Two four years after his return was prolific goalscorer Billy Kee on a free transfer from Scunthorpe in 2015. On the outside, Kee appeared a swashbuckling forward full of confidence as he bagged 25 goals in Accrington's title-winning season, but internally he was facing an ongoing battle with his mental health. When Kee opened up to the world about that in a February 2018 interview with the BBC, what followed over the next two years put Accrington Stanley and John Coleman in the news for all the right reasons. Coleman was able to support his player and friend with the understanding and care he needed, but little did many know that the manager's own experiences in the intervening years between spells at Accrington had helped him relate to and therefore help Kee.

'I went through depression myself when I lost my job at Rochdale, and all of a sudden I had a lot of time on my hands. I was sitting in the house and going through a bit of a bad patch which took its toll on my marriage too, so that wasn't healthy. A lot of things bottle up. You don't expect it, but when I did go through it, I knew how hard it was. I burst out crying at stupid things and just wasn't myself. I wasn't taking any pleasure in anything – my grandkids, playing golf, which I love. I couldn't derive any pleasure from anything.

'Billy was a complex character, but I think it helped him immensely that I understood what he was going through. I didn't just say, "There's nothing wrong with you," which is what a lot of people would think. If you break your leg, people will be sympathetic, but if you have a disease that's very well hidden and doesn't overly demonstrate physical symptoms, it can be as if it's not happening. But at Accrington, everyone was queueing up to help him. Until you know how debilitating it is, until you've been through it, you can't quite grasp it. The fact that I have been through it made it very easy to be empathetic with him and understand what he was going through, understand how much it can knock you sideways and make you feel as though you don't want to get out of bed in the morning.'

Ultimately, Billy Kee retired from professional football in January 2020 due to his struggles with depression, anxiety and bulimia. Stanley agreed to terminate his contract to let Kee spend more time with his family, and his number 29 shirt has since been retired in the forward's honour. So popular is Kee still amongst Accrington fans that a coachload of supporters turned up to watch him play for local semi-professional club Coalville Town against Banbury. At the time of writing, Coleman is still in charge at Accrington and continues to overachieve on a shoestring budget. His player-first philosophy shows no sign of ever letting him or his team down.

* * *

In openly speaking about his own mental health, John Coleman joined what is still a very exclusive club within the world of football management. Martin Ling was one of those paving the way when he opened up about his own struggles in 2015. Ling had taken a break from his role as Torquay manager two years earlier when in the darkest depths of his depression, and although he briefly returned to management with Swindon Town he decided the job was not for him shortly afterwards. Quoted in Michael Calvin's *Living on the Volcano: The Secrets of Surviving as a Football Manager*, Ling spoke about having an 'intolerance of uncertainty' that made a career in football management unviable for him. He suggested at that time that having a history of mental health issues is seen as a 'coffee stain' on your CV as a football manager.

For a few years, the mental health of football managers returned to the backburner in the eyes of the public, but it was brought back into sharp focus by the treatment Steve Bruce endured towards the end of his spell in charge of Newcastle United. A Geordie and boyhood Newcastle fan himself, Bruce faced a targeted and personal campaign to have him removed as manager. Banners were unveiled at home games by fans group Wor Flags, proclaiming him a 'coward' and declaring 'You are not one of us', but the worst of the abuse was concentrated on social media. One supporter messaged Bruce's son, Alex, telling him that he hoped his father would die of COVID-19. Those close to Bruce described him as looking mentally exhausted as things progressed, and when he was eventually sacked, he told the press he was unlikely to take on another managerial role.

The extent of the abuse Bruce had suffered prompted a discussion in the media, with Tony Pulis saying he feared it was only a matter of time before a manager would be physically assaulted. Richard Bevan, the chief executive of the League Managers Association (LMA), weighed in to argue that the personal abuse targeted at managers, prompted by things such as media phone-ins and betting on the 'sack race', needed to be addressed. The whole conversation made you wonder why anyone would want to be a football manager at all. It was the late Tommy Docherty who famously described the job as similar to nuclear war. There are no winners – only survivors.

I spoke to Paul Lambert a few months after he had left Ipswich Town to hear his views on football management and mental health. Lambert, who had taken Norwich from League One to the Premier League with back-to-back promotions in 2010 and 2011, explained that whilst he hadn't suffered with mental health problems himself, he was keen to normalise the conversation around the topic. The Glaswegian had been a team-mate of Neil Lennon at Celtic, a man who has spoken publicly for years about his own battles with mental health. More poignantly, another former team-mate of Lambert's, Paul McGrillen, took his own life in 2009. I asked Lambert what he felt were the main mental health challenges of football management. His response undoubtedly represents the views of a great number of managers in the modern game.

'The game's changed because social media has come into it. I think everybody wants success yesterday. If the players do the job and get the result then everything is great. If you don't win then you have to go to the media and face that side of it. The questions come in, social media intensifies because there's all these fans' websites where they can bounce things about, build up a calamity story and get a manager sacked. When you lose, it can be very lonely. That's when you need good staff around you and good people about you off the pitch as well. They can take your mind off it.

'I did [take results home with me] when I was younger. What changed my mind was I went to see Ottmar Hitzfeld, who was my manager at Dortmund when we won the Champions League. I remember asking, "how do you handle defeats?" He said to just analyse them for 24 hours and let them go, because if you don't it will kill you, it will kill the team, it will kill everyone around you. That's why I changed really … I've always kept to that since. Beforehand, I'd have been a hell of a bad loser.'

Lambert makes it sound easy, but being dragged down into a damaged state of mind after losing on a Saturday afternoon is something so many managers have spoken about, you feel it would be unusual for someone not to be like this. Of course, nobody should be happy with defeat, but when you're getting 'so low it's frightening', as Harry Redknapp admits in his autobiography *Always Managing*, you know something is up. In fairness, Redknapp is not the only one. In *Living on the Volcano*, Aidy Boothroyd talks of nearly cancelling a night out with a leukaemia survivor one Saturday night until his wife forced him to gain some perspective on things. Neil Warnock has described a 3-2 defeat to fellow-strugglers Sunderland during his time as QPR boss as 'like a dagger to the heart', whilst Arsene Wenger has admitted he would sometimes avoid leaving the house for days after a defeat.

Successful managers develop their own coping strategies. For Wenger, it was important to keep at the forefront of his thinking a long-term philosophy and not get too down with any blips that occurred on the way. Sir Alex Ferguson describes a pivotal point during his managerial career as the time he began to indulge in outside interests to take his mind off football. The 13-time Premier League winner discovered that an interest in horse racing, as well as reading books and buying wine, afforded him extra longevity within football management without compromising his focus on the game. Brian Clough went one step further and was known for taking a mid-season holiday around February each year, leaving his coaching staff in charge. It certainly wouldn't be seen as conventional today, but Clough claimed it prevented him from 'going stale', and certainly nobody could argue with his record. Failure to address the day-to-day signs of stress in the job can eventually lead to burnout, as Paul Lambert found out.

'You only enjoy success for a really, really short time. You enjoy it in the moment, but then it's finished and you have to crack on again and try and do something else. The Norwich job … that took me to the limit. I was tired after that. I'd had three years which were relentless. In my third season, I was tired and I needed a break from it. Aston Villa asked me to go in and I said no a couple of times before I said I'd give it a go. But really, even now, I think I should have taken longer out when I left Norwich rather than going right back into it.

'You're working hard all the time, it's always there, it's 24/7. Every day is different. You can go into one session and it's really easy, but go into the next session and it's really tough because some players have problems at home or whatever, or maybe something has cropped up in the media that you have to deal with pretty quickly. So every day changes in football. You very rarely get a rest, other than maybe when the season finishes, in that little period … You have to be ready for that. It can burn you out, definitely.'

The consequences of burnout can extend from mental into physical, showing just how serious it can be. Perhaps most notably, Sam Allardyce participated in a fascinating study during his time at Bolton, in which he was wired up to a heart monitor during a match. The results were so startlingly high that the LMA subsequently brought in a health programme and regular fitness checks for its members. Allardyce required surgery after a health scare with a blocked artery in 2009. Again, he certainly isn't alone, with popular manager Barry Fry suffering two heart attacks during his time at Barnet alone, for example.

The LMA is well aware of both the physical and mental health risks involved with being a football manager, and it has introduced many services since the health programme brought on by the Allardyce study. Originally founded in 1919 as the Football League Secretaries and Managers Association, the LMA has spent most of its existence in a period in which mental health simply wasn't a consideration. A lot has been added in a short period of time, with chief executive Richard Bevan admitting in a March 2021 interview with the BBC that his organisation had been on a 'steep learning curve' with mental health since Martin Ling had opened up in 2015. I contacted Bevan directly to better understand exactly what provision was now available with regards to mental health. His written response, covering several pages of A4, was comprehensive.

Recognising the wide range of mental health challenges a manager can face in the role, the LMA has a defined action plan for each of them. Independent, trained mentors are available to help with self-awareness and emotional understanding, for example, whilst concerns over a sense of managerial identity can be addressed with ongoing career planning support. Mental health is now built into the LMA Diploma in Football Management, with full-day masterclasses on mental resilience a key part of the course. The flagship provision, though, is the 24-hour mental and emotional wellbeing support provided by in-house consultant psychiatrists and psychologists. Members can access this support on a confidential basis, and crucially, so can their immediate family. In focusing on the strains of the managerial role itself, it is easy to forget just how much those around the man in the hot seat can be affected as well. Sir Alex Ferguson, for example, mentions in his autobiography that his wife described the day Manchester City secured the title on the final day of the 2011/2012 season as the worst of her life, such was the strain. More recently, Aston Villa Women head coach Carla Ward openly admitted, when talking about her own split with the mother of her daughter, that she wouldn't want to be in a relationship with a football manager.

* * *

Of course, each manager's experience is unique, and some will breeze through challenges that others really struggle with. Paul Lambert, for example, is comfortable with external pressure, having played in a cauldron of intensity for much of his playing career. Not only did he become the first British person to win the European Cup with a non-British side, he also faced the responsibility of preventing Rangers win their tenth league title in a row having joined fierce rivals Celtic in 1997. At the time I speak to him, Lambert is unconcerned about the fact he is out of work. He has just returned from a trip to Germany, watching sides train and play to learn more about the game, and is still in no rush to dive back into a role without making sure it is the right fit. To find someone who could candidly discuss the challenges of periods without work, I reached out to another Scottish manager in Simon McMenemy.

McMenemy's experiences of being sacked are certainly not typical of a British manager. The axe came down on him for the first time at Long An Football Club in the Vietnamese V-League in 2011. Having been living in a club-owned house, McMenemy was given two months' salary to tide him over in the short term and told to move out. Within days, Indonesian club Mitra Kukar got in touch and told him they would be offering a contract shortly. The trouble was, they seemed to be in no rush. With his resources dwindling, McMenemy and his wife hoped and prayed that something would come through. Luckily, the paperwork did eventually appear, which is just as well given that on the day it did, McMenemy had just $20 left in his bank account. Looking back on it now, he acknowledges the gravity of the situation he was in.

'It was a very nervous time. I remember not sleeping for the best part of two or three weeks leading up to that contract. I couldn't afford the rent for the next couple of weeks if it didn't happen. What you start to learn is how to try to protect against that. You are going to be sacked in your career if you're in the game for a long time. So what are you going to do in between times? How are you going to sustain yourself? Now my little boy is in the world, I can't get into that situation anymore. So that's an added pressure … and you have to mentally develop in order to carry that around with you.'

Introducing McMenemy through a time he lost his job is perhaps a tad harsh. The Aberdonian's first foray into international management brought about the sort of underdog story that you could easily envisage being made into a film. While he was working as assistant manager at

Worthing in the Isthmian League Division One South, a former player of McMenemy's got in touch to recommend he applied for the job as manager of the Philippines national team. McMenemy didn't know much about the job or its requirements, but applied anyway. Six weeks later, he received a phone call and was shocked to hear he had been invited to an interview. In August 2010, McMenemy was offered the job.

McMenemy's first task was to qualify for the 2010 AFF Championship, a tournament for teams in Southeast Asia. A 5-0 win against Timor-Leste in the first of three games was the pivotal moment, with two draws, against Laos and Cambodia, following. With the top three all finishing on five points, Cambodia were eliminated having only won by two against whipping boys Timor-Leste, and so the Philippines were through. Nothing was expected of McMenemy's side in the final tournament, hosted in the football-mad nation of Indonesia. His side were viewed as a hastily assembled group of amateurs, a mix of those playing lower league football abroad and the best players from the domestic league, which typically saw crowds of a few hundred at matches.

It took Singapore 65 minutes to take the lead against them in the first group game, but incredibly Chris Greatwich, the man who had recommended McMenemy for the job, bagged a stoppage time equaliser. Even better was to follow. Vietnam were beaten 2-0 in the second match, a result that was so much of a shock that *Sports Illustrated* named it one of their top ten sports stories of the year. A draw against Myanmar was enough to send the Philippines through to the knockout stages. There, the fairytale came to an end with a 2-0 aggregate defeat to Indonesia, but even that was an incredible experience for McMenemy and his side, with the two matches being played in front of a combined crowd of 158,000 people. His team had gone from nobodies to celebrities in their home country almost overnight, and even now McMenemy is widely credited with kick-starting football in the Philippines.

* * *

Management is a lonely job at the best of times, and the effect can often be exacerbated when managing abroad. Terry Venables, for example, had great success with Barcelona, winning their first La Liga title for 11 years in 1985. He enjoyed his time in Catalonia on the whole, but never planned to spend more than three years there, such was the effect on his personal life. Venables's father was against him going in the first place and had to be convinced by Venables himself demonstrating how quick it was to fly there. His marriage to his first wife then ended as the pair drifted apart, according to Venables's own admission. The initial decision to move home after three years was taken as his daughters were still in the UK, and Venables felt he wasn't seeing enough of them.

McMenemy has his wife and son with him out in Indonesia, where he currently works as technical director at Bhayangkara FC, but this hasn't meant he has been immune from loneliness. 'It can be very lonely, especially in football, being so far away from home. It's difficult, and it takes either a very strong character or a strong environment within your own home – my wife, myself and my son – to deal with it. You don't have a support network, you don't have feedback, you don't have someone you can just chat with and go out for a drink with down the local. A lot of the time with ex-pats, you're thrown into a room and you're friends with people for the sake of having friends, not necessarily because you have a connection. I do find that quite difficult sometimes. To give you an example, my wife picks up men in coffee shops purely so they can be my friend. She'll be chatting to someone who will say they love football and they're from the UK. "Oh, my husband loves football. Maybe you guys can go out and play golf together?" She's done it three or four times, just speaking to random guys in coffee shops so they'll be my friend.'

This sense of isolation is one thing to contend with, but there are also fundamental differences to managing abroad which can present challenges for those who attempt it. John Toshack's autobiography reads like a cultural handbook, with the Welshman having managed in ten different countries. The Basques were often closed off to foreigners, for example, whereas those in Galicia have a sense of secrecy about them. In Turkey, you must deliver instant success or face the sack, whilst his time in Italy was marred by the links his side, Catania, supposedly had to the Mafia. Towards the end of his managerial career, Toshack went to Morocco with Wydad Casablanca and won the title in his first season. However, joy turned to frustration the following season when several of his players were called up to military service the night before a CAF Champions League semi-final game against Zamalek. Wydad were unsurprisingly heavily beaten and Toshack was sacked. Each of these jobs forced Toshack to adopt a new perspective, and certainly anyone who couldn't adapt to such conditions would not have had anything close to the career he did.

For McMenemy, there was a deep sense of injustice to overcome after his Bhayangkara side won an unlikely league title in 2017. Normally, the league winner would qualify for the AFC (Asian Football Confederation) Champions League, but Bhayangkara were not awarded an AFC licence to participate. The reasoning behind the decision was somewhat murky, but McMenemy explained that such disappointments are something you have to get used to if you want to protect your mental health when managing in Indonesia.

'I'm stepping into a new culture. I can try and affect what's around me but I can't change the whole country's culture. If that is something you cannot get your head around, you won't last long here at all. There are little things that challenge you as a person in terms of your morality, your ethics, how you treat people, how you see the world. You get challenged on a daily basis in these areas. It's nothing to do with football, nothing to do with tactics or strategy. It's the relationships you have to build and maintain in order to keep your job and do your job.

'It's a constant battle in your head a lot of the time, to be able to wake up in the morning and go, "yeah, we're doing the right thing here", because there are that many things that can derail you. It's Indonesia, you just have to develop a really thick skin and a roll-with-it attitude, and so long as it doesn't impinge on your morals and ethics, you just treat it as another obstacle and you get on with it and do the best you can.'

It hasn't always been plain sailing, then, for McMenemy despite his successes abroad. The low points have even reached his extended family back home, who received a torrent of social media abuse when McMenemy was in charge of the Indonesian national side. Despite this, McMenemy does not regret that decision taken back in 2010 to leave the quiet town of Worthing and dive into a whole new world in the Philippines. He has often been asked about where he thinks he would slot in if he returned to the UK, but that is beside the point. His wife is happy with the lifestyle they lead, and McMenemy loves the fact that his son is growing up in a multicultural environment in which he is learning that everyone is his friend. Then there is the matter of what he has been able to achieve on the pitch. McMenemy is visibly emotional when we revisit the topic of his achievements in the first international role he took, with the Philippines national team.

'When I've had the experiences I've had around the world, been able to affect football in the way I have, I'm very proud of that and it's a massive motivator for me, because I come from development. I don't come from elite football; I come from giving people opportunities to play football. So, to be able to do that on a national level is a massive motivator and it's not something that I'm willing to give up on right now.'

Chapter 3

Injury

ANTERIOR CRUCIATE ligament. The three words that strike fear into the heart of any footballer. An awkward landing or sudden pivot can result in a tear, which can leave you sidelined for around a year. Suffering such a serious injury once is a huge blow in any player's career, but suffering the same injury twice is nothing short of disastrous. Maxime Biamou, of Coventry City, is one of the unlucky few to have suffered such a fate. His first time, whilst still playing in the depths of French amateur football, set him back for a year and a half and even delayed his studies at university, such was its severity. Thankfully, the surgery required was successful and Biamou was soon on his way, graduating from university and back out on the pitch. Only a few years later, in 2016, his life took a major turn when his agent called, offering a chance to trial at English non-league club Sutton United. A goal in his showcase match helped as Biamou was signed permanently. Just a year later, after starring in an FA Cup run that saw Sutton reach the fifth round before being defeated by Arsenal, he got his big move to Coventry City. Things kept getting better for the Frenchman as the Sky Blues won promotion to League One in the Wembley play-off final, beating Exeter City 3-1 in front of 50,000 people.

However, on 21 August 2018 in a League One match at Blackpool, Biamou landed awkwardly after an aerial challenge inside the opening minute. Straight away, things didn't look right, and the striker was immediately substituted. The worst fears of the Frenchman were confirmed three days later: once again Biamou had suffered a tear to his anterior cruciate ligament.

'I remember the first time because this was the first time I went to the hospital for a few days and opened my body, so it was very hard mentally for me. I remember when I did the MRI and they said I have an ACL and I need surgery, I became white – all my body became white. It was very hard, and I said after my surgery, "If I do it again, I won't play football anymore." When I had this the second time, I was like, "what am I going to do now?" The chance that I had was that I had just signed my new contract three weeks earlier. I didn't really want to do surgery again, but I thought the club will be with me, my family will be with me, I can't stop now.

'I wanted, in my life, to play minimum in League One. It was the goal of my life … so when I had my injury after three games, I was very sad because this was my second ACL. It's a very long injury … you don't know if you will come back strong as before or good enough. That's why you just need to work hard and not think about something like that. Just do your job, do the best rehab, and come back as strong as possible. But it was hard for me to watch the other players play. That season, we had a very good team and I thought I could do something very good for them, scoring goals and everything. It was my chance, but I had my injury – this is football. That's why every time you need to think to be ready mentally.'

A recent study at Brunel University, and facilitated by the Professional Footballer's Association, found that injury had a role to play in footballers seeking mental health support from counsellors in up to 99 per cent of cases. Indeed, 99 per cent of the players surveyed experienced some kind of psychological disruption from injury, which included factors ranging from fears of reinjury to a loss of identity. Given that football entails an extremely high risk of injury compared to the average job, you'd have thought clubs would have provisions for this in place. However, this does not appear to be the case. Of the 75 clubs surveyed, only 37 per cent reported having staff trained in the psychology of injury, and less than 25 per cent had a full-time sports psychologist. Dr Misia Gervis, a leading sports psychologist involved in the study, was frustrated but not particularly surprised by the findings.

'The culture is one where there is virtually no acknowledgement of the fact that injury is a psychological challenge, not a physical one. You ask any of the players; physically they're fine, they understand how to do it, they understand they've got to do the rehab … The difficult things are the emotional changes, psychological challenges, and it messes with them on different levels and in different ways and no one is acknowledging that.

'There will be behavioural changes, there will be psychological disturbances and vulnerabilities, but I don't think there's then the joined-up thinking which basically says, I need some help with this, I need some support with this. What football does is to walk people to the edge of the cliff and it watches them fall off, and when they're falling off, at that point they say, "Ooh, maybe you need some help," or, "Go to the PFA." My point is this: why don't we stop them walking to the edge of the cliff? … then actually the damage is not going to be extensive.'

As knowledge and research over the psychological impact of sports injuries grows, there exists increasing evidence that it's in football clubs' own interests to help their players. Dr Gervis explains that in one of her other research projects, it was discovered that over 90 per cent of athletes experience fear of reinjury. This will naturally impact on performance, but it seems clubs often overlook this. Of course, this is without even getting into the idea that clubs are failing in their duty of care to their players. Having worked as a consultant sports psychologist at QPR since 2015, Dr Gervis is now at Wycombe Wanderers putting steps in place to ensure players get the psychological support they need. She runs with the same core principle that was at the forefront at QPR: any long-term injured player has to speak to a psychologist, with the key being to work collaboratively with physios, coaches and the rest of the staff.

And Dr Gervis is very clear about what needs to happen to normalise psychology in football: 'They need to be just part of the furniture, always around, at the side of the pitch, having a chat. I was at QPR for five years and at the end of it, the psychology programme was so embedded into all of the work of the academy that if anybody's talking to me, it's no different than talking to a coach or a physio.

I'm just part of the team. I have different observations and a different perspective on things because my eye's trained differently and my skill set is different, but it all works together. We should be integrated. I'm in kit. I'm just there, I'm not someone different. I don't come in in a suit and sit in my office.'

Coventry City, to their credit, are a club that have long been ahead of the curve on mental health and sports psychology. They had a sports psychologist as far back as the early 1990s when such roles were virtually non-existent in football. As I sit and chat with Maxime Biamou in his Coventry flat, he describes a framework which helped him through his time on the sidelines. The players have a mandatory meeting with the club's sports psychologist every six weeks, which looks to break down the idea that you only see a psychologist when you have a problem, a misconception Biamou admits to having previously been under. If you have nothing to say, that's fine, and you can simply chat, but many players like Biamou go in expecting little and come out with something of a changed mindset.

During his long spell on the sidelines, Biamou used the time to hone his mental attributes, working with the club's sports psychologist as well as putting significant effort into studying the game. Deep in thought, he casts his mind back to his first season at the club when goals were initially hard to come by. As a striker, the pressure was mounting, with many fans convinced he was not at the level to step up from non-league. Biamou recalls one particularly bad miss, and admits his problem was negative thoughts about the future, specifically what might happen if he kept missing chances. This line of thinking caused him to do exactly that. Speaking to a psychologist has helped him learn to bring his mind to the present, and his goalscoring form has followed naturally. Coupled with some acts of self-learning, including reading the famous self-help book *The Secret* by Rhonda Byrne, Biamou has left the toughest period of his career behind him.

It's refreshing to hear how positively he speaks of a period that would be disastrous for many players. It works for him too – we speak in February 2020, just weeks before COVID-19 shuts down English football, but Coventry City are flying high at the top of the table and are awarded the title on points per game. Having had the ambition before just to play in League One, Biamou has now won it.

That's not to say the nine months out were easy for Biamou, far from it. Injury can affect players in a number of ways, from a natural decrease in levels of endorphins associated with exercise to a fear of reinjury upon returning to playing. Some players suffer from boredom, which can lead to issues with drinking and gambling, whilst another commonly reported factor is the loss of identity.

In Biamou's case, though, the most problematic part of his time on the sidelines was loneliness. Times have progressed since the days of Brian Clough, who famously didn't want injured players he deemed worthless around the side, but players are still often cut off from their team-mates and left to their own devices in their rehab. With his family still hundreds of miles away in France, the situation was even more acute for Biamou.

'I think the hardest thing for me is because I'm French and all my family are in France. I used to be alone, so when I said that to my mum, my mum came to stay with me for probably a week. You feel alone because you're away from the other players. For example, I used to be at the gym to do my job and the other players are just outside, so I used to be alone with the physio. When it's time for lunch, they came, but you don't really see the team normally before every training session. Before training we have a meeting with the manager, but you don't see the manager and don't have the meeting, so you feel a little bit alone. It's probably harder when you come from abroad because you haven't got family or friends.

'Every two months I had a week off to see my family, with two weeks at Christmas. It is very important to have a break sometimes, because if you do exactly the same thing every day, the cardiovascular sessions and upper body sessions, physically it is hard and mentally it is very hard.'

Going on to be heavily involved as Coventry City took on the Championship, Biamou recovered to be a senior member of the squad. His experiences in football are invaluable, and his comeback twice from an ACL injury is something he can share. It's just as well there was somebody at the club to lean on given the abnormally high number of ACL injuries that Coventry had seen after Biamou joined. Along with the Frenchman's ACL tear, there were similar injuries to Daniel Bartlett, Tony Andreu, Reise Allassani, Wesley Jobello and Jodi Jones on three different occasions. It is the unfortunate case of Jones that Biamou chooses to dwell on.

The winger is still young and universally popular amongst Sky Blues fans, owing not only to his talent on the pitch but also his regular work in the community off it. Whilst in rehab for his latest injury, Jones devoted his energies to fundraising for and supporting Teigan Buckley, a nine-year-old girl who was diagnosed with a rare form of brain tumour, Diffuse Pontine Glioma. Every step she took, Jones was there to support her, even having the shape of a scar from her surgery incorporated into his own haircut. Tragically, Teigan passed away in December 2020, but Jones has committed to preserving her legacy, doing a 20km bike ride every day for a month in order to raise money for research into her condition. The ability of the 23-year-old to put things into perspective is as heart-warming as the story itself is heartbreaking.

* * *

Whilst Biamou has been able to recover from his injuries and return to his best, not everyone is so fortunate. Like Biamou, David Busst was plucked from non-league football to sign for Coventry City well into his 20s. However, when he signed from Moor Green in 1992, the Sky Blues were flying high in the Premier League, thrusting Busst into the peak of English football. Making his Premier League debut against Norwich City in January 1993, the defender played 50 Premier League games for Coventry before disaster struck inside the first two minutes of one of the glamour fixtures: Manchester United away at Old Trafford.

A corner was flicked on by Noel Whelan, falling kindly at the far post for Busst, who had got ahead of his marker, to attack. Denis Irwin, on the post, lunged in to block the shot. From the other side, Brian McClair did much the same thing. The result was two forces in completely opposite directions acting on Busst's right leg. The leg had nowhere to go. What happened as a result is widely considered the worst injury in Premier League history, and it took nine minutes to clear the blood from the pitch before the game could restart as Peter Schmeichel went off to be sick.

Busst's injury nightmare was only just beginning. With a compound fracture of the tibia and fibula the diagnosis, Busst needed ten operations in the first 12 days after the injury, but the real issues came when he contracted MRSA whilst in hospital. At the worst point, there was a risk the Coventry man might have had to have his leg amputated from the knee down. Thankfully, it never quite got that bad, though the signs of the damage to Busst's leg are still clearly visible today – he describes it as a 'shark bite'. Nowadays, Busst is synonymous with serious injury in football, but he has no regrets despite the abrupt way his career ended:

'I wouldn't change a thing. If I could go back and not break my leg, I wouldn't. That happened for a reason. I could have broken my leg playing against Bury Reserves at Gigg Lane, but I happened to do it at Old Trafford, which gave me obviously a lot of press and was in people's minds. I had the injury when I was 28. I knew that I would be finishing professional football soon; if I could get maybe to 30 and then probably go back to non-league for five years that would have been great, so I'd probably be finishing my playing career around 35 anyway.

'With me, I always say shit happens in life. You just get on with it and make the positives out of it … Learn from the past and try and impact the future.'

As Busst underwent operation after operation, his priorities were forced to change. Searching for answers in hospital in Manchester, he was eventually told he had been left with a dropped foot due to the damage the MRSA infection had caused to his tendons. This was particularly bad news – if you can't pull your toes up you will struggle to walk, never mind kick a football again. At this point, Busst knew his career was over. It's 25 years on now, but Busst still recalls in some detail the process of learning to walk again and setting small goals on the way to recovery. His biggest motivation was the desire to be able to play football with his kids one day. Thoughts of professional football, and his career in the sport, were out the window.

Bit by bit, step by step, Busst achieved each of his goals. Like Maxime Biamou, he strikes me as an almost impossibly positive person, talking about having to learn how to walk again with the casual air of someone discussing learning a language, or taking up a musical instrument. When I ask him if there was a particular low point, he thinks about it more than when he discusses the positives he's found.

'There were low points. As positive as you want to be and seek the best in everything, there were a couple of days where I was fed up, I didn't want to go to Manchester again, it's that daily routine – the novelty wears off if you know what I mean. And then you're relying on people to put themselves out there. My family and friends were all doing it, which was an absolutely great support mechanism for me, and that's probably what got me through it … Just a couple of times you thought, "oh God, when's this going to end, when am I going to get back to some sort of normality?" Obviously, with me being the main breadwinner in the family, I couldn't show those emotions to my family. I had to be that strong person who had to say everything's going to be OK, so there was responsibility on me to make sure that I wasn't looking backwards.

'Stuff's happened before. You can't do anything about it, no point dwelling on it, so for me it was like, what's my next step? I need to learn how to walk again properly – right, that's the goal. When I've done that, can I do running? Can I do coaching? Can I combine the two? It's all those questions I would be asking myself. That is what I needed to do to get back into and make the best of my opportunity outside of football.'

The point about not being able to show his emotions is interesting, and I prompt Busst further on it. His father was always available to discuss his emotions, he feels, as only he fully understood what he was going through. Twenty-five years ago, venting your emotions was still typically seen as a sign of weakness, not one you wanted to reveal in front of the family you were providing for. Nowadays, Busst feels, this stigma has been largely removed as conversation about mental health has become more common. Perhaps it's a sign of how far society has progressed on the subject of mental health in a relatively short period of time, but there's still a long way to go.

Back in 1996, when Busst suffered his injury, the loss of identity that comes with being a footballer was not the only thing a player retiring from the game had to worry about. Wages, though decent, were nowhere near the levels they are at today, and players suddenly finding themselves out of action were prone to financial worries. Being out of contract at the end of the season, which was only four games away with his club fighting relegation, there was a danger Busst could have suddenly found himself without the means to bring in any money at all – at a time when his wife was pregnant with his second child. Luckily, both Coventry City and Manchester United came together to help him out, as a benefit match was organised at a sold-out Highfield Road on 16 May 1997. A star-studded game saw Paul Gascoigne give Coventry the lead before Eric Cantona, who announced his shock retirement two days later, scored twice to turn the game around. The final say, though, went to Busst, who tucked away a stoppage time penalty to make it 2-2. The money from the game supported Busst for around three years whilst he pursued a career in football coaching. Meanwhile, Coventry City extended his contract for another year to provide him with the financial support he needed.

Had Busst not had this support, he might still have been in a better position than many of his fellow professionals, as he'd had a well-paid job in insurance when he was a semi-professional at Moor Green in the Southern League and the option to return to this industry was always available, but Busst describes it as a 'worst-case scenario'. Having lost out on some of his best playing days through injury, he wanted to remain in football.

'I'd enjoyed the atmosphere being involved full time in football, and I just looked for ways in which I could get back into doing that. Luckily, I had good advice, the PFA helped me as well. I basically had two years of operations. In the second year I started doing my coaching badges and things like that, and then in 1997 an opportunity came to work in Coventry City's community scheme, which is what I'm doing now, and I worked with the academy as well. I ran a team in that and then went on to manage in non-league as well, so I was six or seven days a week involved in football for quite a long period. You can never replace the buzz of playing football whether it's professional, non-league, grassroots, whatever, but I've gone back to playing open-age football. It's all for the fun, mates and things like that, so it's that social side of sport which is more important to me. I even took up golf!

'What I missed the most was going into training and being around the players, and that changed from the day I got injured and was told I wasn't going to play again. That's probably why I kept going with my coaching … and managing and all the other stuff that I've done, like, with communities. It's a replacement for what I enjoyed so much before. I'm fortunate enough to still be in it.'

That opportunity with Coventry's community scheme in 1997 proved to be the golden ticket for Busst, and he still works in the role today. Despite spells coaching and managing in non-league football, where he began his career, it's always been that role that's stuck. As he passionately discusses the scheme's achievements over the last 20 years or so, it's clear to see why. Initially a small operation, Sky Blues in the Community (SBITC) became a registered charity in 2008 and has gone from strength to strength.

Today, they work in four main areas: football, health, inclusion and education. Mental health is embedded into the health side of the programme, and Busst explains that football is an excellent way of opening doors and starting conversations. Lottery funding has just been received for a five-year programme aimed at tackling mental health in males aged 18-plus. With most supporters at games fitting this profile, the fact the programme is run by the football club acts as a carrot for getting people involved. Prior to this specific mental-health-targeted programme, the diet and nutrition schemes often worked in the same way, with part of the sessions simply involving a chat. If ever any help was needed by anyone, the signposting opportunities were there. Ever looking to find the positives from his injury back in 1996, Busst talks of being able to use his own story as a springboard to help others.

'I've done presentations and I've introduced myself and said, "I'm Dave Busst. You'll probably know my right leg better than you know me." It's that sort of thing. It's a great icebreaker between me and a group that I might not have interacted with before.

'Usually, folks will come along, do physical activity, play football and then we'll have a chat about things. They might talk to somebody from the football club around mental health, so, me talking about my experience and how I've had to adapt as a person can be a big help. If I didn't adapt, I wouldn't be doing this job anymore, because it's evolved into a bigger part of communities and social action, and I've had to move with it. And that's important as well.'

The job was a big boost to Busst's mental health back when he first took it, and to this day he continues to give back to the community in a city where he is still universally loved.

* * *

Of all the factors that may play a part in a player's mental health whilst injured, a global pandemic is certainly a new one. Being such a recent phenomenon, there are limited studies into the effects it's had on players, and there are a number of wide-ranging theories. Of course, it varies from case to case – an injured player out of contract at the end of the season was likely to be significantly more concerned than somebody who had just signed a long-term deal. However, Dr Misia Gervis thinks that, in many ways, lockdown might have actually been a relatively good time to be on the sidelines.

'A lot of the challenges for players when they're injured involve being at the club and watching everyone go past them, and feeling fearful that everyone's getting better while they're stuck. But in lockdown, everybody is stuck. So actually some of those feelings do not show up. When you're not pressurised to get back too soon, because no one's playing, you can literally just do your rehab and not worry about it, because there's no team that's being picked on Saturday. Nobody gets left behind.'

Aoife Mannion, of Manchester City and England, was one of the players who found themselves in this situation. The defender was relatively new at City when she felt a sharp pain in her leg after a tackle in a Champions League fixture against Atlético Madrid. Remarkably, she managed to play out the final few minutes of the match before discovering afterwards she had damaged her anterior cruciate ligament. The news was revealed to her in stages, and she specifically recalls the club doctor asking her where she was at the time before delivering the final diagnosis. It was an injury that would rule Mannion out for the rest of the season, just as she had gotten her feet under the table at her new club.

Initially, the swelling around the knee was so bad that the necessary surgery was delayed by nearly two months. Delaying the recovery process might have been a cause of significant frustration for Mannion but instead she smiles and says she feels lucky. After all, if the same injury had occurred a couple of months later, she would have been waiting for surgery as the UK went into lockdown, but she had her operation in December 2019, before the pandemic began and all elective surgeries were put on hold.

Mannion started her post-op rehab with the expert support that comes with playing at a club like Manchester City. The exercises in the very early stages were simple but monotonous – starting with bending and straightening the knee again and developing gradually from there, including the process of essentially learning to walk again. In early March, as coronavirus started to sweep through Europe, Mannion was working on her rehab in the hydro pool at Manchester City's training ground. The opportunity to progress on to the anti-gravity treadmill never came, as the country shut down weeks later.

All of a sudden, Mannion went from having some of the best medical support in football to relying on Zoom and FaceTime for advice. Understandably, she describes the comedown from the training ground to 'sketchy Wi-Fi in the garden' as a tough time, though again references how grateful she is for what her club were able to do for her. Manchester City sent out watt bikes and a comprehensive gym kit to every player, with the plethora of expert staff members always just a call away if any advice was needed.

Extra reassurance over her future was in place due to the fact that her contract, signed the previous summer, was a two-year one. Despite these perks, Mannion readily admits the shift into lockdown was the toughest period on her journey to recovery, describing rehab as a 'war of attrition'. Having moved back to her family home in Birmingham, social isolation wasn't too much of an issue for Mannion, but away from the training ground and exceptional support services that come with it, frustrations started creeping in.

'What really shocked me was that I could put the same intent and focus and attention to detail in it throughout the rehab process but get very different outcomes, and perhaps not be in control of that all the time. I refer to the knee almost as its own entity: sometimes it's behaving and sometimes it's not. If anything, my mindset has kind of shifted towards more of an acceptance of what the state of things are, whereas pre-injury, if you can imagine, I was a player who played at Birmingham who saw their progression getting better, getting more confident, becoming better as a player then moving to City and having the same expectations. It's quite a detachment from life really. That's just not how things work and if there's one thing that the injury has highlighted to me, it is just that life gets in the way, and life happens.'

Over lockdown, as everyone heightened their efforts to stay in touch online, Mannion continued to document the process of her recovery on her Instagram account. A series of photos and videos paint a light-hearted picture of her progress. Looking back on the period where she was most open on social media, Mannion says she almost went too far and shared too much, shining a spotlight into her life more than the vast majority of elite footballers would. However, some of the benefits that brought helped motivate her through the period.

'The only way I could justify it is just to say, if you were inside my head, and you felt how uplifting lovely messages were, it seemed quite natural at the time. I think the main benefit was it just made me feel closer to people because people would interact, and the great thing about being injured is that people have sympathy, so they want to say nice things. It's a shame that's not the case in general day-to-day life really ... There's no bearing from what they say on what you're going to do day to day; that's for the experts and the coaches. But it's just really uplifting. I was surprised at how much energy that gave me.'

When I ask Mannion if she would advise other players to do the same, she is wary of giving a definitive answer. Each player, and each circumstance, is different and it really depends how you feel. Crucially, though, the Solihull-born defender is quick to point out that there is a huge amount of shared experience in each long-term injury suffered by anyone – and so reaching out and learning from the experiences of others is key. Every low point, and indeed every high point, is something that many others can empathise with. When it all comes down to it, you are not alone.

And what of Dr Gervis's theory on the impact of lockdown on an injured player's psychology? Interestingly, what Mannion says seems to support the idea. We talk over Zoom in December 2020, as the country flits endlessly in and out of new restrictions. The one relative constant, though, is the football season, which has been played behind closed doors under the 'elite' classification. The Barclays FA Women's Super League (WSL) kicked off on 5 September, and progressed steadily despite various regional lockdowns. Having been able to work on her recovery with no particular timeline back in the summer, Mannion then had to deal with the frustration of watching games take place without her.

'I think with the start of lockdown, I knew everyone was going through that and so there was a comfort that came from that. I never felt lonely during that time, whereas when I first came back to the training ground it was different. I'd had an idea from the beginning of my injury that I'd be wiped out for the season, but I'd probably be back for the next season. When I came back to the training ground and I became aware … the rehab was going to stretch on for longer than that, there was a real transition period again, getting on board with what reality was.

'Of all of the time of the rehab, whether it was waiting for surgery, just after surgery, or going into lockdown, there was probably a portion of two months there that were much harder for me to process than all of the others put together. My rehab has been just a little bit longer through niggles and aches and pains that have arisen, and so I hope that some of that grittiness will really serve me when I go back onto the pitch and compete.'

Eventually, 498 days since that fateful game against Atlético Madrid, Mannion returned to the field to play the last 20 minutes of a WSL game against her former club Birmingham City. She left Manchester City at the end of the 2020/21 season but before long had signed up with city rivals Manchester United, a relatively new club on the women's football scene having only been founded in 2018, but a side very much pushing towards the top of the table and Champions League football.

It was all looking up for Mannion, but disaster struck again in February 2022 as she suffered another ACL injury. Sadly, it's something of an occupational hazard for female footballers, with research showing they are around four to six times more likely to suffer one than their male counterparts. Similar to Biamou, Mannion has admitted to finding the rehab for this second time tougher than the first, largely because she knows there isn't a promise that everything will go smoothly forever after reaching the end of it. Despite this, she has built up her mental toughness during these experiences and has another supportive club behind her in Manchester United, particularly having previously played for manager Marc Skinner at Birmingham. Less than a year later, Mannion duly made her second return from football's nightmare injury, playing 45 minutes in a friendly against Maltese champions Birkirkara in January 2023. The scoreline, a resounding 10-0 victory, was a mere afterthought for Skinner and United. Deep in a thrilling title race in the WSL, they knew they could now count on one of England's best defenders for the second half of a season that could come down to the wire.

* * *

The one thing Biamou, Busst and Mannion had in common at the time of their injuries was that they were all playing for top-level professional clubs. Coventry City and Manchester City were able to support their players with excellent medical and psychological support as well as the financial security provided by professional contracts. The Premier League and WSL are beamed out to millions all around the world every weekend, but the numbers of players at this level are minute compared to those who play non-league football. When serious injury occurs at this level, players can be left a lot more vulnerable in a number of ways.

Francis Duku is something of a legend in the semi-professional game, having played for 11 clubs over a career spanning more than 15 years. If anyone could claim to have seen it all, it would be him. Having finally retired from playing in 2012, Duku now runs a company called Our Game, which looks to provide a support service for non-league players in the many areas their clubs themselves cannot afford to cover. Now into its 12th year of existence, Our Game is developing the services it provides year on year. Duku's passion for his work is evident, as we talk for hours over Zoom in November 2020.

The inspiration for setting up the business stems from Duku's own experiences in the game. Back in 2000, relatively early in his career, he was still hoping to turn professional with a move to the Football League. Playing for Conference side Gravesend and Northfleet, he suffered an injury in a pre-season trip to Weymouth. The diagnosis made on the day was that he had suffered a sprain – not the worst injury in the world – and Duku was advised he would be back within weeks, so he was confident enough to join his team-mates on a night out that evening. The next day, with the pain getting worse, Duku travelled back to

London with the team, and then with the pain unbearable and his ankle severely swollen the day after, he took himself to A&E. It was only then he discovered he had actually suffered a break and would require an operation.

The operation wasn't the top-of-the-range procedure a Premier League club might be able to afford, and the pins inserted into Duku's leg caused scar tissue that affected his movement. Despite having access to private medical insurance through his job outside of football, the damage was already done, and although the broken leg healed, the effects of the operation left him with reduced mobility in his left ankle for the rest of his career. The dream of a professional career was over before it had really begun. The suffering that resulted from the whole episode is something Duku doesn't want anyone else to go through.

'The shock of being told it was a break rather than a sprain hit me hard, because I had a belief I was going to get back into the pro game that year. So, at first it floored me, but then I've got a kind of practical attitude to a lot of things; I just thought, well, I've got to get back. However, the recovery took so long that it became really, really draining. I remember particularly one game against Farnborough where quite a few of my friends played, and the shock on their faces when they saw me hobbling round the pitch when I was doing some training before the game. I thought I was running, but they told me after that it looked really bad the way I was hobbling. Again, that was a huge setback, but these things I had to deal with by myself, because the club didn't have anything in place.

'I looked at it and thought, there has to be a better way for these guys, for non-league players. They didn't all have the contacts I did, and they definitely didn't have the funding I had with the private medical insurance, which picked up a four-figure bill, so I just tried to build a system to give people that access as well.'

Perhaps the most important service offered by Our Game is income protection for players. At non-league level, many players are paid only when they play, meaning earnings from football fall to zero when they're out injured. Things can easily get even worse for those who earn their money outside of football in jobs where they are self-employed or work on zero-hours contracts, as serious injury can prevent them working. Without measures in place, their income can drop to nothing at all.

In 2013, the FA made it mandatory for clubs to take out insurance for their players. However, the lowest level of coverage provides just £30 a week in temporary disability benefits in the event of injury. Many clubs, already short of money, opt for this minimum-level cover to save as many pennies as they can, with players commonly unaware of the implications until it is too late. Financial horror stories are all too common.

One of Our Game's clients is Michael Charles, who injured his ACL whilst playing in the seventh tier of English football for Met Police back in 2014. The damage was so severe that he couldn't work in his warehouse job either, meaning there was no money coming in. If it hadn't been for Our Game, Charles and his young family would have lost their home as debts racked up.

'Initially, I didn't know what I signed up for with Our Game. I knew it was insurance, but I didn't know what aspects. As soon as the injury happened, Francis [Duku] took a lot of time out with me and explained what I would get. It was three months' pay for my work and the last three months at Met Police, so there was about two grand a month I was taking home from the insurance.'

Charles had heard tales of some insurances only paying out £78 per week, so had been very worried initially.

'I was living with my missus and had responsibilities for bills, so then when Francis explained everything that I was getting, I couldn't believe it – the weight off my shoulders then was just immense. It didn't bring me up to the happiest I've ever been, but it did help with my mental thinking in the future, and it also helped me claim some tax back as well. Non-league footballers travel a lot, you buy your own boots and shin pads and that sort of stuff, so I got money back from that as well. Financially, afterwards, I was very secure.'

Charles never did make it back to that level of football, the injury at the age of 27 simply too damaging, but his finances didn't suffer as a result. Now, with two children and working in recruitment, he is always keen to promote the work that Our Game do, aware of just how much the financial protection helped his mental health. In fact, Charles is a mental health advocate on a number of levels, with a pinned tweet on his Twitter account inviting anyone who feels the need to talk to get in touch with him. Mental health is an area in which he's had plenty of experience, gradually educating himself on the subject as he has grown older and wiser.

'When I was growing up, we didn't have loads of money and all that sort of stuff and things happened. Family members suffered with mental health often. I didn't know it was mental health at the time. I thought you [had to] just get out and get on with it. As people would say, man up and move on. It definitely affected my family and it's affected families that are close to me as well, so I'm an advocate of it.

'I was 27 at the time of the injury, being told my career was over by a surgeon and all you know in life is football at the weekends: it was heartbreaking. I remember coming back from the hospital and my grandad picked me up, and I forgot completely it was his birthday and I was in tears in the car, just being told that I can't play football again. It really, really did affect me and I didn't know what to do. It was heartbreaking, really, really heartbreaking. You know, my specialist subject on *Mastermind* would have been non-league football. It's all I knew. And something that I'd loved for ten years … [then] you get suddenly told it's all over.

'I still think I suffered with real mental health problems for years after because you don't realise how much that Saturday, that Tuesday, that Thursday of training, how much that takes your mind off everything. I don't think you ever fully recover from it.'

Football has not always had a fantastic relationship with mental health, but as society develops to become more aware of it, football has followed. Duku and Charles both admit that throughout the majority of their careers, the line between banter and bullying in the dressing room was blurred at best. Seeking psychological support after injury would be seen as a sign of weakness. The conclusion would be that you weren't ready to return to action, wouldn't be at the same level as before, and this would make you a liability. Thankfully, things have come on in leaps and bounds recently, and the services Our Game offer have progressed to reflect that.

Members now have access to a 24/7 counselling line, and can even access six face-to-face sessions a year for free on top of this. As the stigma over mental health in football has been gradually removed, Duku has seen more and more players take up this offer. Responding to this trend, Duku has developed an app as a first-port-of-call option for players to request support or guidance related to their mental health. With limited budgets at non-league level, this is likely to be the only easily accessible psychological support available to players. As Duku puts it, if a club has a spare bit of money and has the choice between bringing in a counsellor or a centre-forward, they will always go for the centre-forward.

'Regardless of the level, players will tell you that when you're injured, you're forgotten. Because you're not in the squad, you're not travelling on match days, you're not in the Thursday or Friday night pattern of play sessions. There are other things too: if you're a 19-year-old who's come through the system and you're playing for your club and all of a sudden you get injured and all your dreams are taken away from you, it's going to have an impact, I don't care who you are.

'I've found that increasingly over recent times, especially since we've announced we've got this counselling line available. I've had more players ring me up to ask how it works and they've touched on their situation. Now, because mental health awareness is so much better, people are paying attention. There has previously been a line of thinking, sometimes, that people are making a lot of things that are not too serious, but you're not the one who can decide that. You've got to let the individual speak or give them the room to be able to speak, rather than shutting people down, because you don't know the impact.'

Duku hopes that as both mental health awareness and financial education grow, his business will follow suit, and there will be fewer 'bucket collection' stories from when players suffer injury. With non-league players not covered by the PFA in any way unless they have been in the professional game at some point, the suggestion that Our Game might partner with authorities such as leagues or the FA has been mooted, but is not currently on the cards. Instead, Duku is relying on word of mouth and positive reviews to boost Our Game's expansion. He still speaks with a tone of exasperation about the number of players who don't sign up at the start of the season under the mantra of 'we don't get injured', only to come to him and beg for help when inevitably something does go wrong. With the majority of non-league players in the 18–30 age bracket, it's often a case of 'young and foolish'. Having once been in their shoes, Duku is desperate to educate these younger players before it is too late.

Michael Charles may have lost his career when he suffered his ACL injury, but thanks to Our Game he managed to keep the rest of his life on track. He hasn't lost his love for the game either, playing regularly on a Sunday morning with his close mates:

'All you can do is try to score on a Sunday and celebrate in the same way.'

Chapter 4

Retirement

ON 13 September 2015, Marcus Bent hit his low. Heavily paranoid as a result of the cocaine he was taking to 'self-medicate', Bent called the police due to the mistaken belief that there were intruders in his house. When the police arrived at his Surrey home, he answered the door wielding two large knives, which he'd picked up to defend himself against the perceived intruders. Understandably, the officers standing just out of Bent's reach were terrified, and tasered him before arresting him and putting him in a cell overnight. Initially, Bent faced a charge of attempted murder.

Eventually, the situation became clearer and the charge was dropped to affray, with Bent avoiding a custodial sentence. Looking back, the former striker is philosophical, and admits that although he isn't proud of the episode, it helped him get his life back on track. Wading upstream with his mental health during his playing days, Bent was swept away by retirement, losing the anchor of stability that football's routine brought. To fully understand his story, though, you have to start with his playing days.

The football world in 1995, when Bent started his career as a teenager at Brentford, was a very different place to now. Mental health was not given even the slightest consideration, and the suggestion that managers shouldn't criticise players in certain ways would have been laughed at. It was very much every man for himself, and Bent admits he would have given short shrift to the suggestion that his mental health was affected by his career or lifestyle. Bent played for eight Premier League clubs – a record number. Though often described as a 'journeyman', circumstances often conspired against him to keep the regular churn of clubs up. Crystal Palace, Bent's first Premier League club, entered administration whilst he was there, and the manager who then brought him into Port Vale, John Rudge, was sacked not long after the move was completed. Played out of position by the new boss, Bent lasted less than a year at Vale Park before moving on to Sheffield United.

Enduring such a turbulent time as a young player trying to prove yourself would generally be recognised as having some psychological impact these days, but back in the late 1990s, Bent was left on his own.

'I didn't really know what mental health was. I don't think a lot of people did. I think they just thought it was something people complained about and didn't really understand it. You had various players within football trying to take their lives, or drinking, or taking drugs, but nobody really had a plan or a touch on what to do or how to do it. You just got told to "man the fuck up and get on with it". It's hard when you're put into this bubble being a sportsman, being a celebrity, and not being able to reach out to anyone without the public pointing and staring and knowing your business.

'Football can be a bit of a dark world in a sense. You're always in hotels travelling, but then you can't really complain because a lot of people say, "Well, you're on a lot of money, you've got the best life in the world." You end up suppressing it. You kind of just put it to the back of your mind and get on with it. You're scrutinised 24/7, every weekend. You start doubting yourself, then you start thinking what other people are saying is true. I suppressed that, put it to the side, got on with it and moved forward. Eventually, I'd look to come through and prove them wrong. It was always about proving them wrong, when really the focus should be proving yourself right, looking after yourself as number one.

'Towards the back end of my career, it got to the point where I lost the love for football because of the criticism I received, as well as my injuries. But people didn't see that, they just expect you to perform, because you're paid to perform and you're on a lot of money. But at the end of the day, I'm only human.'

Despite fighting mental health battles he didn't even know he was fighting, Bent had a successful career. Prolific spells at Sheffield United and Ipswich led to a fourth-place finish with David Moyes's Everton in 2005. As with many footballers, though, injuries started to take their toll as Bent moved towards his 30s, and he eventually called it a day in April 2012 after a short spell with Indonesian side Mitra Kukar. Bent had earned well throughout his career, and consequently planned to live a life of luxury after hanging up his boots. Holiday after holiday was booked, but they didn't carry the sense of fulfilment that playing football often did. As seems to be fairly common amongst retired footballers, Bent began to lose his sense of purpose.

Academic research on the field of retirement from professional football is mixed. Dr Vincent Gouttebarge of FIFPRO, the worldwide representative organisation of professional footballers, led a study in 2016 that found the prevalence of anxiety and depression in retired professional footballers was far higher than in the general population. This school of thought suggests many former players effectively go through a form of bereavement for their career, which they might arbitrarily assume to be the peak of their lives. XPRO, a charity set up to help former professional footballers, suggests that two in five Premier League players will face bankruptcy within five years, whilst a third of footballers will be divorced within just a year of retirement, factors which can only drive up the prevalence of mental health problems.

The evidence is far from conclusive, though. Dr Gwen Fernandes of the University of Bristol led a study in 2015 that showed very different results. Looking predominantly at players who had retired more than 20 years ago, the study showed no difference in the prevalence of depressive symptoms in retired footballers compared to a general population control group.

'There's a really strong narrative in the literature that constantly talks about footballers being disadvantaged when it comes to mental health outcomes, but when you try and unpick the evidence behind that, I found that it was quite lacking,' she says. 'In general, if you've got a very strong opinion being advocated, like a buzzword or catchphrase, it catches on and really sticks because enough people have said it. There's a lot of messages in the media where if you look at the science or evidence behind it, it might not always stack up. I don't think you can just say, "He's a footballer, he's more likely to be depressed." I think the picture's probably more nuanced than that, and it really depends on the individual.'

When discussing the results of her study, though, Dr Fernandes makes some important points. Whilst her research looks at individuals who have been long retired, the FIFPRO study considers former players who are on average 25 years younger. What the two studies between them might be capturing is a time profile, in which the initial shock of retirement poses some issues for the players, before an adjustment of sorts occurs over time. She speculates as to whether the results of the study repeated for players in the Premier League era would be the same – many of the players in Dr Fernandes's study had other jobs whilst they played football and simply moved full-time into these upon retirement. The money in the game nowadays may well make that adjustment harder, but we don't know for sure until that research is carried out. There's always more to learn.

At any rate, Dr Fernandes doesn't feel that the narrative built by today's media is necessarily a bad thing. She points to ongoing research around neuro-degenerative disease and dementia caused by heading a football, which began as just a narrative itself before being looked into in more detail. A narrative can bring about important conversation, which results in further research and overall progress being made. After all, one former player left to suffer alone with their mental health is one too many.

The importance of mental health awareness is a concept that repeatedly comes up as I talk with Marcus Bent. He mentions several times that he didn't know what mental health was, and therefore was not really aware when things were not quite right. It was this lack of knowledge, and the desire to suppress rather than confront his feelings, that led him further down the path of mental health struggles after his retirement.

'The thoughts that I suppressed and didn't really think about, you think about more when you retire. It can get you down, it did get me down, hence why I tried to suppress or numb the thoughts and disappointment. I questioned myself. Should I have retired so early, should I have done this, should I have done that? I remember being on the bus sometimes during my playing days and other players were crying about their performances. I wasn't really a crier; I was more likely to just put my head down and zone out. I didn't really deal with it or process it; I just got on with it and moved forward. Maybe that was why I hit the floor so hard when I retired.

'Retiring in any job, any walk of life is hard, especially if you've not got anything to do. Retiring at the age of 60 or 70, I think you've lived your life in a sense. You can go and do the gardening and spend time with your wife, go on walks and dog walking. But I think at the age of 35, you've still got a lot of living to do. It's hard to know what to go into when all you know is football, when you've played it from the young age of nine up until 33, and that's all you've known.'

In an attempt to fill the growing void in his life, Bent turned to cocaine. He had never taken it before, indeed looking down on those who did during his career, but figured he had nothing to lose when offered the drug round a friend's house. He describes it as numbing, something to take the edge off feeling alone after retirement. Before long, things spiralled, from using the drug weekly, to daily, to almost hourly. Bent's physical health suffered as he went days without eating, only taking the occasional day off to give his body some respite before going straight back into usage again. This soon culminated in his arrest in September 2015. Bent knows he was fairly fortunate with his sentence, a suspended 12-month prison sentence, a two-month curfew and 200 hours of compulsory unpaid work, and has used the warning as a springboard to turn his life around. It hasn't always been easy, and Bent did relapse, but when we talk in 2021 he has been two years clean. As well as the continued support of his family, Bent cites his weekly meetings with Sporting Chance as key in keeping him on track.

'I found myself hibernating, just away from anyone, not answering my phone, not communicating with anyone. My weight went down, I looked ill, but I only knew I looked ill when I went into rehab. When I was arrested was the scariest moment in my life. That was rock bottom; that really hit me. Even just going to court and thinking about what they were going to say to me, even it going to the press, friends, my family knowing about it; I was at rock bottom at the time and having this go over my head was the worst thing that could ever happen to me. But it made me stronger and pushed me into being clean, so in a sense it was a good thing. I wouldn't wish it upon anyone, but it helped me to get to where I am now. I'm not a bad person;

I was just going through something that a lot of people go through.

'With Sporting Chance … being in there … I found myself. I found I could feel again, I could find my thoughts easier, whilst being in the real world my head was just ticking, ticking, ticking.'

A few months after initially coming out of the rehab programme with Sporting Chance, Bent fell off course and was caught in possession of cocaine at Chessington World of Adventures in 2016. Rather than this being the trigger for another slide into more constant drug usage, Bent instead made his relationship with Sporting Chance closer, which gave him the tools he needed to beat his addiction once and for all. This is highlighted when our conversation is briefly interrupted by a phone call from a Sporting Chance counsellor and close friend of Bent's, ringing to check up on him as he does from time to time. Regular Monday meetings also help keep Bent on track.

There was another immediate effect of the aftermath of his low point that helped Bent's mental health over the next couple of years. His compulsory unpaid work put him in a charity shop in the Surrey town of Epsom, something which Bent initially dreaded. He readily admits his ego initially meant he feared being recognised, but he soon got over this to actually really enjoy the role. He describes it as good therapy, and says that being given a routine for the first time in years was of huge importance. Indeed, Bent loved it so much that once his 200 hours of compulsory unpaid work were up, he volunteered to go back in his own time. He still pops in to say hello from time to time.

Life improved from the dark days of 2015, but Bent faced a big test in January 2019 when he faced bankruptcy. He was a victim of the infamous 'film scheme', which has caught out a number of footballers over the years. The scheme worked by offering tax relief on money invested in films around the early 2000s, with payments on tax delayed for around 15 years. However, HMRC has since deemed the schemes were set up specifically to avoid tax and has looked to claim the money back. Bent admits he has never been academic and, along with the other footballers caught out, didn't understand the ins and outs of how the scheme worked. He was left financially high and dry, unable to pay the money back, and is still dealing with the implications of his bankruptcy.

Given his previous troubles, you might say Bent is coping with the situation very well, but this doesn't mean it's without its struggles.

'Even if I did have the assets I had in my career still, they would have taken it all by now anyway. I look at it in a sense where I've just got to start again and focus on the future, and move forward … It really gets to the bones, it gets to your soul, it affects you at times, your mental health. But I have responsibilities … and stuff that I need to get on with. So I can't keep pondering over it. What will be, will be.'

Money, clearly, is a big issue in football these days, and it's hard to quantify the impact it can have later down the line on the mental health of retired players. Dr Fernandes theorises that it might improve these mental health outcomes, as more players can retire and be comfortable for the rest of their lives, but Bent believes being given huge amounts of money at a young age can ultimately be damaging. He feels he lacked the wisdom to spend and save it appropriately, but perhaps more importantly lacked the support to guide him in this area. If you suddenly gave your average teenager virtually unlimited money and status, with all the temptations around, it would seem unreasonable to expect them to act perfectly sensibly with it at all times. If that money is going to be there, some degree of advice and support needs to be there with it.

As we discuss potential reform, I suggest the idea of locking up a certain proportion of a player's wages in a savings account which they can then access when they turn a certain age, perhaps 23. Bent agrees that whilst he might not have liked it as an up-and-coming young star at the time, he would have been grateful for it now.

Dr Fernandes has other interesting suggestions for the world of football to consider when looking to prioritise the mental health of former players after retirement. She points to the importance of looking at neuro-degenerative disease as an area currently not understood enough, something related to the suggestion that there may be a link between a history of concussion within a player's career and symptoms of depression after retirement. This aside, football simply needs to make sure it is always moving with the times, and has made huge strides in the last 20 years or so.

Marcus Bent is testimony to that. Early in his career, he would have looked at you in ridicule had you tried to discuss mental health in football. Today, he sits and talks with a refreshing honestly on the highs and lows he's faced in his own life, with the ultimate goal of helping those now walking in his footsteps.

'I'm not academic, I wasn't good at school, so the only thing I saw was football; it was always sports for me. What is not taught is that it comes to an end quite abruptly. Whilst you're playing it, you think it's going to go on forever. I wish I'd known what I know now. That's the benefit of hindsight, I suppose. But I'm glad I do know what I know now because I can help the youngsters coming up by telling them my story and speaking to you, and hopefully they listen. If it can help anyone, me telling my story, then I'm grateful for that.'

* * *

Marcus Bent played over 500 games and scored more than 100 goals in his career. He'd made it to the age of 33 when he retired, a decision he had a choice over. Though he faced his struggles after the end of his career, Bent has come through them and can now look back with pride. Not everyone is so lucky. The PFA estimates that 75 per cent of those in the professional game at 16 have dropped out of football by the age of 21. Of the 25 per cent that do 'make it', many more then drop out of the game for a variety of reasons before they can reach the impressive stats that Bent racked up. Angus Beith is one of those who had the talent to earn a professional contract, but the bad luck to be out of the game by the age of 23, left to suddenly work out a new direction in life, having been with Hearts since the age of nine.

Hopes had always been high in Edinburgh for the midfielder, who represented Scotland at youth level and made his club debut at the age of 18. Whenever Beith looked like breaking through fully, though, he was held back by complications around a recurring hip injury: by the time he called it quits, he'd had three operations, all to no avail. It was November 2018, not long after Beith had sealed a move to Inverness, when he was finally forced to draw the curtains on his professional career after feeling pain in his hip again in a routine training session. The timing was particularly frustrating, as his stock had been high following an excellent loan spell at Stranraer, where Beith had scored eight goals in 14 games from midfield. Though he wasn't particularly surprised, having to accept the end of his career once and for all was not easy.

'It was pretty devastating. With my injury it was an ongoing thing, so it was always kind of niggling away at me, and it felt like it was just building and building, getting worse. On the day, I went back to the minibus and just sat there for half an hour, just on my own. That's when I was starting to process it and realise that this was it. Too many times this had happened and it felt worse than it ever had done, so that's when I knew there was no way back for me.

'It was obviously quite raw, quite fresh then. I still felt before that training session that I could get back to a really good level of playing, and felt really positive. As soon as I had that feeling again, and it was the worst it had ever felt, it was pretty crushing. The next two or three weeks were tough because you're processing it mentally, you're starting to worry about what you're going to do next, and thinking, is this really the end for me? I was up north four hours away from my family so although I was in contact with them over text I didn't have that instant comfort with them there. That support network had kind of gone a little bit, not being in the house with them and around them.'

Beith admits that ever since he was young, he had generally been known as 'the lad who plays football'. Having always excelled at the sport, he started to form his identity around it growing up, and always had his heart set on making it professionally. With this suddenly snatched away from him, forming a new identity in the wake of retirement was crucial for Beith's mental health. Luckily, having feared the worst after his second hip operation a few years prior to having to quit the game, Beith had started an online Open University course in sport and football business management. He even had an assignment due ten days after that final training session, which crucially gave him something to focus on when he would otherwise have been at his most vulnerable.

Founded in 1969, the Open University offers flexible learning to students anywhere, not restricting them in terms of location or timings. A part-time honours degree takes six years, but can be done in half the time if studied full time, with the total cost cheaper than a typical university degree at £18,576. Indeed, being below an income threshold, Beith did not have to pay for his course at all. The studying is all online, with a personal tutor assigned to ensure you keep on track. The football world is starting to embrace this form of learning more and more, with players studying there including Eric Dier, whilst Manchester United reportedly encouraged their players to take up courses during the initial COVID-19 lockdown.

For Beith, starting his studying journey has been life-changing.

'Starting my Open University course really helped me because it gave me another focus, and I started to creep out of that football identity that I'd had since I was younger. I was beginning to form a brand-new identity, starting to plan ahead for things, and that was really important for me.

'I think it can serve people well during their careers as well, because having that other focus takes away some of the pressures of football. If you're going through a bad period, I think a lot of players will go home, a lot of them will live on their own as well, and they'll be thinking about their bad performances, about everything they did wrong. That just builds up and isn't very healthy at all, so having that other focus actually serves you well.'

Another player who took an Open University course having dropped out of the professional game in their early 20s is James Bransgrove. His story is unique, though, in that he actually chose to tear up his contract at Colchester United and instead pursue a career in business. Despite, in his own words, only being 'a random 21-year-old back-up goalkeeper in League Two', the media coverage on Bransgrove's retirement was very high-profile, with the story featured on the BBC Sport website and making the back pages of the *Scottish Sun*. The 6ft 5in goalkeeper knows just how unusual it is to walk away from a dream career, but he has no regrets.

Perhaps the signs were there that Bransgrove was not destined to play professionally when he quit Leyton Orient's academy at the age of 11, not wanting to train three times a week, having started secondary school that year. He spent most of his teenage years playing Sunday League football with his mates, featuring as a centre-forward as much as a goalkeeper, before joining Isthmian League side Waltham Abbey's youth squad aged 17. Before long, he had progressed to the first team and was quickly snapped up by Brentford, before signing a professional contract at Colchester United, closer to his home, in July 2013. Featuring in a double-winning youth side and being called up to the Scotland U21 squad, you might assume Bransgrove was loving life in the pro game, but just a few months after that international call-up, he had quit the game altogether.

His realisation that football was not for him was gradual, though he explains the one tipping point was when he came off the pitch after a 6-1 hammering against Bristol City and found he didn't really care. The next day, he faked a knee injury to get out of training, finding that he had no desire to be there. I put it to Bransgrove that staying in professional football at that point could have affected his mental health:

'I would have thought so, because even up until the time when I wasn't training and I'd faked this injury, I was still going in every day and it was starting to feel like a chore. I could see how that could accumulate and then if I had been playing games thinking, I don't want to be here, I'm sure that would have had an impact. I must admit when I told the club I told my goalkeeper coach first, and we both started crying! I think he started crying in shock and because he was so upset, and then I started crying, not only because he was but I just felt a weight off my shoulder then – that's it, I'm free. I'm certain it would have had an effect on my mental health, you're right.'

One of the main reasons Bransgrove decided enough was enough with professional football was the strict and inflexible schedule it imposed on him. A keen cricket fan, he would play under a fake name for the first few games of the season, hoping to avoid repercussions should he suffer a broken finger or similar injury. This wouldn't be possible for most of the summer, though, with pre-season training on the football side starting again in early July. Holding down a professional football career required major sacrifices too, with Bransgrove missing out on boozy nights out with mates and having to stay obsessively on top of his fitness, even when he was on holiday. The game itself was not an issue for Bransgrove, who still plays semi-professional football for Saffron Walden Town in the Essex Senior League, with the fixtures all on the goalkeeper's doorstep. With the standard considerably lower than League Two, Bransgrove has been able to take it a bit easier and has even been known to do a 'leg day' at the gym on the morning of a match, something he admits you could never get away with at Colchester.

Unlike many that drop out of professional football in their early 20s, Bransgrove had a clear plan in place for the future. He was already 18 months into his business management course and fancied a few months off to travel the world after completing that, envious of his schoolmates who were now living the life at university. As it happened, Colchester chairman Robbie Cowling offered Bransgrove a job with one of his other businesses straight away, setting his former player on the path towards the accountancy career he desired. Having now graduated and started work in a full-time accountancy role, Bransgrove is keen to emphasise the importance of education for all up-and-coming footballers, in case their dreams don't work out as planned.

'It's phenomenal; the Open University's been great. I think now education is becoming more widely accepted within football, as a lot of players are realising they do need something to fall back on. Football is a horrible industry, put it that way. Some of the team-mates I've played with in the past, you see some of the things they're doing now and just feel a bit sorry for them really. There's still time obviously, but you think if only they'd done something when they were 18, what a different position they'd be in. I advocate anyone to do it within the game at any level, because you can't play football forever.'

Indeed, both Beith and Bransgrove argue that football's authorities can do more to promote education to all players. The Scottish PFA never followed up with Beith after the initial post-retirement call they'd set up with him, triggering the ire of Beith's father in particular who thought they could and should have done more. Angus himself thinks that maybe they didn't follow up as they knew he was fairly well prepared for life after football, but does worry that not everybody would be in this relatively favourable position. Interestingly, his main concern is for those who reach the peak of their career before suffering a serious injury, rather than for those like himself who are forced out of the game young. Beith had time on his side, he feels, whereas a career-ending injury at the age of 28 might be harder to adjust to. Thinking out loud as we discuss what can be done, he suggests an obligatory plan set up by clubs or the PFA themselves, to start focusing the minds of players once they reach that age.

The policy suggestions of James Bransgrove are not dissimilar to Beith's. Accepting that the PFA might be stretched to put a plan in place for every single one of its roughly 4,000 active members, he suggests targeting those forced out of the game in circumstances they haven't planned. Discussions of life after football might be stalled by the sport's attitude to mental health in general, which remains behind the times as a result of the macho atmosphere typically sought in the dressing room, and a funnelling towards education may be a practical way to start tackling this issue. Both Beith and Bransgrove agree that when a player is released, the club doesn't typically take an interest in that player's wellbeing. Hearts and Inverness, though, were notable exceptions.

In the summer following his retirement, the two sides put on a benefit match for Beith at Tynecastle Park, helping raise a bit of money to tide him over as he studied his Open University course. The following year, Robbie Neilson came in as Hearts manager and offered Beith a role as an analyst for the first team. At first, filming the training sessions rather than being involved in them was tough, but he soon adapted and is now really enjoying the role. Indeed, looking back on his whole experience, the former Scotland youth international takes a philosophical view.

'The feeling of sitting around and not doing anything, it wouldn't have given me a sense of fulfilment. After that initial few weeks, I started to process that was the best thing for me; I needed to do something that was going to actually benefit me in the long run. There was a sense of relief a little bit that I'd put that [first few weeks] behind me, and I could now focus on what was next from there, which was getting my Open University degree finished, starting to do a little bit of coaching, and just personal growth in whatever way possible; doing things I hadn't done before, like reading books.

'I feel like I've become more of a resilient person off the back of the whole situation. After my second operation, I took action and I felt like it was time to start thinking about what was next potentially, given the worst-case scenario was that I might not be able to play anymore. It forced me into looking at what was next, and from there I've grown as a person.'

With Bransgrove now in his dream job and able to devote more time to the sport he really loves, cricket, both he and Beith act as good role models for young players. Their stories haven't been without struggles; in fact, some struggles are to be expected, but in switching their identity away from football and having another focus, they're both happy in what they're doing. Retiring young might signal the end of your career in football, but it does not signal the end of your life outside of the game as well.

* * *

Of course, the Open University is not the only place to go for an education, and the PFA is not the only place a player can access support. Sometimes, it takes someone who has been there and knows a situation inside out to provide the perfect service. Robbie Simpson is that person, the all-action striker finding himself stranded without a club at the magical age of 28 highlighted by Angus Beith. Simpson, always a keen mathematics student, was in theory relatively well prepared for life after football. After signing for then-Conference side Cambridge United in June 2006, they allowed him to finish his degree whilst playing for the club, skipping training and only driving down for matches at the weekend. Simpson scored 17 league goals for the mid-table Cambridge outfit before moving to Coventry City at the end of the season, where he scored on his debut and played the full 90 minutes of a famous 2-0 win against Manchester United at Old Trafford.

After leaving Coventry the following year, though, Simpson spent the next six years of his career in League One with Huddersfield, Brentford and Oldham. He fancied a move back up to the Championship, given he had now reached the peak of his career, and a stunning goal against Liverpool at Anfield had put him in the shop window. Hopeful of one final big move, he left Oldham at the end of the 2012/13 season and waited for an offer to come in. That offer never came.

'It was a real tough time. I was just training on my own at home really, waiting for the phone to ring with an offer. I went back to clubs who did offer me a contract at the start of the window and they just replied with, "Well, no, we've got someone else in now, we've spent our budget" – there really was nothing … Even though I had a degree behind me, I didn't know what I wanted to do.

'Because I always thought I was going to carry on playing football at the same level, if not higher, my lifestyle was still the same. We still had a mortgage to pay, so I was still spending at the same rate I was when I was earning a good income, when I was earning nothing! So, it was a real tough time financially but also mentally not having a job. My wife would go to work and say to me, "What are you doing today?" and I'd be like, "Well, just going to the gym again to do some running, it's all I can do." Keep fit and hope the phone rings! It's not a way to live really. I just didn't feel in control of my future at all, so it really did get me thinking.'

Having been dreaming of a Championship move just months before, Simpson was faced with the very real prospect of having to retire from football altogether instead. It took until November for him to receive an offer, a short-term contract at Leyton Orient, and whilst searching for a club, Simpson realised just how many people were in the same position as him. The PFA website has a 'transfer list' visible to members with a list of players currently out of contract. Browsing through this as the season got underway without him, Simpson found no less than 300 other players all in the same position as him.

They say that out of adversity comes opportunity, and the tough position Simpson found himself in got him thinking. If he was anxious over his future, despite the degree he had behind him and the money he had saved up over the years, how would the other 300 be feeling? The support from the PFA left a lot to be desired in Simpson's eyes, and there was next to no chance of a player's former club offering any support. There was a clear gap in the market, and a significant number of individuals who could really use the support.

'For some reason, I thought about those other free agents more than myself really. It got me thinking that something had to be done to help in this situation, because I know and I've seen team-mates of mine retire and really struggle with their mental health, and with their finances. I guess I kind of put it to the back of my mind whilst I was still playing, but when I actually experienced it or had a little taste of it, it really hit home to me and actually thinking back to those players that I know struggled, I know what they were going through now. Rather than thinking of myself and my future career, having really seen the gravity of the situation, I felt I needed to set something up to help in this kind of situation for everybody.'

The result was a platform called LAPS – Life After Professional Sport. It works on the principle that not only do sports people need help after retiring, but businesses need help in their recruitment process. A career in professional sport gives you a unique set of soft skills that can help you in any role: a natural drive and determination, the ability to deal with setbacks, confidence, working under pressure – the list goes on. As we discuss the merits of the model over Zoom, Simpson tells me the initial inspiration from the recruitment side came after he heard the story of an Olympic rower earning three promotions in three months after starting a new job outside of the sport.

Simpson makes it very clear he makes no money from LAPS, with his full-time income coming from his job as a financial advisor, whilst he also manages National League South side Chelmsford City. Membership of LAPS is free and is available to any professional sportsperson, current or former. The platform's key feature is a placement service and job board, where businesses can advertise jobs and approach athletes they feel might be a good fit. The benefits can be reaped before a player has actually retired, with education opportunities signposted on the website, and a particular focus on part-time learning that can be done alongside a professional career. A wide-ranging advice section helps the athletes as many do not know which direction they want to go in after a life of professional sport, whilst a video interview section picks out stories from former professional athletes who have successfully transitioned into life after sport, to act as role models and provide inspiration for others. Prior to the COVID-19 pandemic, LAPS had branched out even further to deliver careers workshops to academy level players. As of March 2021, when Simpson and I spoke, the platform boasted over 4,000 members.

Many players talk of missing the adrenaline of football after retiring, but for Simpson, any time somebody thanks him for the work he's done with LAPS, 'it feels like scoring a goal'. Consultations with various other parties have highlighted just how much the platform is needed. A Professional Players Federation report, picked up on by LAPS, estimates that only 30 per cent of professional sportspeople choose when they retire. Often, injury catches up with them or they find themselves unexpectedly on football's scrapheap, as Simpson himself almost did back in the summer of 2013. With the majority, then, not in control of their future, Simpson thinks it is vital for everyone to have a back-up plan. Whilst working with the Sporting Chance Clinic on the mental health side of things, Simpson was told that they estimate 70 per cent of their clients come to them because of issues brought about by retirement. A staggering figure, it really hit home to Simpson the scale of the issue he had set out to tackle.

'There are lots of reasons why people suffer mental health problems, lots and lots of reasons, but I believe LAPS helps with one aspect of that, and that is preparing them and giving them other interests and other passions to make a career out of. A lot of mental health awareness currently is around after the event has occurred. Let's try and help stop people having mental health problems in the first place. They might suffer mental health problems anyway because their dream job, what they love doing, has come to an end, but LAPS can just ease that burden a little bit.

'I believe we're doing a great thing. One of my former team-mates that I spoke about, I called him up the day LAPS launched, I said to him, "I've just launched this website, I'd love for you to become a member and log on and have a look, and just let me know your thoughts," because he was one of the people I had in mind throughout the whole process of setting it up. He called me within an hour in tears, and I was welling up as well. He just said, "I wish I had this during my career, I wish someone had told me that LAPS existed and forced me to go on it every day." He said it really helped him. The minute I got that feedback from him was the minute I knew that what I'm doing and what we've set up is a really good thing, and we need to try and continue it.'

Chapter 5

Addiction

EVER THE entertainer, George Best once described himself as the 'first football celebrity', believing it was he who kicked off the media frenzy that exists around the lives of professional footballers today. He may well have a point, but it was largely because of his off-field antics rather than his mercurial genius on the pitch. For years, his drinking was almost celebrated; indeed, fans still sing about 'going on the piss with Georgie Best' today, but behind the façade the Belfast man himself admitted to being restless and lonely.

His Manchester United side, one which had won the European Cup just six years earlier, were relegated in 1974 and Best's own top-level career was over by his mid-20s too as he spent the rest of his playing days flitting between the likes of Stockport County, Dunstable Town and Cork Celtic. The drink caught up with Best once and for all in November 2005, as he passed away due to complications surrounding a liver transplant he had required three years earlier. At his own request, he had a picture of him published in the *News of the World* showing him dying in his hospital bed, with the double-page spread warning, 'Don't die like me'.

Despite all of his flaws, Best will quite rightly also be remembered for the footballing ability he possessed in spades during his good times, and to follow in his footsteps on the pitch at least was the goal of many growing up. One of those was Kieron Brady, a Glaswegian who burst onto the scene as an exciting 18-year-old at Sunderland, helping them to promotion to the First Division in 1990. A crowd-pleaser, his first goal for the club was from an outrageous bicycle kick, and a winning goal at Bradford City a week later was crucial as his side chased promotion. Despite all the early promise, though, it never did work out for Brady. A rare vascular condition in his leg forced him to retire from football in 1993, at the age of 21, and he descended into alcoholism in the subsequent years.

As time went on, it became less and less easy for Brady to convince himself that he did not have a problem. An intoxicated Brady sparked a security breach at Number 10 Downing Street when he swore at the Prime Minister Gordon Brown, setting alarm bells ringing and failing to impress the group he was in attendance with. His neighbours regularly heard Brady singing Irish songs in the early hours of the morning on his way home from drinking sessions that would last anywhere between five days and two weeks. He eventually reached a low point when considering drinking aftershave because he had woken up without any alcohol in the house and had no money to buy any more. Since 12 June 2009, Brady has not touched so much as a drop of alcohol. He now works for SP Bespoke, a treatment provider for others suffering from alcoholism, and does not shy away from his past. Similar to George Best on his deathbed, Brady wants others to learn from his lows, but also his successes in giving up alcohol for good. Wearing a baseball cap to complement his beaming smile, Brady looks healthy as he discusses the drinking culture during the time he played football at the top level; a time you might assume sent him on his way down the path to alcoholism.

'The drinking culture when I played was very prominent, and not only accepted by the management and coaching staff but often prompted and encouraged by them too. At Sunderland, once a month on a Wednesday we would go to a local restaurant after we finished training at about 1pm. We would have something to eat, and then we would drink until about 2am or 3am. That was organised by the club and would involve the manager, the coaches and all of the playing squad. On top of this, players would also go out on a Saturday night and drink a lot, sometimes a Sunday too. Despite the broad cultural acceptance of it, nobody could argue that that type of behaviour was conducive to being a professional athlete. I could guarantee you that at the same time, people like Linford Christie and Daley Thompson, both well-known and respected athletes, were not going out and treating their bodies with such disdain.

'Sunderland were not unique, I believe players at other clubs were doing likewise. Then of course at the end of the season you would go away traditionally to one of the Spanish hotspots like Magaluf, and over the course of five days to a week you would drink repeatedly. Some people would be more sympathetic to that, given it's the end of the season and you have several months off, but nevertheless

I doubt you would find any within the medical fraternity who would put forward the notion that doing that would have medium – to long-term benefits.'

Sunderland certainly were not unique in their drinking culture at the time. Perhaps most infamous was the Arsenal 'Tuesday Club' under George Graham in the late 1980s and early 1990s. Including two current recovering alcoholics, Tony Adams and Paul Merson, amongst its alumni, the premise was simple. With no training on Wednesdays, the players would be free to go out and drink as much as they pleased, with no repercussions the following morning. This might have seemed like a bit of harmless fun when the idea was first conceived, but the damage is clear in retrospect. Adams admitted that his alcohol consumption caused him to feel 'empty' even after the incredible final-day title win over Liverpool in 1989. He was sentenced to four months in prison the following year for a drunken car crash, going on to increasingly turn to drink to cope with the pressure he was under to perform on the pitch, until finally getting sober in the mid-1990s.

Both Merson and Adams played the occasional game still drunk from their exploits the night before as alcohol gained an increasingly strong grip on them. It was Merson who publicly came out as an addict first, after developing a cocaine habit that brought him to his knees. Adams followed with his public admission a year later, and writing in his 2011 autobiography, *How Not to Be a Professional Footballer*, Merson notes that his own story enabled his captain at the time to seek help himself.

Sadly, not everyone who fell into addiction has found their recovery quite so straightforward. The legendary

Kenny Sansom, capped 86 times for England, has been in and out of rehab throughout his life, battling an alcohol addiction that he acknowledges stopped him playing for England even more times than he did. Back in 2016, he appeared in an interview on ITV's *This Morning* in which he said he couldn't see a future where he wasn't drinking. He tragically added that he just wanted to 'forget about things', describing himself as a 'coward' who wanted to 'get away from life'. Further attempts at sobriety have followed, but these are sadly juxtaposed with voyeuristic clips appearing on the websites of tabloid newspapers showing him staggering around the streets, having reportedly failed rehab. You have to wonder how much the culture at Arsenal led Sansom down this path.

Kieron Brady, though, does not buy into this argument. With his own addiction, you might think the drinking culture at Sunderland at the time in addition to the trauma of early retirement from the game due to his health condition would be nailed-on causes of his descent into alcoholism. Brady himself disagrees.

'I believe that I've been predisposed to the illness of alcoholism from the day I was born. I suppose that coming from a family where the illness of alcoholism has been somewhat consistent and affected many, some people would regard me becoming an alcoholic as something of an inevitability. I'm often asked if I believe I'm an alcoholic because I had to stop playing football at such a young age. As much as there may have been times in the past when the temptation for self-pity may have been particularly empowering, the honest answer is no. Whether I'd been a footballer or not, I still believe that alcoholism and I would have come into collision at some point in my life. What life events often do is dictate and determine when that collision will be. If people have a period of adversity, as I did when I had to stop playing football at 21, I was able to justify and defend my use of alcohol as some sort of coping mechanism.

'Alcoholism is an illness that at source is about how we think. The drinking just comes afterwards. As strange as it may sound, the one thing excessive alcohol use can't cause is alcoholism. It's alcoholism that will cause excessive alcohol use.'

When you examine some of the stories of football's most notable alcoholics in the 1980s and 1990s, it looks like he may have a point. Brady argues that the common thread that runs through every alcoholic is a feeling of 'soullessness'. When I ask him to explain further, he refers back to his own personal experience. Despite his extroverted nature and talent as a sportsman from a young age, a feeling of not fitting in, or not quite belonging, gnawed away at the Glaswegian. He refers to alcoholism as an illness rather than an addiction, but an illness where there is nothing wrong with you physically. The issue, then, must be to do with the mind and the soul.

Not all of them refer to it directly as soullessness, but a lot of football's recovering alcoholics do talk of similar feelings to the ones Brady experienced. Tony Adams, in his first book, *Addicted*, calls alcoholism a 'disease of the personality' and says he could see it in himself from a young age. Football itself was like an addiction to him in his youth, as he always desired more and more, and he talks of a feeling of emptiness when he couldn't play. For a young Adams, this manifested itself in panic attacks around the age of 11, brought on by feeling like there was a void that needed filling when it was too dark to go out and play football in the winter months. Adams's team-mate at Arsenal, Paul Merson, was drawn to drink as he found it would lessen the effect of his own panic attacks. For both of them, the long-run result of trying to use alcohol to numb feelings of anxiety was to generate a vicious cycle whereby the situation only got progressively worse.

Perhaps the most striking case of a footballer's 'soullessness' linked to alcoholism is that of Paul McGrath. Alongside Adams, the Irishman is undoubtedly one of the best defenders English football has ever seen. Despite the prominence of his drink problem at the time, McGrath was voted the PFA Players' Player of the Year for the 1992/93 season, the inaugural season of the Premier League in which his side, Aston Villa, finished second. McGrath was well into his 30s at the time, and rarely training due to his knee injuries, but his achievement is even more remarkable when you consider the issues he faced off the pitch. Indeed, manager Ron Atkinson had been prepared to let him go at the start of the season after McGrath turned up to two friendlies drunk, but changed his mind after the centre-back put in some impressive performances at the start of the season. Villa physio Jim Walker helped limit the damage McGrath could do to himself during the season, though he did still go absent without leave before a home game against Liverpool.

Like Adams and Merson, McGrath's problems with alcohol can be traced back to his childhood. He grew up in a series of orphanages with his father absent, and admits to becoming institutionalised, despite the often poor conditions. His first drink, on a youth team tour of Germany, triggered feelings of 'liberation', but McGrath had a mental breakdown not long after and spent a year in hospital. Though recovering enough to have a successful football career, the man who was immortalised on an Irish postage stamp in 2002 was stricken with a terrible shyness and imposter syndrome throughout his career, regularly turning to the bottle to try and overcome these feelings. Even with his national side, where McGrath was often one of the biggest names in the squad, he notes in his autobiography, *Back from the Brink*, that he often felt like 'a fraud' and would lack the confidence to mix with the other players. Alcohol gave him this confidence, a means to get through, but it wouldn't stop there as he 'drunk to oblivion' instead.

Being on a genetically predisposed, interminable slide into alcoholism might sound like a dystopian nightmare for those on that path, but it also might help with recovery. After all, it takes away the element of guilt and blame that haunts so many. Recovery is very much possible, as Kieron Brady proves, and he talks of how a key part of his own recovery is extending a hand of friendship, support and experience to others. His work for SP Bespoke provides a perfect platform to do this, and Brady is able to use his knowledge of the ins and outs of alcoholism, as well as the secrets of sobriety, to help others through their own problems. He knows the damage that can be caused, and the value in escaping the madness.

'The great thing about SP is that because of our own experiences, we're very understanding of this being a family illness. I'm the only alcoholic in my house, but I wasn't the only one suffering from alcoholism, because my poor wife, who's stood by me throughout my misadventures, was suffering as a result. If somebody lives with an alcoholic long enough, they will develop their own neurosis around it, because it's just such a painful, horrific existence. I went through a lot of it drunk. My wife went through it stone-cold sober. So you then ask yourself – who's actually suffered the most? My poor wife didn't know when the next phone call was coming to say that I was in a hospital, or a police station, or a morgue. I owe it to her now to do my best to remain sober for the rest of my life, and the way I remain sober for the rest of my life is helping to get and keep others sober.

'In essence, I'm paying it forward. I'm not paying anything back to the people who helped me, they've only asked that I go and pay it forward to others. It's something that mercifully I enjoy, and it is for me the very essence of a healthy, pure and spiritually well recovery. I took a phone call from a father several months ago who was very emotional but wanted to express such gratitude for the help I was able to give to his daughters. Scoring my first goal and having thousands chant my name as a teenager was incredibly rewarding, and what I'd worked towards in my childhood, but in terms of something that's pure and affirming, and something that enhances your self-worth and the value that you contribute towards people in your community, it's incomparable to being able to save people and give them life.'

Finding such emotionally powerful work is a testament to Brady's recovery, though the COVID-19 pandemic has meant opportunities to get hands-on with helping people haven't been as prevalent as he would have hoped. SP Bespoke works by taking into account the stigma some people may feel about seeking treatment in their local area and the mixed success of a 28-day rehab programme, and looks to find a solution with the best elements of both. Confidentiality is assured as Brady and the team go out to people's homes, giving them intense one-to-one therapy to help them detox without having to go anywhere they fear they might be recognised in the local community. Unsurprisingly, this wasn't easy to get approval for during the pandemic, though Brady still looked to help as many people as much as he could, whether on a professional or informal basis.

Brady is unlikely to see many current professional footballers come in for help. Far from the drinking culture of the late eighties and early nineties, drinking at all in football is now generally frowned upon. The English top flight, once made up of almost exclusively British players, is now diverse and rich with different cultures, virtually none of which include drinking as a primary activity. Sports science techniques and constant physical monitoring mean players can't get away with heavy drinking anymore, and alcohol consumption in public will typically be picked up in an instant by the tabloid press, a legacy of the 'football celebrity' culture created by George Best. That's not to say that footballers won't be alcoholics, as Brady points out, and there are concerns over the players who might fall into heavy drinking once their regimented training days are over, but, for the current pros, another dangerous form of addiction is now endemic in the game.

* * *

On Tuesday, 15 March 2005, Kevin Twaddle sat at home, ready to take his own life. He was stuck in a gambling hell, a cycle of bet and regret, bet and regret, until the money ran out and he went home with nothing. His footballing career was over, and a decent career in the Scottish leagues at that, but all his earnings were gone, and had been gone for years. Since he was a teenager, Twaddle had been a slave to gambling; what seemed an initially benign force had developed inside of him after an accumulator win at the age of 13, and had grown to take an invasive icy grip around his heart. Now he was powerless, and suicide felt like the only way out.

Looking back over the last 15 years, some of the lows that Twaddle stooped to in order to keep gambling were morally shocking by his own admission, but that's what addiction does to you. Lying, stealing and manipulating are all a means to an end; that end always just being the ability to place another bet. On one occasion, early in the tall and athletic winger's career at St Johnstone, Twaddle told his friends and family he would sort them out a corporate box to see him play. Instead, he told them the box was cancelled and used the money they had given him, £12,000 in all, to back his own side to win. St Johnstone went 3-0 down after 15 minutes, and the money was effectively gone. Not even fending off punches from his furious would-be corporate box punters acted as a wake-up call for Twaddle.

As he progressed in his career, ending up at a Motherwell side challenging for European football in 1999, the money that Twaddle earned went up and up, feeding his gambling habit further. Things were so bad that the Edinburgh-born man confesses to never playing well at Ibrox, as it was the only ground in the country where the live scores from around the division would come up on the scoreboard, and Twaddle would be distracted as he tried to track the success of his coupon. He ended up in significant debt to many of his team-mates, few of whom seemed keen to help him despite his obvious issues, and even stole money from his family before reaching that low point in March 2005. The guilt and remorse had taken a hold of him.

In the end, Twaddle saw through the darkness, ultimately kept alive by the thought of the family that had stood by his side despite his struggles. Whilst his recovery was not immediate, Twaddle was soon on a path towards getting his life back.

'I still went on gambling for another three months after my suicide attempt. I needed the help, I could admit that I was powerless over gambling but I couldn't accept it. Three months later, I remember my girlfriend at the time sitting next to me in a taxi, saying I'd done all these amazing things in life but had nothing to show for it. It came from someone I cared about, and those words just really hit home to me. It was a weird experience, like an out-of-body experience, like my body just drained through the taxi seat. I went home and opened my heart, and spoke to my mum, my dad, my sister. I just broke down and said, "You know what, I need help."

'On 5 October 2005, I walked into Gamblers Anonymous and it helped change my life around. It was on the previous Friday that I'd decided to go, but on Saturday and Sunday I was still betting on horses, betting to lose.

This is very common among compulsive gamblers as well, you get to a point where you don't even want money, it's not about the money. I was putting these bets on and still sitting and thinking to myself, I've got this meeting tomorrow and it doesn't matter what anybody says or what anybody does, nothing will ever be able to stop me gambling unless I'm dead. I walked in the door for the first day and wow … I just didn't know there were other people like me, to give me that strength and courage and hope. I had never had that hope before. To have that hope from so many people who were doing so well helped change me.'

As a professional footballer suffering from gambling addiction throughout his career, Twaddle is far from being alone. Research from EPIC Risk Management, an independent gambling consultancy, estimates sportspeople are around five times more likely to develop a gambling addiction in comparison to the general population. Research from the Professional Players Federation has similar findings, with footballers and cricketers being three times more likely to develop gambling problems than other young men, a demographic who are themselves more at risk than the average person.

To better deal with this trend, Sporting Chance launched their Gambling Awareness, Treatment and Education (GATE) programme in 2020. This was rolled out in the wake of the fact that around half of the clients treated for an addictive disorder at the clinic the previous year presented with gambling problems, with the numbers continuing to rise as the country went through lockdown. As a result, there has been a notable increase in demand for education around gambling from clubs, keen to avoid their players falling into the kind of problems that plagued Kevin Twaddle throughout his career.

Chris Murphy is the gambling education facilitator at Sporting Chance, tasked with producing seminars and other forms of learning that will stick in the minds of vulnerable young players in particular. Murphy has his own experiences of gambling, having been an addict since the age of 17. His addiction swallowed him quickly, to the point where Murphy was thrown out of college and never got the chance to take his A-Levels, as he was absent from lessons so much. The devastation caused by his habit reached a point where Murphy decided he was going to try and win back all the money he owed in one go – or take his own life. Within 20 minutes, he had lost everything. Thankfully, Murphy survived his suicide attempt when he accidentally tried to overdose on his housemate's hay fever tablets rather than his sleeping pills. He has been able to give gambling the elbow, aside from a few brief relapses which Murphy points out are not atypical in the recovery of a gambling addict, and at the time we speak over Zoom is now two and a half years without a bet.

Given Murphy is also the communications manager at Sporting Chance, as well as having a separate role with the Professional Darts Players Association, I'm grateful for his time as he explains to me why gambling-related issues are so prevalent amongst professional footballers.

'We think that psychologically there might be something in the competitive nature of a professional sportsperson that gambling serves more than any other addiction. There's that need not to be beaten, trying to beat the bookie, trying to beat the machine or roulette wheel, whatever it is. It's certainly prevalent in some of the clients that we see, who have got extremely competitive natures. In truth, though, I think it's a mix of a few things. For example, the environmental factors of being in professional sport, the unique types of stress people experience, might contribute. The amount of downtime footballers get and the money they earn gives them more time and means to gamble than the general public.

'I do also think that the environmental aspect of being exposed to gambling is a big part of it. I would be really interested to see a study done on football fans, to see if they are also more susceptible to gambling addiction, as players are. They're exposed to it all the time as well, whether they're watching it on TV or in the stadium, or getting notifications on their mobile phone or whatever. We're concerned about the pathway footballers can go on when they come into treatment for gambling addiction at Sporting Chance; [they] have really good intensive work, are put in a good place, and then we're sending them back into that environment.'

The fact that danger lurks for footballers in the form of both their genes and the environment they work in hammers home the importance of a good education programme, and the young players just starting out in the game are often the priority. Murphy sees gambling as something that can pose a problem for anyone with little warning, as young footballers are thrown into an environment where gambling is seen as normal, with the logos of gambling companies often plastered around the stadiums of the clubs the youngsters represent. Many academy members, when asked what their first perception of gambling is, will say 'winning money', when the truth is the exact opposite. Bringing home the facts, and the real-life horror stories so many addicts go through, is a key part of ensuring everyone knows exactly what's what.

All the education sessions Murphy runs are designed with the audience in mind, to make sure the message hits home. Kevin Twaddle tells me that he never had any sort of education on gambling whilst he was playing, but with the mindset he had at the time he wouldn't have listened anyway. Sporting Chance's seminars look to relate to the players, and will often include the personal story of someone like Twaddle or Murphy to show that gambling addiction can affect anyone, and the consequences can be severe. An audience of younger players may be asked to use some introspection and see if they can recognise any addictive traits already present in themselves. For example, a young player staying up late at night to play the Xbox or PlayStation even though it affects them at training the next day may be showing parallels with someone addicted to gambling. Giving the warning at this early stage may help any more serious habits developing.

The GATE programme goes beyond just education, with an open letter written to sport's professional organisations expressing concern about the relationship between those sports and the gambling industry. Linked to the concern about sending recovering gambling addicts back into a sport rife with gambling, Sporting Chance called for the reliance on gambling funding for advertising and sponsorships to be gradually reduced. The charity also argued that social responsibility monies from gambling systems should be paid into each sport's welfare system, with governing bodies such as the Football Association then providing a strategy for how this money should be used, based around the four pillars of education, protection, awareness and treatment. Already renowned as one of the best treatment centres available to sportspeople, Sporting Chance's rehab programme has been further developed to offer 28-day residential courses exclusively for gambling addicts. The nationwide network of therapists means each player can arrange a next-day consultation with someone half an hour from their club or home.

Kevin Twaddle has been into clubs to talk to young players about the perils of gambling. Having seen what the game was like throughout his playing days and through to today, he is not impressed with how football has recently further embraced the gambling industry despite all the pain it has caused to so many.

'Football for me has lost the love of the game. It's not the football I used to know. Football is a gambling industry now. I'd have been jailed for some of the things you can bet on now. Billy Davies used to say to us at Motherwell, "Take the centre, put the ball down in the corner flag, and then we start the game from down there." You can bet on the first throw-in now. I have no doubt I'd have ended up in jail, because my addiction was so bad that I would have done anything to get money. I'm so glad these kinds of markets weren't there at the time.

'I went into a club a couple of seasons ago, when William Hill were sponsoring the Scottish Cup, to talk to a kid who was really suffering from gambling addiction. He got awarded man of the match and won £500 in vouchers for William Hill. I could have come out of there crying, it was so sad. How a gambling company can be allowed to sponsor Scottish football is just beyond me. Football is a lifestyle now that is unfortunately rife with gambling. If you went across Scottish football and banned everyone who had a bet on a Friday or Saturday night then you wouldn't have any football, it's as simple as that.'

Football's uneasy relationship with gambling has often extended down to the individuals suffering from it. Keith Gillespie, of Newcastle United at the time, infamously lost £47,000 in one day in October 1995, followed by a further £15,000 the next day as he chased his losses. The seeds of his addiction were sown during his earlier spell at Manchester United, whom Gillespie had joined at the age of 16 after moving over from Northern Ireland. Gillespie's gambling habit was common knowledge at the club's training ground, the Cliff, but nobody challenged him on it. On the contrary, club staff asked Gillespie to enter their pools coupons for them when he went to the bookies, allowing him to keep some of the winnings if they came in. Unsurprisingly, Gillespie's addiction continued to develop to the low of what he calls 'Black Friday', referring to that October day in 1995. John Hartson fell into financial ruin during his time at West Ham because of his gambling addiction, but manager Harry Redknapp would take him to the greyhound racing where the two of them would gamble. Whether Redknapp knew the extent of Hartson's problems, or indeed whether Hartson understood his own issues, is not clear.

Twaddle himself was never challenged on his gambling habit by any managers or team-mates, and looks back with regret that nobody tried to get him back on track. Though gambling is regarded as the 'hidden addiction', not being quite as obvious as an alcohol or drug problem, Twaddle has no doubt that it significantly influenced his career. He recalls signing for Greenock Morton and being told by manager Billy Stark that he was embarrassed to have been able to sign him too easily, with clubs like Celtic would-be suitors if it wasn't for the reputation Twaddle had acquired from his gambling problems. He even turned down a move to Norwegian side Lyn Oslo during the peak of his powers, as there was very little gambling available in the country. When Twaddle was on the pitch, his off-field financial woes were never far from his mind, and he admits that football never truly offered him the vital distraction that it offers so many.

When I ask Twaddle why he thinks nobody challenged him on his gambling, given the benefits to his performance that it would likely have brought if nothing else, he tells me it was probably largely down to the times. Mental health awareness around the turn of the Millennium was not what it is today. Many of his managers, as strange as it seems now, simply would not have recognised that Twaddle had a problem. Though he is hopeful that the situation has changed significantly, Twaddle recognises that it can be hard for players to come forward and confess to a gambling addiction, given that betting on any football match is illegal for professional footballers, creating something of a Catch-22 situation for anyone who wants to stop but needs help in doing so. The 18-month ban placed on Joey Barton in 2017 may act as something of a deterrent for footballers to come forward, certainly publicly, though the option of confidential support from an organisation such as Sporting Chance is still available.

Now older and wiser than in his playing days, Kevin Twaddle shares the desire of both Chris Murphy and Kieron Brady to help others with his own problems. His 2012 autobiography, entitled *Life on the Line: How to Lose a Million and So Much More*, was one step towards doing this as he aimed to lay himself bare, showing that gambling addiction could be managed. In this book, he notes that he simply cannot ever put another bet on again, and should he ever go back down that road he would be 'gambling with his life' once more. In fact, Twaddle did relapse briefly in 2016, something he is now open and honest about. Going through a tough time in his personal life, with his wife suffering a miscarriage, he once again fell victim to a phenomenon he describes as 'manipulative and horrible, something that prays on the low and vulnerable'. Knowing addiction to be an illness rather than a negative character trait, he has been able to forgive himself and move on.

Now back on track in his recovery, Twaddle has recently completed a 12-step recovery programme unrelated to his gambling issues, following another low point in his mental health in January 2020. The course, which is based around the principles of addiction recovery, is designed to help people who don't like what they see in the mirror change who they are. Personality traits Twaddle concedes to having had, such as laziness and selfishness, are banished and replaced by principles such as compassion, kindness, humility and gratitude. Like his recovery from gambling, these cannot be taken for granted and Twaddle has to work on them each day, but he is overjoyed with the difference he has seen in himself since starting the programme. He now sponsors others through it, taking particular delight in seeing the progress his mentees make in their own personal journey. More than anything, though, Twaddle was motivated to take up the course through the love for his daughter. We finish the call with the former flying Motherwell winger expressing immense gratitude to those who gave a previously 'hopeless individual' that message of hope, allowing him to feel a true love and warmth towards his wee girl that he describes as 'the greatest gift in the world'.

* * *

The scourge of gambling addiction has extended its toxic hold in football far beyond just the players, perhaps unsurprising given the extent of advertising and sponsorship in the game now. At time of writing, 34 of the 44 Premier League and Championship clubs have a gambling sponsor or partner. The English Football League itself is sponsored by Sky Bet, and the game has started to see the situation get even more ludicrous, with crass stunts designed to promote the gambling industry. Paddy Power's controversial 'save our shirt' campaign saw them put a huge sash over a Huddersfield Town shirt when the kit was released, only to reveal that in fact the shirt would carry no sponsorship at all as they declared a campaign to 'unbastardise' football shirts. Trying to position themselves as the good guys, it felt more like a clever ploy to make themselves stand out amidst the deluge of gambling advertising in football, and Huddersfield themselves were put under an FA investigation as a result. Derby County's signing of Wayne Rooney, agreed in August 2019, was controversial due to its association with betting company

32Red. Rooney wore the number 32 on the back of his shirt, at the same time a 'record-breaking' sponsorship deal with 32Red was announced. They were accused of doing it to get around the rules preventing betting logos being placed on children's shirts, though of course both denied they had done anything wrong.

The gambling industry in Great Britain makes around £14bn in gross profit each year, but contributes less than £20m to pay for research, education and treatment on gambling addiction. By contrast, the industry spends roughly £1.5bn a year on advertising – around 75 times the research, education and treatment amount. With such shocking spending statistics, it is left to organisations such as Gambling With Lives to assess and mitigate the damage.

Gambling With Lives is a charity set up by the families of young people who have lost their lives as a result of suicide linked to gambling addiction. Initially a campaigning organisation, they have expanded to provide a support service for bereaved families and an education programme, as well as having a research project looking at gambling-related suicide. The growing body of research from various sources on their website makes for an upsetting read. A 2018 study from Sweden which tracked over 2,000 people with diagnosed gambling disorders found that this group had a suicide rate a shocking 15 times higher than the general population. Applying this rate to the number of people with a gambling disorder in the UK gives an estimated number of 550 gambling-related suicides in the UK each year. This means gambling plays a part in around a tenth of suicides, yet only two per cent of gambling addicts in the UK receive treatment. The situation looks pretty dire.

I spoke to James Grimes from Gambling With Lives and the Big Step, one of the charity's campaigns. It looks to raise awareness in the fight against gambling advertising and sponsorship in football by hosting a series of walking events. At the time of writing, Grimes has just finished walking from Scotland to Wembley with Euro 2020 about to kick off, in one of the biggest events yet. He talks to me about the importance of their campaign as the gambling industry continues to ravage the lives of so many.

'It might be a clichéd thing to say, but the best form of treatment is prevention. Whilst we don't have the ability to pluck people out of the water, we shouldn't be throwing so many in. I think getting rid of the advertising would stop a lot of people getting to that place, because it's not just about people who are struggling with gambling, it's about people who haven't even heard of gambling yet. A line of defence we're getting from the industry is that advertising doesn't impact behaviour, but for you to ever be a gambler you have to know about it, and how do you know about it? The advertising. So of course there's a link. You've got complete saturation of advertising at the minute. Wolves vs Burnley in the Premier League was on BBC iPlayer last season, Chris Wood scored for Burnley and in the following ten seconds the word 'bet' could be seen 63 times. Nobody can tell me that level of advertising doesn't cause football fans to gamble.

'Gambling advertising creates a complete exaggerated perception of normalisation. It creates a sense that everybody is doing this, that this is a thing you should be doing, that you'd be weird if you weren't doing it. Gambling is so normalised that it's entrenched in the way you socialise. You don't just go to the match, you go to the bookies before. It happened to me too, I thought that it was me who had the problem because everyone else I'm seeing on the adverts is doing this completely normal, fun leisure activity whereas I've managed to turn it into a really dangerous addiction. Of course now I know it's because we're got addictive products, predatory marketing and a dangerous environment. There's nothing normal about that.'

Grimes has now gone over three years without a bet, after an addiction story similar to so many. He grew up a massive Peterborough United fan, describing football as his life. Unfortunately, at the time he was growing up, the 2005 Gambling Act deregulated the industry and opened the floodgates of gambling advertising. Grimes describes gaining access to online gambling at the age of 18 as being the turning point, and with the accessibility in his pocket he lost thousands, leaving him having to lie, borrow and beg just to get food to eat. The responsible gambling narrative only served to make things worse, as it suggested to Grimes that he was completely at fault for his addiction. If other people could gamble responsibly, why couldn't he? It might not be immediately obvious, but all the 'responsible gambling' adverts around today, the 'when the fun stops, stop' narrative, actually cause more harm than good. They are the wolf in sheep's clothing of the industry, and for Grimes they brought him further towards suicidal thoughts.

Aside from the responsible gambling narrative, Grimes is particularly critical of fixed odds betting terminals (such as slot machines and casino games) and in-play betting in football. The research available on the Gambling With Lives website talks about the addictiveness of different products, and within football it is in-play betting that is the most harmful. Grimes explains that addiction is made worse by the speed at which you gamble, and the more opportunities you have to gamble, the more addicted you become. If you can place a bet every five seconds, you lose the ability to think rationally about what you are doing, and chasing your losses becomes much more hazardous. In-play betting isn't quite on the same heinous level as casino games, which are rigged to extract millions from people whilst luring them further into the clutches of the industry, but within football it is a particularly dangerous area. Mind you, that's not to say the rest of the industry is exempt from blame exactly.

'Not at any point in my addiction did I ever really feel like the industry was wrong or doing anything bad, even when they were giving me VIP tickets to go and watch Premier League football matches. One company let me deposit £18,000 over two days, which was basically my nan's inheritance money, and spin it all on roulette. Not at any point did that company ask me if I could afford it, if it was my money, or if I was OK. Instead, they put me on a gold VIP scheme, gave me free bets, free spins, bonuses. At the time, you think that you're the villain, you think you're the person that's done this to yourself. But there was no accountability or responsibility from the industry at any point, not one gambling company ever asked me if I could afford to bet the money I was betting. Instead, they did the opposite and incentivised 12 years of addiction.

'I received no education on gambling, I had absolutely no idea that the industry does what it does and it could lead to the things it did. My role with Gambling With Lives is head of education, and we are creating and rolling out an education programme we are quite proud of. We think it's unique because it's completely independent from the industry and determines where the harm is caused. The harm is caused by the products and the practices, and the environment. Traditionally, gambling-based education has been about individual responsibility and resilience, words like that. We're saying you need to be made aware of the true risks, the technicalities of products, and give children critical marketing skills, so when they do unfortunately see gambling adverts, they know it's all bullshit. I think a big part of recovery for people is understanding what the gambling industry is all about. They need to know that products are addictive, and you can't win. They need to learn that 60 per cent of profits come from just five per cent of players, so the more you gamble, the more addicted you become, and the more likely you are to be in that five per cent of people that provide so much of their profits. I think if people knew that, they would think twice.'

If the stigma around gambling in the UK is bad, the Premier League clubs promoting gambling on their shirts and in their stadiums should cast their thoughts over to China. A lot of Premier League clubs have gambling sponsors which include Chinese script and the lucky number eight, looking to reach the Chinese market even though gambling is illegal in the country. Many of these sponsorships are done via 'white label' agreements where minimal background information is required on the brands being promoted. This can lead to farcical situations – in June 2021, Norwich ditched their new sponsorship deal with a somewhat sketchy online casino BK8 after the company's sexualised advertising was revealed online. It would appear that background research on the company, aimed at the Asian market but based in Malta, was limited or simply hard to do. The likes of Laba360 and OPE Sports, who sponsored Huddersfield and Burnley respectively in the Premier League, no longer have functioning UK websites.

The real issue comes for those in China who are drawn in by the advertising, with an estimated 300 million followers of the Premier League in the country. Due to gambling being illegal in China, anyone who starts on the path and develops an addiction would be more likely to be jailed than given support. This also means the true scale of the problem remains almost completely unknown, though the vast sums spent on advertising and sponsorship by gambling companies targeting the Asian market suggest it is unlikely to be insignificant.

At the time I speak to James Grimes, there is an ongoing government review of the 2005 Gambling Act, with the hope that changes to advertising and sponsorship regulations could prove significant for the welfare of those in both the UK and China, as well as the other 186 countries where the Premier League is televised. The review follows a July 2020 House of Lords report which recommended banning Premier League clubs from having betting logos on their shirts, as well as preventing any gambling advertising being featured in or near sports grounds. Chairman of the EFL, Rick Parry, was one of those to lead the argument against a potential gambling advertising ban, saying it would cost the EFL £40m a year in lost revenue. With clubs still suffering from the pandemic, he argued it would cause financial meltdown.

Grimes disagrees with Parry. He points to a list of clubs who don't have gambling sponsors and are doing just fine – the likes of Luton Town, Swansea City, Tranmere Rovers and Forest Green Rovers to mention a few. Similarly, Wigan Athletic, Bolton Wanderers and Macclesfield Town have all carried gambling sponsors in recent years and struggled financially, Macclesfield even going out of business. His argument goes beyond just the money, though. With so many suicides each year linked to gambling, clubs have a responsibility to the community they represent to limit the damage. Carrying a gambling sponsor promotes gambling to young fans, and in doing so you are failing them and the community. They're powerful words from Grimes, on a topic he is clearly passionate about, and with good reason too.

Despite all the evidence and tragic real-life stories that can be seen all around, Grimes was not confident of a positive outcome from the government review at the time we spoke. His pessimism with regards to advertising, marketing, and sponsorship proved to be well founded. The review resulted in the publication of a White Paper in April 2023, which prioritised a crackdown on online gambling above other measures. Key reforms included a mandatory levy on industry revenues and restrictions of online casino games, but there was nothing targeting advertising or sponsorship. Despite this frustration, Grimes is not about to give up the fight. He is hopeful the football industry will gradually change without needing the law to push it into doing so. League Two club Forest Green Rovers came out in May 2021 to publicly back the Big Step campaign to end all gambling advertising and sponsorship in football, with EFL clubs Luton and Tranmere since joining them in this pledge of support. In April 2023, two weeks prior to the release of the government review, the Premier League committed to ending gambling sponsorship on the front of shirts from the 2026/27 season. Grimes hopes more progress will follow and is philosophical as I ask him where he thinks we'll be in ten years' time.

'The negative is that I think we'll still be dealing with the fallout from this current situation, and the advertising's not going to go away overnight. I'd like to think in ten years we'll have safer products, slower products, affordability checks, better customer interaction, a greater number of better treatment services, independent education and a statutory levy on the industry so they pay properly for research, education and treatment. I hope we'll have a complete end to gambling advertising so we return to a place where gambling is tolerated and not promoted.

'In ten years we'll watch highlights of last season's Premier League and see a match where one team had LoveBet on their shirt and the other team had Fun88, and we won't believe that we allowed it. We'll look at it and go, "What were we thinking? How did we ever allow this to happen?" I genuinely believe that.'

Chapter 6

Social Media

AS LONG as sites such as Twitter and Facebook have existed, there have been questions about the ethics of running, and making money from, platforms which are so addictive. However, it wasn't until the Netflix documentary *The Social Dilemma* was released in January 2020 that the shocking details of just how social media platforms can manipulate users psychologically were laid bare to a large number of people. The film featured a number of former employees at a whole host of large social media companies, each carrying a stark warning on the industry. Tristan Harris, former design ethicist at Google, spoke about the whole university discipline of 'persuasive technology' – exploiting human weaknesses to cause you to be addicted to your phone. Chamath Palihapitaya, former VP of growth at Facebook, talked about how the company essentially tries to work out how to manipulate you as quickly as possible and then gives you back a dopamine hit, to ensure you stay fixed. Beyond this, the algorithms used by social media companies to give you suggested videos are feeding fake news and extremism to the point where democracy and the very fabric of society are under threat. So, what chance have footballers got?

Professional footballers are by no means your average user of social media. Cristiano Ronaldo, for example, is able to earn over a million dollars for each of his sponsored posts. With nearly 500 million followers across Instagram and Twitter, it was reported in June 2020 that the Portuguese icon was able to use his extreme talent to bring in a total of £41.7m from Instagram over the previous 12 months – more than he earned from actually playing football. Even in the lower reaches of the EFL, professional footballers will typically have thousands of followers and won't be short of interactions after a game. Their posts won't be sponsored and certainly won't be bringing in much money, but social media does offer a unique way to interact with the supporters who care so much about the club they play for. Unfortunately, when things aren't going well the mood can quickly turn, and the persistent refreshing of a Twitter or Instagram feed brings only the sort of negativity and abuse that seems to routinely afflict a football team that have lost three or more games on the trot. It can be vile.

As social media becomes more mainstream amongst the younger generations of footballers, its effects are starting to become clear. Ted Smith, a promising former England U20 goalkeeper who played for his boyhood club Southend United, quit professional football at the age of 24 in April 2020, admitting he had fallen out of love with the game. One of the main factors behind this was social media abuse he received after any mistake he made. In an interview with the local newspaper, Smith remembered one particularly traumatising game, away at Bolton

Wanderers, where the criticism and abuse he received after dropping a cross to cost his side two points meant he really struggled with having to go out and play the next week. Despite deleting his social media accounts, he was aware of the comments on there and Smith eventually quit the professional game altogether. Over in Australia, talented Tasmanian midfielder Josh Hope walked away from professional football, saying the social media abuse he was receiving was seriously affecting his mental health. At its worst, someone online threatened to kill Hope if he gave away another penalty, with the former Melbourne Victory player feeling terrified of making mistakes on a match day as a result. The performance impacts of just using social media, before you even get onto the abuse, were quantified in a January 2020 academic study in Brazil which showed that players who used social media sites before a match experienced slower reaction times in that game as a result of a slowed speed of information processing.

In the modern game, football clubs are keen to garner every small potential performance gain, and so are beginning to be more aware of the pitfalls of social media. At the top level, players' contracts often include clauses on social media, but these typically only prevent a player posting something that will bring the club or player into disrepute and put them in breach of Premier League or Football League rules. Beyond this, personal social media use is a murky area and that is where Matt Himsworth comes in. Himsworth, whose main background is as a media lawyer, heads up B5 Consultancy, a company which helps clients get the best from themselves, with player care a key pillar of their work. They aren't recruited by clubs for commercial gain, as Himsworth explains, but to care for the human side of players and staff. Himsworth himself acts as a trusted advisor to a number of Premier League and Championship clubs and players and therefore knows social media and how it affects the best players in the country very well.

'We live in a world where people will happily ridicule super-talented human beings and do it in their faces in stadiums. Nobody's going to stop them, and that's what football players have to come to terms with. Neco Williams is a great example, someone who has achieved in his short career something that you or I could only dream of, but he currently receives incredible abuse. We are all wracked with self-doubt, we all suffer from imposter syndrome. We get strength when we surround ourselves with people who love us and want to help us, but when you're a footballer you're also surrounded by the entire football-loving public, which is the majority of our country. There are some hugely unkind things that are said. When it sounds like an enormous noise, it can become irresistible and can become that player's established reality … When your form is bad, it's difficult to get out of that cycle and then when everyone's telling you your form is bad whilst you are already doubting yourself, it's absolutely huge.

'The other thing that's worth noting is how social media is designed. It's designed to give us these dopamine fixes, and with a young player, the dopamine fix is very, very strong because they get a lot more likes than we do, a lot more responses, a lot more comments, etcetera. They get a lot of validation as well. We did a report on a player recently, an under-23s player. He was liking and retweeting validation tweets that his username wasn't mentioned in. He's been doing a vanity search, seeking out his name. From the actions I see from the lads, they really care about what people say about them on social media, even though they might deny this ... I don't believe them when they tell me it doesn't impact them, that they can just ignore it, because I have seen so many players that have been impacted.'

Neco Williams temporarily closed down his social media after receiving a volley of abuse following a mistake he made against Lincoln City in a League Cup tie. Liverpool were 5-0 up at the time of his error and ended up winning the game 7-2. He isn't the only high-profile player to have shut down his accounts. Three Aston Villa players – Anwar El Ghazi, Henri Lansbury and Kourtney Hause – all simultaneously deleted their social media accounts after a League Cup defeat to Stoke City in October 2020. Martin Odegaard deleted his social media accounts after joining Arsenal, whilst his team-mate at the time, Bernd Leno, said he stopped reading social media after being told to 'do it like Enke' online. Robert Enke, a leading German goalkeeper, took his own life in 2009 after a battle with severe depression.

With such shocking abuse sadly now not atypical, Himsworth is unequivocal in believing top-level players should run their social media through a third-party company. The desire to avoid a barrage of abuse occasionally conflicts with the supposed need to appear 'authentic' to supporters in posts. Gary Neville in particular has called on footballers to run their own accounts and has been critical of PR firms doing it on their behalf, but Himsworth disagrees. He gives the anonymous example of one of his 'superhuman' clients who opened up and admitted to being seriously affected by social media abuse, and says this sort of thing is more common than we might think as supporters. Indeed, quite often when a player misses a game through a 'knock' or a 'niggle', it can be something mental-health related. Players may be able to avoid things printed in the press itself, but they are amplified on social media and will always find a way back to the player in question unless somebody else is reading and dealing with their comments and replies on their behalf. Crucially, though, the man behind B5 Consultancy says all players who use an external PR firm should work with the people at that company, to bring a message and drive through their accounts. Himsworth cites Jordan Henderson and Marcus Rashford as ideal examples of where players have set out a strategy from their hearts to promote allyship and social justice.

It's not always that simple, though. An October 2020 post from José Mourinho's Instagram account shows his Tottenham Hotspur side sat around in the changing room immediately after a victory, with each of the six players in the background on their phones. Most footballers would tell you that it's commonplace, particularly amongst the younger players. With so much free time afforded to them after training and on long coach journeys to away games, many players will use social media purely for something to do. Though seen as a bit of fun and a way to fill the time, it can leave them vulnerable. Knowing this will always be the case to some extent, B5 have a number of services to give as much protection as possible to footballers who do choose to run their own accounts. Himsworth is helped by Fraser Franks and Leigh Nicol, both of whom have played football and experienced social media abuse themselves.

'You can divide what we do into a few categories. One is education, which is crucial. We're looking to develop a culture of three behaviours that we talk about regularly: being risk averse, respectful, and defensive. The youngest age group we speak to is the under-9s, where they shouldn't be on social media but unfortunately a lot are. A lot of them even have parents who run social media accounts for them, which we don't encourage or believe is a healthy thing. We deliver them real-world stories from our experiences of players who have had problems online through their own mistakes or the abuse and negativity that comes with it. We run these sessions regularly and education is really important.

'We also give players support when needed. We will help them from the most insignificant and minor thing to the most serious. It might, for example, be something like getting back into a hacked Instagram account. It's quite taxing mentally when you've got a criminal in your Instagram account and you've got a public profile. It could be that we help them with situations in relationships that are going wrong. It could be communications that they've had where screenshots are taken and communications have been leaked and are going viral online, up to the top end of me offering my help and support as a lawyer in relation to media stories. Leigh [Nicol] and Fraser [Franks] are two people who have lived the same journeys as the players we talk to. Fraser's experience of his mum replying to people that were criticising him on Twitter and having to explain to her that it doesn't help a big, hard centre-half who's playing lower league football – they're good experiences for us to help the lads to understand. I can talk the technical side of working with top Premier League players, but to talk about what it feels like is an important element of what we do as well.'

Of course, the majority of footballers are not in a position to hire someone to do their social media. In divisions where the pay is more modest and life more down to earth, if you have social media, you have to run it and deal with any criticism or abuse you face. Robbie Thomson has had a solid career in Scottish football, though not hitting the dizzying heights of the likes of Rashford and Henderson. We chat in November 2021 with Thomson at Raith Rovers, the club where his father, Scott, famously saved a Paul McStay penalty in the shootout to secure his side the 1994 Scottish League Cup. Thomson junior is particularly keen to discuss mental health, as the academy he runs in his time away from professional football, Pro Performance Goalkeeping, has a partnership with the Chris Mitchell Foundation, named after the Scottish footballer who tragically took his own life at the age of 27 in 2016. Each of the coaches that work for Pro Performance have taken a mental health awareness course through the SPFL Trust, which helps them spot any signs of mental ill health in the kids they coach. It is this raising awareness of mental health that is key, and Robbie Thomson is keen to normalise conversation on the topic by discussing his own day-to-day challenges despite never having been diagnosed with a mental health condition. Aged 28 at the time we talk, Thomson has matured now, but accepts social media was an influence on his mental health earlier in his career.

'When I first signed as a professional, Twitter was rife, and I remember when I was younger competing with all my mates and the boys in the team on who's got the most followers, who's got this, who's got that. Because it was so new, everyone was really naïve in a way. It was like a competition; you were just so engrossed in it.'

After joining his local club, Falkirk, he started to receive abuse. 'They're quite a big, well-supported club, and on social media they've got quite a big following. When I first signed there, we had a bit of a purple patch, we got into the play-offs and it was all good and rosy. Then we started the next season and results-wise we dipped … and I remember seeing negative comments on social media from fans.

'Your brain's natural response is to focus on that negative. You might have ten really good, positive comments and then you get one saying you can't come for a cross or something like that and it sticks with you. In the heat of the game, I would never be thinking of that comment, but in your day-to-day time as footballers you have so much time to yourself … you're checking Twitter or whatever … and of course it doesn't make you feel good. People will say, "I don't get bothered by it," but naturally it does bother you.

'That could be anyone in their work. If Sandra in your office says you're crap at your work, it doesn't make you feel good. Any sort of negativity isn't going to really help you.'

The learnings from Thomson's testimony reflect one of the key pieces of advice for any footballer given out by Matt Himsworth. He reiterates throughout our conversation that it is important for players to use social media as 'an outlet, not an inlet', meaning they shouldn't be using it as a form of validation. There will always be negative comments and that is what the mind will naturally focus on. Therefore, if you are using platforms such as Twitter or Instagram as a means of feedback on your performance level, you will never reach a good conclusion and your confidence will suffer as a result. Performances on the pitch will then suffer, prompting more criticism in a vicious cycle which can only be broken by avoiding the unnecessary and unhelpful criticism that can be freely found online.

Now one of the more experienced heads in the dressing room, Robbie Thomson has weaned himself off Twitter and Instagram and now typically uses the platforms to promote his coaching business rather than getting hung up on what other people think about him. However, football as a whole is trending very much the other way, he says. The younger generation use social media more than ever before, to the point where Thomson finds it 'alarming'. The goalkeeper was part of the Cowdenbeath side that were relegated from the Scottish Championship in 2015 and claims you can see a mile off in a dressing room bereft of confidence when players are searching for something to try and make themselves feel better. Of course, with results poor, the reality is they are only going to end up feeling worse for it. Thomson himself describes a spell of his career whilst on a promotion push with Queen of the South, where he would 'play the game about four or five times' in his head before he went out onto the pitch. It got to the point where Thomson would be entering the field with his mind focused only on avoiding mistakes, rather than concentrating on what might go well for him.

So, how did Thomson overcome this mindset and the contribution that social media made towards it? Like a wise guru looking to share his teachings, he tells me of his 'lightbulb moment' that he feels every footballer should seek to take advantage of.

'I probably initially just rode the wave and tried to fight through it for a spell. Eventually, I started working with a sports psychologist and ever since I did that it's been mentally so much better for me. I never seem to focus on any negativity. Even if I do see anything now, I've got the tools in my toolbox to deal with it, whereas a lot of players would see abuse and be affected by it. Probably the first bit of advice I got from the sports psychologist was to block any negativity I see, until I learnt the skills to cope. The worst thing you can do is search your name on Twitter. It's hard trying to resist the urge to do that, because it was almost part of your routine after a game. The second piece of advice was that these people's opinions don't matter. You realise Jimmy down the road who goes for a pint with his mates does not understand goalkeeping. It's important realising whose opinions count to you.

'There's still the stigma around mental health of, "He's weak" or, "He works on his mindset, that's weak." That just needs to be flipped. If you work on your psychology, you're stronger than everyone else who's not working on that. If you've got the skills and you've got the strategies to deal with mistakes or with negative social media, you're a better player than the person next to you who doesn't know how to do it ... You'll take a dip at some stage and you need to be able to deal with it. I think having the skills from a sports psychology point of view has 100 per cent helped me mentally, even away from football.'

Thomson is hopeful that as sports psychology becomes more ingrained in the game at the top levels, it will filter down throughout the football world. He notes that from a goalkeeping perspective, seeing a sports psychologist is considered almost normal now, particularly around the topic of dealing with mistakes. The Raith Rovers man is keen to see football as a whole make continued progress in its attitudes towards mental health, including around social media. After all, social media is not about to go away any time soon, and to avoid the 'mental health epidemic' Matt Himsworth refers to when speaking about social media, both awareness of the downfalls it can bring as well as the coping mechanisms that can be used to mitigate these downfalls are more important than ever.

* * *

I was fortunate enough to get a ticket for the final of Euro 2020, spending the equivalent of several weeks' wages in the hope of seeing England win their first tournament of my lifetime, indeed, the first tournament in my dad's lifetime. Like the majority of the 67,173 strong crowd (plus the thousands more who gained entry illegally), I watched on devastated as Italy triumphed on penalties to extend our 55 years of hurt, but the overwhelming emotion as I queued for hours in the rain on Wembley Way after the game was one of pride. Our young side had brought excitement to a country that had hardly seen any live football in the last year and a half due to the perpetual lockdowns that had ravaged the nation's morale. For a few glorious summer weeks, there had been a real feel-good factor and the country had come together. Waking up to the headlines the following morning, all that changed.

It wasn't a detail I was thinking about at the time – I'm sure very few fans inside the stadium were – but the three England players who missed their penalties all happened to be black. Jadon Sancho, Bukayo Saka and Marcus Rashford had been sent a deluge of racist abuse on social media, with this grim reflection of society being the main news headline for days to come. It was all depressingly predictable.

Sadly, discriminatory abuse towards footballers on social media is nothing new. Analysis commissioned by the PFA, in collaboration with data science company Signify Group, looked at more than six million posts aimed at footballers on social media between September 2020 and May 2021. They found more than 1,700 abusive posts, which works out at more than six per day. This data only looked at posts sent in a public forum, with the worst of the vitriol often reserved for private messages sent to players. Previous research by the PFA showed that around half of online abuse was directed at just three players – Raheem Sterling, Wilfried Zaha and Adebayo Akinfenwa – all notable for their visible support of the Black Lives Matter campaign around the time of that research in the summer of 2020.

These numbers are so vast that it's easy to forget the human impact, the mental health impact, of each of these cases. Look into some of the stories, though, and the disheartening picture becomes clearer. In July 2020, Wilfried Zaha posted screenshots of sickening abuse he had received on Twitter, the messages referencing the Ku Klux Klan, with the perpetrator threatening to come to Zaha's house if he scored. A 12-year-old boy was arrested in connection with the abuse. Zaha later gave an interview to CNN on the subject, saying he had started to avoid social media, as he was afraid of what other abusive messages he might find in his inbox. He expressed a deep frustration at how footballers are often treated as though they are immune to mental health problems, and spoke of hiring a life coach to help him manage his emotions.

It is perhaps difficult as a white Englishman who has never been racially abused myself to understand just how it feels, but there is no shortage of comments from black footballers past and present that really hammer it home. Marvin Bartley, the former Burnley and Hibernian man who now has a role as the Scottish FA's equality and diversity advisor, has repeatedly warned of a potential suicide in the football world due to social media abuse. He can remember every single piece of abuse he has received, but the toughest element was seeing the effect racist abuse on social media had on his family. Bartley fears that players who receive this type of abuse, aware of the impact it can have on those close to them, may end up internalising the pain and lacking a support network as a result. With this in mind, he always makes an effort to reach out to anyone who faces racist abuse online.

Speaking in a May 2021 BBC documentary on social media racism in football, Troy Deeney talks about how hard it is to read racist comments wishing his six-year-old daughter dead. What's more, if he were to react to this then he would be seen as the bad guy, given his status. You can be as strong-minded as you like, or tell yourself that what happens online 'isn't real' and doesn't matter, but it's impossible to imagine that sort of thing not affecting you. And for Deeney, it's something he has to face almost daily.

In February 2021, I spoke to Iffy Onuora, then working for the PFA, on the subject of online racist abuse in football. Glasgow-born, Onuora carved out a successful career in professional football after securing an economics degree from Bradford University in the 1980s. Both sporting prowess and brains run in his family, with sister Anyika an Olympic bronze medallist and brother Emy an academic and the writer of *Pitch Black*, a fascinating book which looks at the history of black footballers in Britain. At the time we speak, Iffy Onuora is set to move to a new role with the Premier League as head of equality, diversity and inclusion. A key part of his role is to work with social media companies to try and reduce abuse, as well as supporting players who are victims of such abuse. The day prior to the interview, Anthony Martial had a number of racist comments left on an Instagram post after Manchester United were held to a 1-1 draw against West Brom, highlighting once again the scale of the problem. It's something Onuora is fully focused on as he looks to protect the wellbeing of the footballers in the Premier League, and further down the pyramid.

'Even if you're strong-minded, it [abuse] can still seep into you, but it's got to go somewhere. It's like a pressure cooker, whether it manifests itself in your relationships with friends or family or your partner or whatever, that anger and frustration that's come from somewhere else gets directed at somewhere. So it's going to have an impact, especially if it's repeated. Even if you manage to hold it together then perhaps as a person you become a bit more cynical. You become a little bit more inward-looking, you're not as engaged, you could become a bit more suspicious and guarded.

'In a big way or little way, that abuse has to have an impact on people. We could see that at a really tragic level. You look at a celebrity like Caroline Flack taking her own life – God forbid that happens to a footballer, but we can never discount it.'

With racist abuse directed towards footballers now so common, most clubs have developed some sort of protocol for supporting their players when it occurs. As Onuora suggests, this won't always be a one-size-fits-all method, as different players will react in different ways. Young players receiving this type of abuse for the first time, for example, may require more support than the seasoned pro who has unfortunately become used to it. This isn't to say these more experienced players shouldn't be checked up on, though, as a 'straw-that-broke-the-camel's-back moment could come at any time after sustained abuse. One of the biggest challenges in supporting the victim can be around reporting the abuse, with screenshots of any comments typically not sufficient for action to be taken. It can take days to get comments removed from the platforms before you even get into the trials and tribulations of taking legal action. As well as the clubs themselves, support is also available from the likes of Kick It Out, the PFA, and the Premier League, as Onuora explains:

'The PFA has a wellbeing department. Michael Bennett heads that up and he has a network of people he can direct players to. As a hands-on approach in the equalities department, including what's happening now with Anthony Martial, one of us will reach out to the PFA delegate and try to speak to the player. Sometimes, in fact, a lot of the time, the players just don't want to speak. They just want to either give a shrug of the shoulders or get on with it … but some do, so I've actually personally called a lot of players over the last few weeks, months and years just to offer our support. I normally give them the speech: "Listen, these guys are sad people in their rooms, tapping away at a keyboard jealous of your achievements as players, don't lose sight of that." But I guess it's probably easy for me to say that, I'm not the one getting abuse. That's all we can do at the moment: offer support and hopefully further entrench support from higher up along the way.'

Much of the remainder of our conversation centres around what more social media companies can do to protect the mental health of footballers receiving this abuse, by stamping it out as much as possible. In fact, it's clear that the responsibility of companies such as Meta and Twitter goes far beyond just protecting the players themselves. A Sky Sports News survey orchestrated by YouGov in August 2021 showed that 46 per cent of the 516 Black, Asian and Minority Ethnic football fans surveyed felt racist abuse online also caused an increase in racist abuse in stadiums, while 73 per cent were concerned about receiving racist abuse themselves at a game. Clearly, the visible online abuse of top footballers is affecting more than just the players the comments are aimed at. The mental health considerations for these platforms should involve wider society, making tackling the issue even more of a priority.

As to how social media companies can do this, though, it isn't as simple as it seems. Iffy Onuora argues for an identification system for social media users to hold them accountable, and certainly isn't the only person to have called for this, but it is an idea that has received constant pushback from the companies themselves. Not everyone in the UK has a form of ID, Twitter have argued, and forcing people to produce this identification to stay on the platform would exclude these people, many of whom are from disadvantaged backgrounds.

Then there is the argument that anonymity should be a right on social media, particularly to allow the expression of personal opinion without the threat of persecution in countries with less liberal civil rights. Another suggestion is using some sort of software to identify where slurs have been used and remove them immediately, but any automated tools can't pick up on the context of a message. The use of banana or monkey emojis may not always be racist, for example. As explained by Fadzai Madzingira, working for Facebook at the time she gave an interview to the BBC on the matter, the use of some slurs may be in a context whereby the words are being 'reclaimed' by marginalised groups, and therefore automatically removing posts and messages with these words would be more harmful than leaving them up. There doesn't appear to be an easy solution to the problem, though Matt Himsworth of B5 Consultancy is sceptical that the likes of Meta and Twitter have the motivation to tackle the issue of racism on their platforms.

'Their responsibility is as huge as the profits they're making from their platforms. So Meta and Twitter are the two huge players, they have effectively come to every single country in the world and dominated and become hugely rich as a result of it. Do I think they are doing enough? No. The reason they're not doing enough is because their platforms thrive on interactivity. Every time someone racially abuses someone, there's always a reaction, so therefore Twitter sees spikes when players are racially abused. Effectively, their platforms are run by robots and algorithms, so therefore they see profitability in racism, and that is a real shame. I worry that they're not doing enough because they don't see it as commercially profitable to do enough. But that said, there are so many pressure points and they care about their reputation and do more when their reputation is threatened. We've had some good conversations with Meta and Twitter and they've improved their tools, for instance.

'The one thing that they could do to almost eradicate hatred on the platform is to introduce proper verification of identity or make them paid-for platforms. But they're not going to do that, because that would end their platforms effectively commercially. Let's say Twitter said, "We're going to verify all of our users now." The number of users would probably shrink to around five per cent of their current users. It would be like saying to Amazon, "stop selling 95 per cent of what you sell" – they're not going to do that. In an ideal world, we'd go back to year one and we'd realise at that point that actually everyone needs to be verified on this platform. Otherwise, it's not going to be safe. And now it's too late.'

The mental health of footballers may be a priority of clubs and organisations such as the PFA, but it can be challenging to make any tangible progress if the social media platforms themselves have other priorities. The significance of the mental health impact on footballers of discriminatory online abuse has been repeatedly raised: a PFA statement from January 2021, said: 'We have been at crisis point with this issue for two years. Racism causes trauma, and online abuse presents a significant risk to people's mental health and wellbeing.' The statement blasted social media companies, saying it appeared to be 'a choice by the companies running the social networks' to allow abuse to remain online. A similar statement was issued after the Euro 2020 Final in July 2021, while the Premier League and EFL temporarily boycotted social media in May 2021.

Little progress seems to have been made, but Iffy Onuora urges the football world to keep the pressure up on social media companies. The collective strength of the football authorities is important and has prompted companies such as Meta and Twitter to take notice and release statements themselves. The football industry may not be able to directly compete with the social media giants in terms of turnover, but its global significance is enough to worry them and prompt them into potential action. The boycott of 30 April to 3 May 2021 saw accounts with a combined following of nearly two billion temporarily come off social media, sending a powerful message and prompting further conversation on new tools that could be introduced to protect footballers from abuse. However, the main hope as far as tackling social media abuse goes still seems to be in the form of the Online Safety Bill.

Published in draft form in May 2021, the Online Safety Bill looks to bring into law a regulatory framework for content that appears online. The rules are to be enforced by strict punishment, with the bill proposing fines of up to ten per cent of a company's turnover as well as having managers face criminal liability where there are failings. Discussion in Parliament on the contents of the bill was often emotive, with Rio Ferdinand explaining that he had seen family members 'disintegrate' after he received abuse online, with it being particularly hard to explain to his children what was meant by the monkey emoji in the context it was sent to him. Ferdinand added that he had spoken to an anonymous gay footballer who was advised by a lawyer not to publicly come out due to the potential effects the resulting social media abuse would have on his mental health. There was also much disagreement over the proficiency of platforms such as Twitter and Instagram in removing abusive comments. Representatives from Instagram argued they were largely on top of it, with director of public policy Tara Hopkins saying 95 per cent of 'hateful content' was removed from the platform proactively. Evidence from Imran Ahmed of the Center for Countering Digital Hate showed a very different picture, saying 94 per cent of the accounts that had sent racist messages after the Euro 2020 Final had not been removed by Instagram.

It remains to be seen just how much of an impact the Online Safety Bill will have [it was still passing through Parliament at the time of writing], though the harsh punishments proposed for failing to comply should at least provide the incentive to work towards a solution for the big social media companies. Certainly, Iffy Onuora is hopeful, feeling that the bill will force responsibility onto companies which have previously refused to shoulder it. Other media, such as film, television and radio, have a regulator, argues Onuora, and so it is about time the law was adapted for social media companies too. In the meantime, one of the main ways of tackling abuse and deterring others comes via the legal route, though this can often be a challenge to the mental health of footballers in itself, as Matt Himsworth explains.

'It's not easy at times, but the people that send abuse with impunity really shouldn't be doing it with impunity, because you leave a muddy footprint everywhere you go on the internet. One of the challenges of a criminal prosecution is ensuring the police devote the necessary resources to it, and understandably the police are under-resourced in these times. We have made a report to the police for a particular player who doesn't have huge resources, so he can't afford to fund it himself. We have a crime number and it's under investigation, but we haven't had much of an update since. So it can be slow.

'This is unfair because it puts the onus on the victims, but what is really important is that victims are prepared to follow through on prosecutions. I know there have been some football players who have been racially abused or otherwise abused and then they've found that they need to give a witness statement and cooperate with the prosecution, and might even need to give evidence in court. The prosecutions often finish, because you need a victim to prosecute it. There have been other players, such as Romaine Sawyers, who should be really proud of themselves. Romaine clearly said, "Enough is enough, I will cooperate with this," and those prosecutions were successful.'

The case of Romaine Sawyers provided a new and more encouraging precedent for prosecutions over online abuse. His abuser was jailed for eight weeks following an investigation by PC Stuart Ward, the UK's first dedicated football hate-crime police officer. Sawyers spoke out following the verdict to encourage all footballers to report any abuse they receive, saying the case had deeply affected him, but he was hopeful the prison sentence for the abuser would act as a deterrent to other would-be keyboard warriors. The prosecution of a man in Singapore in June 2021 for sending death threats to Neal Maupay will hopefully set a precedent for those abusing Premier League footballers from overseas, where it is thought 70 per cent of abusive content originates from. Despite Sawyers' words of encouragement, however, many players opt not to prosecute when abused, as they try as much as possible not to engage with the comments and messages at all. As most top-level professionals have an agency running their social media accounts for them, this acts as a buffer against the mental impact abuse can have. Pushing for a prosecution might be considered to be in the best interests of society as a whole, but who can blame someone for choosing not to engage with the vitriol constantly appearing in their inbox? Ultimately, the best strategy for dealing with racist abuse will come down to the victim on a case-by-case basis. What is clear is that more needs to be done by social media companies, and indeed society as a whole, to crack down on this sort of abuse and protect the players receiving it before the tragedy predicted by Marvin Bartley becomes a reality.

* * *

With the abuse of footballers seemingly constantly in the news, it is easy to focus exclusively on the negativity around social media, forgetting that there are benefits too from utilising platforms used by around 4.5 billion people worldwide. Marcus Rashford, for example, reached national hero status by using his Twitter account to pressure the government into extending their free school meals programme into the 2020 summer holidays. Not content with this, he used his social media to coordinate a massive effort across business and community organisations to provide food to families and children in particular who might be struggling. Such were his achievements that the Manchester United and England star's use of social media was added to the GCSE Media Studies curriculum. Rashford continues to use his Twitter account to tackle child food poverty, often responding to messages from children and their parents backing his cause, making their day in the process. He has spoken about how grateful he is for the platform provided by Instagram and Twitter and has suggested these positives of social media should be promoted as part of the mission to tackle online hate.

Jordan Henderson uses his presence on social media to help promote the good mental health of his followers. The Sunderland-born midfielder had previously considered deleting his accounts due to the levels of abuse aimed at both himself and his team-mates, but instead decided he could make a bigger statement by remaining online and handing over his account to the Cybersmile Foundation. The anti-cyberbullying charity partnered with Henderson to post resources providing support to anyone suffering from poor mental health as a result of comments online, as well as looking to educate the general public on the topic. Henderson was also part of the BT Sport *Hope United* campaign, which had a similar aim to the Cybersmile content, and he was shortlisted for the British LGBTQ+ awards for his allyship, partly conveyed through social media. Across the other side of Stanley Park, Everton legend Neville Southall is known for opening up his Twitter account to charities and marginalised groups to raise awareness of real-life issues, including mental health. He also regularly dedicates part of his day to reaching out to those who are struggling with their mental health and have asked for a conversation. As noted in his autobiography *Mind Games*, he finds it 'heart-warming' that he can help in this way.

Chris Kirkland too has opened up his private messages to anyone following him on social media who may be struggling with their mental health, all too keen to help, given his own struggles with anxiety and depression. Kirkland's troubles stemmed from an inherent dislike of breaking from routine, coming to a head during his time at Sheffield Wednesday. The 6ft 6in former England international had spent the six years prior to joining Wednesday at Wigan Athletic, living in the same house and with largely the same routine as his five years preceding that at Liverpool. However, when the time came to move on for the good of his career, Kirkland didn't want to uproot his family from their Greater Manchester base and opted to commute the 60 miles to Sheffield each day for training and matches. The time on his own caused his mind to play tricks on him and Kirkland fell deeper and deeper into depression. Though never seriously considering suicide, he does describe a feeling of 'not wanting to wake up' and his wife, Leeona, describes 'losing her husband' for the four years Kirkland was at his lowest ebb. Having received counselling through the PFA, and after attending a residential clinic at Parkland Place when suffering from a relapse in 2019, Kirkland is now in a much better place and has the tools to deal with any tough days he may experience. With this knowledge, he is keen to raise awareness of mental health and help others where he can.

'I started to withdraw myself, not answering calls. When I got home from training late, I didn't want to speak to anyone outside the house. But obviously it got to a real bad way. I didn't know what was going on because it's only really been the last 18 months where mental health has come to the forefront. You turn the TV or radio on every day and there's something about mental health. It's great how it's being publicised. I just got to the point where I knew that I needed help. It's the old cliché: it really was a big weight off my shoulders. You bottle everything up, telling yourself "I'll be OK next week, tomorrow I'll be fine, I'll snap out of it myself," but not really knowing what it is until you get professional help. You realise that these feelings are normal … you shouldn't be ashamed of yourself.'

He felt that by speaking out he could encourage others to follow suit. 'I was probably the first footballer to publicly come out and speak because I was in a better place then and knew it would help a lot of people … I opened up my Twitter direct messages during the first lockdown because I'm an active person. I can't just sit down and do nothing, that's when my mind starts. I knew we were going to be stuck in the house for a while, so I thought there's going to be people struggling as well, let's do some Facetime calls. A lot of the calls have been really good, a lot have just wanted a chat, feeling a little bit down, but then there's the ones that have been really tough as well, ones that have shook and upset me. I try and guide them to the right services, tell them, "It's OK, there's people that can help you," and give them the confidence to make those calls. But on the whole I've enjoyed it. I'm still doing the calls now and I'll continue to do so if somebody needs a chat.'

Opening up his messages to those in need isn't Kirkland's only social media initiative. He is among those attempting to develop new, alternative apps. Footballers Tom Cairney and Joshua Windass have worked to develop OPON, with the main differentiating feature being that all users must be identity-verified to tackle abuse. The app Kirkland has helped to launch in collaboration with entrepreneur Jack Knowles takes it one step further and looks to eliminate more of the issues associated with mental health issues derived from conventional social media. YAPA, which stands for You Are Perfect Always, contains no likes, followers or even photos in an attempt to strip itself back to pure communication. Specifically focused on mental wellbeing, users can post messages in which they set their background colour depending on their mood. Anybody who posts a series of five negative messages will be contacted to ensure they are OK, with local support services also signposted. More recently, sections for meditation and fitness have been added to help users stay on track with their good habits for mental health. In keeping with the football theme, YAPA sponsored the shirts of Colne FC of the Northern Premier League West Division for the 2021/22 season, the club where Kirkland is the goalkeeper coach.

There is a sound logic behind the approach taken by YAPA. A 2020 study from the US led by researchers at the University of Texas at Austin employed a practical experiment which showed teenagers who received fewer likes on social media felt more strongly rejected and reported more negative thoughts about themselves. A further study found that those teenagers who were most affected by having a low number of likes were more likely to show symptoms of depression. The detriment of making unhealthy social comparisons due to images on social media is also a known issue, to the point where a law was recently passed in Norway requiring all 'influencers' to declare what edits they have made when posting photoshopped or modified photos. A reported leak in September 2021 suggested Facebook (now known as Meta) had data showing Instagram exacerbated body issues for one third of teenage girls going back to 2019.

Kirkland himself is a critic of traditional social media, despite recognising its benefits. He deliberately stayed off it during his playing career, only signing up for Twitter and Instagram in 2016, but did see team-mates suffer from reading comments they received towards the end of his playing days. When I ask him what his advice to current players on the matter would be, Kirkland sighs.

'Social media is poison. I made a conscious effort not to go on when I played, so I've only come onto it recently, but I came on it for different reasons: to publicise mental health and try to use it for the positive. It's tough because a lot of footballers use their influence to the good, a lot do some amazing work for charities, but there are also those keyboard warriors who will come after people and abuse people. People have got to be held accountable now. Telling someone you wish their kids and family were dead on social media – you've got to be talking jail sentences … It won't stop everyone doing it, but I guarantee it will stop a hell of a lot. People might say, "They're not murdering anyone, they're not doing serious crime." Well, they are, because people have committed suicide because of the abuse.'

YAPA, by contrast, is perfect for a footballing environment, according to Kirkland. If players set their moods in the morning, their coaches would be able to see straight away how the boys and girls under their command were feeling and could check in on them if necessary. The design of the app allows this exchange to be kept discreet, with the information left to the individual most responsible for looking after the players' mental health, perhaps the club head of wellbeing or player care. Those players repeatedly reporting a positive mood could even have their routines shared as a best practice story.

Chris Kirkland continues to keep mental health at the forefront of his mind. He is now an ambassador for Parkland Place, the residential clinic where he received mental health support when struggling in 2019. The role is particularly rewarding for Kirkland, who regularly travels back to the North Wales clinic to speak to the guests there, all the while giving the message that if a former Champions League winner and England international can speak about his mental health then so can anyone. To keep on top of his own mental health, Kirkland stays active and is part of Walking And Talking Charity Hikers (WATCH). Including other former professional footballers such as Mark Crossley and Dean Windass, the group aim to raise £50,000 for mental health charities and the NHS, culminating in climbing Mount Kilimanjaro in 2023. His work on YAPA is another string to Kirkland's already impressive bow, and the benefits to society are already becoming clear to see.

'It's brilliant what Jack [Knowles] has done. If he'd said he wanted to charge people, I wouldn't have got involved, but from day one he said it would be free for everyone. Obviously, I'd just come out and spoken about my mental health, so I was at a stage then when I thought, this could really help people. So it just seemed the natural and the right thing to do at the time. It's not for praise … it's just I got help when I needed it and it's helping people that need it now. It's gone out all over the world and we get emails literally saying we've saved people's lives. There are emails from people that have really been struggling, saying that they see a way out, they see there is life for them to live. Getting emails like that, yeah, it upsets you, but it makes you feel great knowing that one person has found the courage to ask for help.'

Chapter 7

Academy Football and Those Who Don't Make It

AT ANY given time, there are around 12,000 young boys in English football's academy system, many believing they're on the path to the big time, to the bright lights of the Premier League and the fame and riches that come with it. The reality is somewhat different. Fewer than one in 100 of these boys ever make a first team appearance, and 500–600 will be released each year, the majority between the ages of 13 and 16. Overnight, their identity is essentially torn away from them and they are cast into the harsh reality of the real world, left to fend for themselves. It's no wonder the effect on the mental health of these boys can be catastrophic.

The discussion around mental health in the academy system was brought back into focus with a tragedy in October 2020, when Jeremy Wisten took his own life. The 18-year-old had been released by Manchester City in May of the previous year after suffering with injury problems and had struggled to find a way back into football. Friends described him becoming withdrawn as the months dragged on with Wisten unable to find a new club, to the point where he wouldn't even play 5-a-side football with his mates, and turned down an opportunity for a trial at League Two club Salford City. His devastated parents called for more support for players who are released from academies, as well as mental health education for parents to support their children.

In Michael Calvin's 2017 book, *No Hunger in Paradise*, Manchester City's academy head of performance at the time, Grant Downie, appears to almost predict the tragedy. Speaking to Calvin, he admits to being worried about the danger of players being rewarded too early, only to be cast off and left lost without the comfort blanket of their football career still around them. Manchester City, thorough in all that they do, operate with a relatively advanced welfare arm, with a team of five staff specifically dedicated to player welfare, but still could do nothing to prevent the Jeremy Wisten tragedy. He was not the first boy to take his own life after rejection at academy level, and sadly is unlikely to be the last. The inquest into the 2013 suicide of Josh Lyons, released by Tottenham Hotspur several years earlier, highlighted the impact of that. Assistant deputy coroner Dr Karen Henderson said, 'I find that it's the single most important factor. To build up hopes of a young man and for them to be dashed at a critical age. To have no support for that letting-go seems to be adding cruelty upon cruelty.' In March 2021, 20-year-old Matthew Langton leapt to his death, an inquest ruling the death as suicide. Langton had struggled with his mental health for a lengthy period, but this had worsened following his release from Mansfield Town. He had been in the academy system, initially with Derby County, since the age of seven. The death of Per Weihrauch, aged 32, in October 2020, would not immediately point to a struggle with being let go at academy level, but the Dane had struggled throughout his life with not living up to the huge potential he showed at the academies of Ajax and Chelsea. He took his own life 12 years after leaving Chelsea, where injuries had stopped him progressing into the first team despite his immense talent.

With so many boys in the system, and so few of them making it through to the first team and the professional game, the ultra-competitive nature of some academies has resulted in an abundance of horror stories coming out. In 2020, a 15-year-old Premier League academy player was given a nine-month ban for doping offences. He kept Somatropin, a banned growth hormone, in a fridge at his academy digs where he had just moved from his family home. It appears that this player was so desperate to make the grade for a scholarship at age 16 that he had no qualms about taking the banned substance to enhance his prospects. Instead, the nine-month ban he faced will surely seriously damage his chances. Questions were raised over anti-doping education, which is typically only given to players aged 16 and above and on a scholarship programme. With the intense pressure to make it that far, by that stage it could already be too late.

Going further back, former Fulham academy player Max Noble brought to light the shocking treatment he faced whilst at the club. Noble was persuaded to leave school early, before he had taken his GCSEs, with the promise of a professional contract three years later. However, suffering with injury problems, he was given painkilling injections by staff before training and games. Unsurprisingly, Noble ended up with severe tendonitis in both knees and needed significant surgery to rectify this. Fulham, rather than paying for the treatment after the damage they had caused, released Noble at the age of 18 and cut off all contact with him, leaving him to pick up the pieces alone. On top of this, Noble spoke of suffering racist bullying at the club, with the white players in the dressing room often given preferential treatment. Speaking to *iNews*, Noble admitted his depression and anxiety became so bad after his time at Fulham that it nearly killed him, and he was not the only one, with five friends he knew through football ending up in prison and one attempting suicide. He now runs an informal support group for others like him who have experienced mental health problems as a result of their time in the academy system and their post-academy experience. Noble's strength of feeling is clear, and he describes the academy system as 'grooming' and 'an abuse scandal'. Fulham launched an investigation into allegations of racism, bullying and threatening behaviour at their academy in the wake of Noble's comments, and it would appear that situations like this are generally becoming rarer as the football world wakes up to mental health.

However, even if a young footballer has the time of his life at an academy, with no complaints at all, many still struggle with their mental health after leaving. I spoke to Ben Marlow, who played for West Ham from the age of eight until being released 12 years later. He tells me hasn't spoken much about his mental health before, but is aware of how much of a problem it can be for those like him who see their dreams broken when on the verge of being realised, and so is keen to share his story in the hope it might help others going through the same thing. Now working as a gardener whilst also playing semi-professionally for Bishop's Stortford in the Isthmian League Premier Division, Marlow had a rough idea he would be let go by West Ham back in 2015. Injuries had blighted his scholarship years, but the midfielder was still confident in his abilities and backed himself to find a new club before long. A failed medical at QPR and an injury sustained in a trial match at AFC Bournemouth meant it never turned out that way, and as Marlow spent longer and longer without a club, his mental health started to suffer.

'I remember at the time [of being released by West Ham] I didn't feel too bad, because I was kind of expecting it. I thought, "OK, this is an opportunity to go to a new team, to get a fresh start". It was only afterwards, when obviously I experienced all the rejection, that it hit me. I always put on a brave face, like a lot of people do. You get an ego when you play football, you think you're a footballer, you put on a front. It's all the things surrounding it as well, your family, the outside pressures. Obviously, when you get released, you're not earning any money, so you've got people in your ear saying, "Are you going to stop, are you going to look for a job, how are you going to go to this trial if you've got to pay for the hotel?" All this kind of stuff. So, you go to trials and in the back of your head you're thinking, "shit, I need to get something here". You put more pressure on yourself, which ultimately means you're probably not playing to your best standard.

'I always just used to say to people that I was fine, but when I was on my own in my thoughts I used to think, "shit, what am I going to do?" You feel like you're letting people down. If a team said no, I was more worried about telling other people that I didn't get in than myself. I didn't want to let other people down, people like family that tell me I'm going to do well, and all the people that put effort into helping me. It just all hits you at once, I went through six trials and then I remember just thinking, "fuck". It's a horrible feeling.'

Marlow is certainly not alone in his experiences. Dr David Blakelock of Teesside University conducted the first study to quantify the levels of psychological distress experienced by players after their release from academies, the work being published in the *Journal of Clinical Sport Psychology* in 2016. Though not experiencing any significant mental health difficulties himself, Dr Blakelock's research is partially inspired by his own experiences in football – he played at youth level for Newcastle United and Nottingham Forest but didn't quite make the grade, instead pursuing a career in psychology. Dr Blakelock tells me of mixed experiences during his own time in academy and centre of excellence football. It was, on the whole, an enjoyable time and taught him the importance of hard work, but new staff coming in at Forest whom Dr Blakelock did not get along with spelt the end of his time there. Despite his success in the academic world, he does admit to experiencing unpleasant thoughts and feelings from time to time that involve the idea of underachieving and disappointment.

Dr Blakelock's findings suggested that released players had an increased risk of developing clinical levels of psychological distress, citing examples such as depression and identity crisis or confusion. The paper and Dr Blakelock's subsequent research papers on the same topic discuss several key factors that may make the mental impact of release worse for certain players. One that clearly stands out is the concept of young boys developing an athletic identity – in other words, seeing themselves as 'the footballer'. This is often exacerbated by the fact the boys in academy football are often in their identity-forming years whilst there, meaning they can experience an identity foreclosure of sorts. All this means it can be hard to come to terms with having to leave this all behind and try and integrate into the 'real world'. It's something that Ben Marlow can certainly relate to.

'Because it's all you've been doing all your life, you think, "I'm just going to play football for the rest of it". All through school, everything was, "Ben plays football". That was it. Because you're just known for doing it, not many people think that you're human. I've seen that in one of Marvin Sordell's interviews, that you're not known as "Ben the human being". You're known as "Ben the footballer", which is a role that you feel you have to keep up. It's quite a big role, and when you find yourself, like I was, labouring on a building site for a year after being at a pro club for 15 years, it's quite demoralising and it does affect you.

'When I was working on that building site, I reckon that was probably the eye-opener really. You go in, in the freezing cold of winter, waking up at 6.30 in the morning and finishing at about 4.30, lugging bricks around all day and that kind of stuff, like you're the bottom tier of the building site, labouring. That's when it hit me properly. When I failed the medical at QPR I was still at the top of my game, and I just remember crying for the whole drive home on my own. Six months later I was on the building site. I was like, "how can it go from there to there so quickly?" But that would be when I was by myself. When there were other people around me, I'd be like, "I'm all right, I'm fine".'

Around three years after leaving West Ham, when Marlow feels he 'hit rock bottom', he did seek help. His time with the east London club's academy meant he was a lifetime member of the PFA and was therefore able to take advantage of their counselling service. Talking about his mental health is not something that comes naturally to the Bishop's Stortford midfielder, but he found it was much easier when speaking to a professional. Though Marlow stresses that mental health issues never fully go away, he now understands what triggers him to feel down and how he can prevent it. The main thing, a common theme across football, is ensuring he stays level. Marlow admits after a good game he used to think he was 'the best thing since sliced bread' but would crash and feel worthless after a poor showing. Now, he is able to see the bigger picture and use the last performance as motivation for the next, no matter how he played. He uses his experiences and new-found knowledge to help educate the younger players at the club for whom he now plays, where players regularly join on loan from academy sides.

Marlow stresses he has no hard feelings towards West Ham and doesn't want to criticise them in any way. In fact, he reserves specific praise for his coaches, the likes of Mark Phillips and Nick Haycock, whom he feels he could pick up the phone to at any time. However, it is notable that the club itself did not provide Marlow with any follow-up or support after letting him go. It raises the question of what clubs should be doing for the young players they release.

This is something inherently answered in Dr Blakelock's 2019 research paper. One key consideration in this should be the coping style of individual players. Some young players may show problem-focused coping strategies, using a practical approach to try and minimise the damage and loss of being released if they cannot avoid this career outcome. For example, they may search proactively for a new club or enrol on an educational or vocational course to progress in other areas of life. Others may be more prone to avoidance coping: essentially acting as if their release from their club has never happened by attempting to escape from any unpleasant thoughts associated with it. It is this form of coping that is commonly linked to problems such as substance abuse. The 2019 research paper showed a strong correlation between avoidance coping and increased psychological distress after release, whilst players who habitually use problem-coping strategies are generally better off. Though genetics and personalities may partially influence a coping strategy, it is something that can be shaped by the player's environment too. As Dr Blakelock explains, helping players learn to deal with rejection in the right way whilst still at the club may help set them up for the rest of their lives.

'I suppose each player's journey is like a fingerprint, very individual. What we could do is have a psychologist assess them and try to formulate and develop a shared understanding about what key factors could increase the risk of adverse mental health outcomes and what could protect against them. This in turn might act as a blueprint about what might be helpful to change and guide any intervention or development. For example, if a player engages in avoidance coping and has a limited social and support network, interventions could be implemented to enhance coping and support to protect against adverse outcomes. The key factors will vary so it will be beneficial to review players on an individual basis.

'It could be helpful to have staff try and assess players who are potentially more prone to engaging in avoidance coping both for their development as players and to try and reduce their risk of mental health difficulties after they're released. It could be helpful to foster more adaptive types of coping such as problem focused coping and regulating emotions. If players are going to face difficulties on and off the pitch, they're going to have to be able to deal with difficult emotions on and off the pitch as well.'

But what about after the player has left the club? Dr Blakelock suggests that clubs simply have additional provisions to track and monitor the mental health of their former academy players. Should they identify that anyone is having a difficult experience, the club can step in and provide them with the right psychological support or formal therapy. With the latest Premier League TV deal worth £10.5bn to the division's clubs over three seasons, money should be no object at least for those at the top of the football pyramid. Dr Blakelock also emphasises that even if every club employed this policy and operated it effectively, there would still always be a few players that can't be reached. After all, clubs could offer exemplary support but some players may simply choose not to engage with it. Ultimately, society as a whole, rather than just the football clubs involved, should take responsibility for the duty of care towards young boys who may well be vulnerable, having almost tasted the fame and riches of professional football, before having the dream snatched away. Just in getting that far, they will be sure to have transferable skills that can be well employed elsewhere.

Research into the mental health of youngsters released from academies is very much still ongoing, with plenty yet to learn. The next broad phase, according to Dr Blakelock, is looking at interventions for players, whether that be preventative or reactive. Within the general population, the guidelines for treating depression-related symptoms typically point to either cognitive behavioural therapy or interpersonal psychotherapy. Seeing how generalisable these methods are to released players would be a helpful next step in protecting their mental health. Another interesting consideration is that Dr Blakelock's findings of released players suffering from higher levels of psychological distress than those who were retained looked at players released in the 2011/12 or 2012/13 seasons. Since then, mental health and psychology have been treated with greater importance so players may experience enhanced psychological development compared to previous cohorts. It could be that as this trend continues, the risk of mental health problems developing in players after they are released falls. It is certainly not a time for football to get complacent, though, with the tragedy of Jeremy Wisten showing just how serious the damage can be. The sport must always prioritise the mental health of those who are sold the dream but never quite reach it.

* * *

For those who struggle to come to terms with being released at academy level, one of the first considerations, whether conscious or subconscious, can centre around money. The training ground is full of relatively young men with huge sums of money, all of which is clearly visible for the impressionable young starlets looking to make their way in the game. It is not uncommon for bright young talents who haven't even broken through into the first team yet to be offered thousands of pounds a week just to be retained. Several clubs, including Tottenham and Liverpool, have looked to cap the amount players up to the age of 17 can earn at £40,000 a year, but past this stage the limits are removed. For a player on the verge of making it, the prospect of earning big money very quickly is taken for granted, not a concern at all. When they are released, the chances of earning this sort of big bucks fall pretty much to zero. Players usually find that whatever they do immediately after, they will be taking a significant pay cut.

Having desired – even expected – these riches for so long, it is no surprise that some former academy prospects go to desperate lengths to try and maintain the lavish lifestyle they envisaged. Statistics from 2015, presented in a *Vice* article, show that 147 ex-professional footballers were in adult prisons, with the vast majority convicted of drugs offences. There has also been tragedy on top of this shocking statistic. In 2009, Reece Staples, tipped as the next big thing during youth spells with both Notts County and Forest, died in police custody when a bag of cocaine he had tried to smuggle into the country burst in his stomach. Staples had reportedly been struggling to come to terms with the 'failure' of being released, having had so much attention when he was younger. He fell under the influence of an avaricious girlfriend who persuaded him to make the drug-smuggling trip to Costa Rica which ultimately cost him his life.

Ellis Myles is one of those to have faced time in prison having previously been at a top-level academy. Living in Leicester his whole life, it was a dream when the attacking full-back signed for Leicester City at the age of 14. He secured a scholarship there, but with no U23 side back in 2012 to bridge the gap between the youth side and first team, Myles was let go. With the ambition of running out for his boyhood club now ended, he was left wondering what to do next.

'You give so much of your time, the scholarship was full time and before that you give so much effort … it's like you've been blowing up a balloon for years and then someone just lets it all down and you're back to the start. I think that's the best metaphor for it, that exact feeling. Some people can get their balloon and blow it back up, and some people can't. I was unsure whether I wanted to go again, unsure if I wanted to keep playing football. It was a scary thing for me, when I first got released and went into essentially the normal world. I'd never had a job before, I'd relied on football and that was it.

'When I was at Leicester, I enjoyed the persona of "I play full-time football". Other people see you as the guy who plays full-time football and is going to be a footballer. As soon as I was released, I started thinking, "what if I get a normal job and people see me?" I was worried about what other people thought, so I was like, "people are going to see me in Tesco and they're going to say they thought I played football". I was scared of people asking that question and confronting me. I felt a bit embarrassed. I know a lot of people won't admit it but now I've grown up and look back on other mistakes I've made and you live and learn and grow. But that was a big thing for me, other people's perceptions of me.'

By his own admission, Myles was from a tough part of Leicester, to the point where the club actually requested he move into digs and away from his family home when he signed. On the whole, football is renowned as a sport that gives opportunity to many young working-class boys, and Myles is certainly not the only boy to have left behind an area of high crime to try and escape through football. The beautiful game is, of course, a traditionally working-class sport and for many young boys from council estates represents a shot at the big time. Whilst private and grammar schools may look to paint a high-ranking CEO as an idol, those being idolised in areas like Myles's are invariably footballers, the likes of Gary Lineker and Emile Heskey. Indeed, Ellis Myles turned out for the same youth team as Lineker – Aylestone Park – before signing for the Foxes.

Myles and both his parents were keen for him to relocate away from some of the pitfalls of life back at home. For four years, Myles lived with 16 fellow Leicester players, describing it as the time of his life, but at the age of 18 his release meant he was left to return home, to the environment he had been so eager to escape just a few years earlier. Myles acknowledges he made a mistake in mixing with some of the faces he'd left behind previously. Unsure of how to make money, and with fears over how he would be perceived by others by working in a 'normal' job, Myles had an alternative route, an illegal one, on his doorstep. Crime didn't pay for him, however, and two years after leaving Leicester City, Myles was caught in possession of 30 wraps of crack and heroin. He was jailed for 33 months.

In an interview with football blog *More Than a Game* in June 2020, Myles was asked to identify the highs and lows of his time in football. Most people would assume a spell in prison for drugs offences having been released by your childhood club would be a pretty strong contender for a low point, but that wasn't the response Myles gave: in fact, far from it. The defender, who was kept on the books at non-league Stamford AFC despite his time behind bars, actually describes his time in prison as his high. But why? Being able to sit and reflect on his life allowed him to learn about himself, and know he was going to come out as a better person. It changed him, said Myles, adding that he didn't believe in lows, so long as you learn from them. It's certainly an incredible mindset to have, and something I quizzed Myles on as we spoke over Zoom.

It wasn't always easy. When he arrived in prison, an article written about his football career was printed out and left at his door. People would come up to him wanting to talk about his career and what had happened since, meaning no harm, but every day reminding Myles of where he was now compared to where he could have been. Embarrassed by the attention, he describes 'something clicking in his head' as he went on a personal development drive, eating as healthily as possible and hitting the gym every day. Speaking to people facing stretches of 20 years or more gave Myles an important sense of perspective, and meant his year inside didn't seem so bad anymore. With the help of some friends he met in prison, and the unwavering support of his loyal girlfriend, the former Leicester City man was able to come out the other side feeling much better than he had when he was sentenced.

Having been through all that emotional trauma, Myles feels he can help more than just himself with his experiences. With his knowledge about how the system works, or in some areas doesn't work, he has some strong ideas on how to help others who may find themselves in similar positions to where he was in 2014.

'When I was at Leicester, I remember people used to come in and do talks. They'd be footballers or retired footballers and they'd talk about their lives or careers. But I always feel like those people were all successful or doing things in their career to be proud of. There was never somebody like me, somebody who had a bit of adversity.

'I like to think I was a pretty normal child growing up, I never thought I'd see myself where I did. When I look back now, it's like it all just happens so fast. Maybe I could just take time out to go and talk to the younger people. There are people growing up in bad backgrounds that do manage to get out, and there are loads of people that don't get out. You just need someone in between. Other people who are telling you what's good and bad haven't done it, so people don't want to listen. That's the issue. If I go and tell someone, "right, listen, prison isn't the place for you, you won't like it and you won't enjoy it", compared to someone who hasn't been there or done it, who are they going to listen to? I'd like to think probably me.'

Like Ben Marlow with West Ham, Myles has no complaints about Leicester City as a club, although again he notes there was no aftercare when he was let go. I ask what he would change if he could alter one thing, and his response is instant and unequivocal – the education process. The scholarship group at Leicester City had to do a qualification with their football, and so were automatically enrolled into a sports science college course. Myles doesn't criticise the course itself, but feels it wasn't the right fit for him and indeed many other teenagers who face release from professional football. When these dreams are shattered, the last thing a lot of those let go want to do is stay in football or sport in general for a career. Myles himself was unsure as to whether he wanted to continue playing football, so a career in the area was never on the cards. He wishes instead he'd had the option to study a trade, an electrician's course or plastering course, for example, which would have given him the practical skills to start afresh. It's essential, according to Myles, to drill into young heads the fact that there are always options, and they should be encouraged to explore these. Myles didn't have any options when he was let go, describing it as 'like trying to walk again'.

Now aged 28 and playing for Brackley Town in the National League North, Myles has done a solid job of rebuilding his football career as well as his life as a whole. Having been kept on by Stamford throughout his time in prison, the right-back took a step up to sign for Brackley in the summer of 2016. Straight away, his new side made headlines by knocking League One Gillingham out of the FA Cup in a thrilling replay which finished 4-3 to the non-leaguers, but the best was still to come. A fine run in the FA Trophy saw Ellis Myles and Brackley reach the final at Wembley. With a crowd of over 30,000 in attendance, Myles came off the bench as Brackley equalised late on to force extra time, before triumphing on penalties to win the competition for the first time in their history. It represented a clear footballing high for Myles, a vindication of his efforts to return to the sport after his year in prison.

Myles now has a wise head on his shoulders and tells me of his desire to always help the younger players in the squad. His football with Brackley is on a part-time basis, something which can be seen as a nightmare when you still dream of making it pro, but Myles tries to explain that it isn't bad at all, indeed, quite the contrary. Working as well as playing football part time means he earns an overall wage similar to an average League One player, and is able to use training and games as a stress release tool from day-to-day life. Even if he was offered a professional contract in the National League, the division above where he currently plays, he would be unlikely to take it. Just weeks after we talk, it is announced on Twitter that Myles and his long-term girlfriend, whom he credits as being the biggest help in keeping his mental health on track, are expecting a baby. By coincidence, I had asked Myles if he would let any of his potential future children play in a top-level academy themselves. He would be sceptical, he says in response, but would let them do it and try to guide them with the knowledge he has picked up. As we close the interview, a fascinating conversation in which both of us learn a lot, Myles reflects on the importance of education around mental health.

'I just feel like for me, for the mental health side, I think I don't understand it enough. I maybe could have been suffering from it, or still am suffering from it, but because there's no understanding about it, I haven't felt the need to speak to anyone or pass it on. It's a tricky subject, everyone tries to tiptoe around it because everyone's unsure, or maybe we just don't understand. I feel like it's a good topic, it just needs people to talk about it, but some people just want to laugh it off because they don't understand. I was one of them. I have had tough times and when I came out of prison, I was anxious, worried, and in a bad place.

'When I look back, I've had that same feeling a lot of times before but never understood it. Maybe I needed to speak to someone or needed some sort of help from when it first happened. If I had had that help when I got released, would I have felt the same way the second or third time? That's one of the main things for me, trying to nip it in the bud early, these feelings. The quicker you nip it in the bud, later on down the line you might have the same feelings but you know how to deal with them.'

With hundreds of kids let go by professional football academies every year, and the numbers ending up in prison shockingly high, there is a great significance in Ellis Myles speaking out. Able to articulate his thoughts and experiences in a relatable way, if Myles can find opportunities to preach the advice he has talked through with me, he will help countless youngsters realise they are not alone in their thoughts, and that there is no shame in conversation around mental health.

* * *

In 2019, a photo swept the internet, sparking a great deal of debate. It showed a group of very young children, their faces blanked out, dwarfed by their two coaches stood either side of the group. It wasn't the picture itself that prompted conversations, though, more the caption accompanying it. It read, 'Manchester City FC. Under-5s Junior Academy Elite'. It was alleged, off the back of this leak, that the Sky Blues were dividing their under-5s into three ability-based groups. Of these groups, only the elite were treated with official kit. The club hit back, saying the children involved were only there to take part in fun sessions and were not registered with the club. The photo itself was taken as a souvenir for the children and their parents, and should not have found its way into the public domain. Nevertheless, the criticism was understandably vociferous. Nick Levett, head of talent and performance for UK Coaching, raised his concerns over the wellbeing of the children in the photo, and indeed those in the lower ranked under-5s squads. He pointed out that it would be easy for these kids to start to build their identity around being a footballer before they even reached double digits in terms of age. By this point, many would have been released along the way, leaving them vulnerable to mental health issues whilst still young children. On top of that, the children in the lower ranked teams are effectively being told at the age of four or five that they are not good enough, which shouldn't be something kids have to comprehend at that stage of their lives, certainly not in what is billed as a fun activity. Though there are fears this will become more common as English football's academy system seemingly engages in a race to the bottom in recruitment practices, not everywhere around the world is following the same example. A year after the Manchester City Under-5s scandal, Bayern Munich scrapped their under-9 and under-10 teams, indicating that they thought children would benefit more from learning at their local club without the additional pressure to perform that comes from being with one of the biggest clubs in Europe.

The farming of young children treated as financial assets in English football's endless pursuit of profit was first made possible in 1997, when the FA Charter for Quality put the responsibility of developing players from the age of eight upwards on football clubs themselves. Prior to that, the schools system was the primary way for children to be scouted, and an FA School of Excellence, run at Lilleshall in Shropshire for the country's very best players. Initially, Howard Wilkinson's 1997 reforms offered some protection to the kids they were looking to develop, and indeed one of the ideas behind the changes was to prevent young footballers from playing too many matches for school and local club sides. Small-sided games were introduced, where previously kids had bizarrely played full 11v11 matches whatever their age group, and there was a drive to increase the number of qualified coaches involved in junior football, including implementing codes of conduct and better methods of screening. Crucially perhaps, academies themselves had strict recruiting rules and could only sign players from within their local area. This all changed with the advent of the Elite Player Performance Plan (EPPP) in 2012.

Thought up by six of the richest Premier League clubs, the EPPP was effectively forced upon their less illustrious counterparts in the Football League by threats from the Premier League to withdraw funding for youth development if the proposals were not accepted. A compensation structure was drawn up for the transfer of young players, but the money involved at all levels was peanuts for the top clubs (and not much more for those at the bottom of the pyramid), meaning that in practice there were few barriers for young talents to move to the biggest clubs, who were now able to more easily hoard players. As a consequence, it is not uncommon to see kids as young as eight lumped with huge pressure on their shoulders as they become the sole reason for their entire family to move halfway across the country, for what is ultimately a slim chance of making it as a professional footballer. The ease with which the biggest clubs can acquire players means many of their young talents may even struggle for game time. There have been implications for those smaller clubs who lose their best talents for pennies as well. Hereford, Wycombe and Yeovil all disbanded their academies as EPPP was introduced, citing it as a direct reason. Salford City, Brentford and Birmingham City have since followed.

There are some redeeming features to the Elite Player Performance Plan, admittedly, but there are still clear welfare concerns being raised. The reforms make it compulsory for category one and two academies, those of the top clubs with the most money being invested, to have a full-time welfare and safeguarding position. However, category three and four clubs only need to fill this role on a part-time basis and can double-hat with their head of education. Talking of education, it is compulsory for scholars to take a qualification with their football, but often this is just a sports-related BTEC, which as Ellis Myles explained, often has little practical value for those ultimately let go by their clubs.

As far as producing talented footballers goes, it would be fair to praise the academy system that exists in England. Performances in major tournaments are on a general upward trend under Gareth Southgate, driven in part by exciting young talents such as Phil Foden and Bukayo Saka, who joined Manchester City and Arsenal at the ages of four and seven respectively. However, whilst the success stories are plastered across the back pages and beamed across worldwide television, the collateral damage of the academy system is often hidden out of sight and out of mind.

Howard Wilkinson himself, the man whose reforms instigated the creation of the academy system, spoke out in 2017 in an interview with *The Guardian* calling for reform, saying clubs take too many boys in and do not give them enough opportunity to play. This creates high release rates, he recognised, and mental health difficulties in many children and teenagers as a result. Given the nature of the academy system, it is unsurprising that so many wellbeing concerns are raised by players, parents and staff involved with it. Historical allegations of racism and child abuse have sadly dominated the headlines in this regard in recent years, though there are plenty more 'day-to-day' cases to be dealt with too, often simply involving clubs neglecting the mental health of their young players, past and present. It is fair to argue the sport as a whole does not always deal with these situations as best it can, as Pete Lowe of PlayersNet said to me in an hour-long interview on the subject:

'Does the game pay enough importance to these types of issues? No, it doesn't. The game's reactive, it's not proactive. It would turn round and say, "That's not true, is it, because we've got the Elite Player Performance Plan," etcetera. Really? Is that what the Elite Player Performance Plan does? It's just an audit process. They've admitted that themselves. They say in documentation that I've seen that it's a process of making sure clubs have policies and procedures in place. But policies and procedures, with respect, have never taken care of somebody's health. And what happens when policies and procedures don't work? What do you do then? That's a question I've asked at high levels in the game and you never get an answer, because they don't know the answer to it, plain and simple.

'Football thinks it's got all the bases covered. I've used the phrase many times, that when you mark your own homework you only ever get the grades that you want to see on the piece of paper in front of you, but the grades you give yourself don't necessarily reflect the talents and abilities you show. Football marks its own homework. We have met with a leading chief executive (who was in place at the time) of one of the governing bodies, who asked us to put a business plan to them and we did. It became obvious to me in the end that they never considered that business plan with any seriousness whatsoever. In the three meetings [with them] … they asked us for all types of details, and yet here we sit today and we still wait for an official answer from that governing body to that business plan that was put in front of them about three and a half years ago. I find that astounding.'

PlayersNet was founded by former Manchester United and Wigan Athletic player Simon Andrews with the goal of providing an independent support service for players and parents who have issues inside of clubs, and are frightened of going to the clubs and governing bodies themselves in case it is held against them. Lowe, himself a director at PlayersNet for over five years now, explains that it is this aspect of independence which is so vital, as not only does it give the people the organisation helps peace of mind, but it is also the only thing stopping football from 'marking its own homework'. The cases they get involved in range from contractual disputes to issues around injury and responsibility for care, right through to alleged racism. For example, around the time I speak with Lowe, the news story breaks of the FA investigating racist abuse at Cardiff City, after a 14-year-old alleged his team-mates made monkey noises towards him and rubbed bananas into his clothes. The young victim, who was allegedly told to clean himself up and get on with it by a member of staff at the time, was being advised by PlayersNet throughout the investigation. For all their good work, PlayersNet receive no funding from the PFA, FA or Premier League, instead having to look elsewhere to keep their non-profit, voluntary organisation running.

Don't underestimate the positive effect PlayersNet has had in the years it has been in operation. Simply put the name of the organisation into a Google search, and you will find numerous stories in which they are credited with effectively saving the lives of several young former footballers struggling to find their feet, having been let go by their clubs. One recent example, detailed in a Joe.co.uk article, talks of one player left utterly lost having been released by his club when he thought he was destined for stardom. He sat down with PlayersNet, who were able to point him in the right direction for a career in wealth management, and he is now happy in his work as a financial advisor. In many ways, PlayersNet filled the aftercare gap where the player's former club did not step up to the plate.

When I initially contacted Lowe, I asked him for an interview primarily on the subject of what clubs can do for young players after they have released them. Not one to sit on the fence, Lowe came back to me and told me I was focusing on the wrong thing. The main way clubs can protect young players after they have been let go is to deal with them properly whilst they are still at the club. In fairness, Lowe would know. His first youth development role was with Oldham Athletic in 1992, when the Latics were founder members of the Premier League and pulled off a remarkable great escape, winning their final three games to ensure they would remain there the following year. Lowe moved on to near-neighbours Manchester City in July 2000, being involved before and after the big-money takeover of the club in 2008. He reflects with pride on his time at Manchester City, where many good young players were developed, but first and foremost Lowe always had his principles to ensure the wellbeing of his players at the forefront of his mind.

'Released players now seems to be the in-vogue topic. I ask myself why it's really an in-vogue question if I'm honest with you. There is a process that should be in place inside of clubs that starts to kick in when players aren't quite meeting the standards for the club they're registered at. It should kick in with naturality … with the skill set of the people who are working with those players, so they start to say the right things … well before it's actually happened, and so when the news is actually delivered it's not a cataclysm in a player's life. He was expecting it. It's not a catastrophe in a parent's life – they were expecting it. They can plan for the future.

'What this all comes down to is the messages you give to players on a daily basis. No player should be told he's going to make the grade. I tell you one thing that happens too often in the game, we use the word 'great' too often. It's such a false word, it's untrue. Let me just give you some examples: "Son, you've had a great game today. You're a great player. That was a great pass." Why don't we just understate it and turn round and say, very simply, "Well done"? If I had one strength, that would be the one I pick out for myself going back to those years as a coach. I tried to understate everything so the players understood they'd done very well, but that was what had happened then. What happens next then becomes important. And so, giving players messages that "You're going to make the grade." Really? Are you that good that you can tell what player is going to make the grade? There should be no false promises made, because making false promises is an easy way out of a problem. And so, what we should be talking about is … the process we go about to release players.'

With his knowledge and years of experience, Lowe frames the problem in a different way to the popular media view but makes a lot of sense. Another thing he is passionate about is his hatred of using the word 'elite' to describe players in the academy system. There aren't any 'elite' players in the academy system, merely players with potential. Calling someone elite before they have advanced through to the first team would be giving the wrong daily message and set the player up for mental health problems further down the line if they don't make it. Lowe's theories on constantly preparing a young academy prospect for the possibility they don't make it don't negate the need for aftercare, but addressing the cause of the problem rather than trying to pick up the pieces after the damage has been caused seems a very common-sense approach. But this best practice is not always visible within academy football, hence the high rate of mental health difficulties amongst players that Howard Wilkinson refers to when calling for reform. As Lowe puts it, common sense is not always that common.

Our conversation moves on to how the perfect environment to look after a player's mental health can be brought about. We both agree that the academy system is like the rest of football – results-focused. In this case, the end goal is the production of players for the first team, or to be sold on with a good resale value. With the football side the number one concern, there is a danger of the mental wellbeing of young boys being neglected. The chance of this happening all comes down to the culture within a club as a whole, a relatively abstract concept in itself, which Lowe explains comes from leadership. During a visit to South Africa on behalf of Manchester City, Lowe heard the story of Nelson Mandela and considered how he could apply the teachings of the first post-apartheid president of South Africa to his role in football. Mandela considered himself as akin to a shepherd, with those following him his flock of sheep. He would tend to stand at the back of the flock, letting them have responsibility and feel in control. However, when required, he could step to the front of the flock and protect them from danger.

In a football sense, Mandela's model requires staff who have a massive curiosity about the people they work with, and can build a rapport with them. It's about knowing people's backgrounds, their triggers, and what places them under pressure. When their mental wellbeing is under threat, the coach can step to the front of the flock and protect them, with this support continuing after the player has left the club in question. This isn't just the responsibility of one or two people, and sometimes a title can create a problem, as Lowe explains. A head of welfare may be the person ultimately responsible for welfare at a football club, but that shouldn't mean other people negate their responsibility towards welfare. The culture of wellbeing needs to permeate throughout the club, with everyone stepping up to the plate. Some top professional clubs have taken steps towards promoting this culture in recent times, particularly as the conversation around the mental health of young footballers gains more focus. Swansea City's safeguarding and academy operations team is 18 people strong, and the club have also partnered with non-profit organisation Beyond the White Line (BTWL) to provide their players with mental health and wellbeing support. In the wake of the Jeremy Wisten tragedy, it was notable that it was a Swansea City player, Ali Al-Hamadi, who felt comfortable in speaking up and discussing mental health challenges the academy system can pose whilst still in the system himself. It was reported in August 2021 that Tottenham were recruiting a mental health and emotional wellbeing manager to work with young players, and Liverpool have an alumni project to track and look after former academy players after they have left the club. All these things show clubs taking an initiative and going beyond the policies and procedures in place, which Lowe argues is crucial in promoting the wellbeing of young footballers.

Even if clubs are on top of their player care in-house, external pressures and the nature of football's big bucks industry can still pose problems along the way. Football's race to the bottom in recruitment standards of young players was highlighted in a September 2021 BBC *Panorama* documentary which alleged that leading agent Aidy Ward broke FA rules by signing underage players. These FA rules forbid the offering of deals to players before the year of their 16th birthday, but the documentary exposed a series of leaked emails and messages purportedly showing Ward's agency, Colossal Sports Management, breaching these rules. A number of parents of children under the age of 16 came forward and said that Colossal had been in touch to offer their services, whilst it was also alleged that Ward paid a parent £10,000 for their child to join his agency. Ward had also apparently asked one of his former clients, Raheem Sterling, to speak to a 15-year-old as part of an attempt to sign him. It is understood that Sterling at no point spoke to any players about agents, and would only give aspiring players advice on football matters.

Whilst the case of Aidy Ward and Colossal Sports Management made headlines due to their financial clout and high-profile clients, realistically it is unlikely he is alone in making illegal or simply just unethical approaches to young impressionable players and their parents, many of whom are economically challenged at the time. A survey from *The Athletic* spoke to more than 20 top football agents under the condition of anonymity. When asked if agents were breaking rules around minors, not a single one of the surveyed agents said no. One of the agents admitted the process was essentially 'grooming', whilst another lamented how, if you did follow the rules, you would never pick up a promising client at 16 as they would already have been signed up to another agency illegally. FIFA deregulated football agents in 2015, scrapping the licensing regime and entry exam that had existed, making it far easier to become an agent as a result. This allowed the opportunistic an open door to pay the £500 required and register as an intermediary, hoping to make a quick buck in whatever way possible. Stories of agents approaching boys as young as ten on social media are common, as countless individuals compete to attract whatever young talent they can find. If an agent finds the next top player at the age of 12, this kid will be worth millions to them in ten years' time in commission on transfer fees and in negotiating new contracts. If the child turns out not to ultimately make it, the agent loses very little. All this presents a significant danger to these young players and their families, as they try to separate the good agents from those trying to exploit them for their own financial gain.

The problem of the 'meal ticket syndrome', in which kids end up being used as a way to make parents money, is particularly acute as agents continue to prowl. It is often hard to blame the parents in this situation. With the sort of money that can be offered, if somebody is living on the breadline it can be hard to turn clubs and agents down. There have even been anecdotes about parents of promising young footballers being offered jobs at the club where their child plays. If the child is released, the parent will also lose their job. It's a ruthless world, and the pressure it puts on a child at a young age is intense. Football effectively becomes a job for that child from a very young age, and so it is no wonder so many lose their hunger and drive in football, as Pete Lowe points out during our conversation. It is not always just agents who break the rules, and clubs can occasionally be complicit too. In 2017, Liverpool were banned for a year from signing academy players from other clubs after being found guilty of offering inducements to a 12-year-old Stoke City player and his family.

If George Best was the first footballing celebrity, then Sonny Pike was quite possibly the first football child star to fall foul of the meal ticket syndrome, with the main perpetrator in this case his own father. Shooting to stardom before he even reached his teen years around the time the Premier League was just starting up and the media's interest in football was skyrocketing, Pike trialled at Ajax for a week before spending time at Chelsea. However, the mental health troubles that resulted from his experiences led a teenage Sonny to the verge of suicide, as feelings of worthlessness engulfed him when his football dreams were shattered and his relationship with his father ruined. His 2021 autobiography *My Story: The Greatest Footballer That Never Was*, is written as a stark warning to parents whose young children are caught up in the cut-throat world of football today.

Sonny's father had harboured dreams of being a professional boxer but had to give these up when Sonny was born, to look after him instead. The story that follows is essentially brought about by Sonny's father attempting to live his broken dreams through his son's footballing career, whilst also keeping a keen eye on the pursuit of profit. With Sonny's talent evident from an early age, his father was quick to support him in his footballing endeavours but would always focus on the difference between winning and losing, rather than emphasising that football for his young son should be something to enjoy. As the goals Sonny scored began to stack up, interest started to grow in the local press, which was blown up by his father to extreme proportions. Put Sonny Pike's name into YouTube, for example, and you will find a clip of his appearance as a guest on *Fantasy Football League* in 1996. A week-long trial with Ajax was marred by constant intrusive media attention, starting at 5am on the final day of that trial, affecting Sonny's performance as a result. Not even his son having a panic attack due to the constant presence of cameras and media men in his life convinced his father to wind down the attention slightly.

Ultimately, his father signed up with the infamous agent Eric 'Monster' Hall, with Sonny set to be the subject of a documentary which he thought would talk about his footballing ability. Instead, it was about the poaching of players by football clubs, and Sonny was banned from playing football for a year after an FA inquiry. Sonny didn't know he was doing anything wrong, but was also signed for Leyton Orient at the time he was playing for Chelsea, breaking FA rules. Rubbing salt into the wounds, those forms at Orient had been signed by his dad, when it ought to have been only his mother who had legal responsibility to do so.

In the wake of the fallout around the documentary, Sonny's father disappeared. He eventually returned only to ask Sonny to engage in more media work, which he refused to do. His father told him, 'I ain't got a son no more then,' and the pair have not spoken since. Having survived the mental health lows that followed in the ensuing years, Sonny is now married with children and talks in his book about being desperate to learn from the mistakes of his own father. He reflects that there is currently a large 'burden of expectation' on kids in academy football due to the commercialisation of the sport, as well as the rise of social media. When his own son was asked to play for a Premier League academy, he was sceptical, but let him go ahead, safe in the knowledge he could use his own experiences to look after him. He emphasises it is important that kids have a focus outside of football as well to avoid having everything too soon – something he terms as 'Sonny Pike syndrome'.

The challenges faced by kids today are of a different nature to those faced by Sonny Pike, though the root causes are very similar. It is unlikely one single child barely into their teenage years would face the media attention Sonny Pike did, but the temptation of financial benefit to their parents will heap pressure on the shoulders of hundreds of kids across the country. It is vital that agents who do break the law and approach underage players are punished accordingly, and that clubs are reminded of their responsibilities in recruitment practices. Parental education, too, is key. Ultimately, when things go wrong, it is always the child who suffers the most.

Speaking to Michael Calvin for *No Hunger in Paradise* the week before he was appointed manager of the England first team, Gareth Southgate admitted his fears over the 'commoditisation' of children. With this intrinsically linked to the high amounts of money young players can earn, he expressed his support for some sort of financial reform, whereby players under a certain age are automatically entered into a bond scheme. Some of their wages beyond a certain level would be locked away until they were older and wiser, with the hope of preventing money and fame going to their heads at a young age. Pete Lowe, of PlayersNet, agrees. However, despite the common sense intrinsic to the idea, he doesn't feel there's a way it would ever be practically implemented, with some form of legal challenge always likely to prevent it. For the young fish coming through into football's big pond, the issue of premature riches is one for them, and indeed their parents, to deal with, as Lowe points out.

'There is no question that some who get too much too soon lose drive, they lose hunger. There is a danger that what we do is project all the types of riches onto young players and what they see the game as being is a payment method for them, not a game that they can play to be recognised as a major talent in. Money always creates the problem, let's not hide behind the bushel and say that it doesn't. Of course, you get families who chase the best deals for their sons. But are the best deals the longer contracts that are given, without there necessarily being great money on the contracts at the start, or are the best deals the shorter contracts with fantastic money, yet no career at the end of the contract? So, money will always be an issue. It will always create problems. It's how it's handled by the people who want to give it out, how it's controlled, how the message of it is delivered, and how and when it's delivered.

'Parents have a huge role in their child's development, and those clubs that want to keep parents at arm's length because they think they're trouble-causers and messers and goodness knows what, with respect and in my opinion are missing a fantastic opportunity to bring into the coaching environment somebody who can help solve problems for the football club. I remember a football club from years ago who used to have a sign on the pitches, and I found the sign incredible. It simply said: "Strictly no admittance to parents beyond this point", or words to that effect. Can you see the message that's being delivered? You're just sending a message to them that actually, they're not that important, when really they are.'

With their children likely to face so many challenges on the way, and the landscape constantly changing, it is vital that parents are given as much help as possible to support them. The FA and Premier League do provide education to academy players and their parents about the murky waters of agents, but this is just one facet of a complex set of challenges facing them. It is notable that Jeremy Wisten's grieving parents called for more education for parents to support their children with their mental health throughout their academy journey. Evidently, the football world needs to heed this call and ensure plans are in place for all stages and aspects of a child's time in academy football, from starting out, learning to deal with agents and financial considerations, right the way through to the reality most boys in the academy system face – being released. For all the concerns raised over wellbeing, the academy system is not going away. Football is a multi-billion-dollar industry watched by billions across the globe, and to develop the best talent, kids will be coached and developed from a young age. This is fine, but the game must learn to recognise and deal with the negative externalities, the side effects, that come from that. One death is one too many, and it is imperative that football learns from the Jeremy Wisten tragedy to prevent anything like it happening again.

Chapter 8

The Coronavirus Pandemic

WHEN IT was announced that Arsenal manager Mikel Arteta had tested positive, the football world knew. Arsenal's trip to Manchester City had already been postponed, owing to the fact Olympiakos owner Evangelos Marinakis, who had met several Arsenal players following their Europa League tie, had tested positive for the virus. For weeks, as the COVID-19 pandemic started to take hold on the continent, football in the UK staggered on, heeding the government advice at the time – or rather the lack thereof. Indeed, on the day Arsenal's fixture in Manchester was due to take place, Wednesday, 11 March, Liverpool hosted Atlético Madrid at a sold-out Anfield, even though the situation in Spain was weeks ahead of that in the UK. Two days later, the inevitable was confirmed, and the Premier League, EFL, Women's Super League and the Women's Championship were all postponed until 3 April at the earliest.

Below this, the National League staggered on for one more weekend, though five of the 11 scheduled games were called off anyway with a number of players and staff members from various clubs self-isolating. The atmosphere at the last games standing was somewhat bizarre – at Sutton United's 1-1 draw against Hartlepool, the crowd, though larger than usual as neutrals flocked to see one last game before the impending shutdown, were muted as supporters tried to work out the context of the game. What might happen next? Any hopes of a late play-off push from either side looked set to be rendered irrelevant, collateral damage in the wider fight to protect the health of the nation. The National League, along with the grassroots leagues who had also kept playing for one final weekend, finally gave up on Monday, 16 March. A football wouldn't be kicked in the UK for another three months, when Aston Villa and Sheffield United played out a 0-0 draw behind closed doors in the Premier League.

When Prime Minister Boris Johnson finally announced a full lockdown a week after the last of the football had been suspended, the nation was only just starting to grasp how much things were set to change. With the population largely confined to their own homes, permitted out only to exercise once a day and to shop for essentials, a huge mental health impact was understandably feared. Up to 11 million people were put on the government's furlough scheme, leaving them temporarily not working with many fearing future redundancy as the economy suffered from lack of activity. An Institute for Fiscal Studies report, published in June, found a significant rise in mental health problems as a result of the pandemic and subsequent lockdown. Research conducted by Mind in June, towards the end of the initial lockdown, found that 66 per cent of adults and 75 per cent of 13- to 24-year-olds with an existing mental health problem said it had got worse during lockdown, and 22 per cent of adults with no previous mental health issues now said their mental health was poor or very poor. The Centre for Mental Health estimated 500,000 more people in the UK would need mental health support as a result of the pandemic. With footballers' lives completely disrupted, they certainly were not exempt from this.

One of the many leagues affected by the pandemic was the FA Women's Championship, which was officially terminated early on 25 May with the title being awarded to Aston Villa ten days later. There was still great uncertainty at this point as to when the league would start again, and the players of each club were forced to deal with this as best they could. Research on the UK's general population showed females to be a more at-risk group in relation to suffering mental health conditions related to COVID-19, and this was reflected in a FIFPRO survey that came out in April 2020. The survey, which looked at a sample of professional footballers worldwide, found 22 per cent of female players compared to 13 per cent of male players reported symptoms consistent with depression. Chelsea Orme is the club psychologist at Lewes, one of the sides playing in the Women's Championship. Her expertise in the subject, as well as her experiences working with the squad over lockdown, mean she's aware of just how significant the mental health impact of the COVID-19 pandemic is when we talk in October 2020.

'Everyone is suffering; the pandemic is definitely not discriminating against anyone. It's a new and uncertain situation with a lot of physical isolation. Seeing friends, seeing family, doing all the things you take for granted, and then it's suddenly gone. I think, though, that people have started to realise how much they rely on physical interaction and connection for their positive mental health. Then you add the extra anxiety of the health risk or bereavement and you've got two prongs of a very extreme situation. You've got the physical health side and then the social isolation side: the two combined is going to affect your wellbeing in some way or another.'

Across the division, and arguably women's football as a whole, Lewes are one of the clubs best equipped to deal with the psychological challenges posed by the pandemic. As well as having a psychologist, there is also a welfare officer at the club to make up the wider mental health and wellbeing team. This is something of a rarity in a side where the majority of the players are only semi-professional. Community owned, the club themselves are perhaps best known for becoming the first club in the world to commit to equal pay for the men's and women's teams, and have a reputation for always putting their players first.

As the country went into lockdown, the mental health and wellbeing team worked even harder for the players. Weekly quizzes were organised over Zoom to keep the players in touch, and they were also all engaged in daily videos with different focuses, the idea being to maintain a visual connection. On top of the fun stuff, players were regularly asked what their key learnings from the lockdown period were, and there was a focus on staying fit, given it wasn't until late May that it was known for sure the league wouldn't finish. The squad were even able to take advantage of a couple of the players' other talents – personal training sessions were put on by a few members of the squad involved in that line of work, whilst midfielder Emily Donovan entertained the squad with her ukulele skills.

Connectivity was key, but the processes in place went beyond just that. The club assessed every player's and member of staff's risk on a number of factors, including physical, psychological and financial risk. The holistic approach to this considered several variables, from their living situation to the job they did, and included regular consultation with the mental health and wellbeing team. The end result was that Lewes were always on top of the situation, and were able to offer support to those who needed it most. It's this sophisticated approach to mental health that was one of the key factors in attracting star striker Ellie Leek to the club.

'I think the difference is Lewes actually put you first as a person, and then as a footballer. There's not that much money in women's football so a lot of clubs feel that pressure and can't really treat people the way that people probably feel like they deserve, so you do just become a number and a player in a lot of environments.

'I can't speak highly enough of Chelsea [Orme]. Having Chelsea as a sports psychologist just for us, knowing it was confidential, was great, and she would always check in and just text us. If we wanted to chat, we could just chat. It was completely on our terms. It did take me a while to build that trust and open up more to her, but we have a really good relationship now. I speak to her most weeks.'

Leek was a relatively new signing at Lewes when lockdown hit, having only joined the club in January 2020. It might have been considered a rocky start after the manager who brought her in, Fran Alonso, left the club just four days later, but Leek still managed to begin to establish herself under new manager Simon Parker. However, before she had really had the chance to get going, the season was abandoned. All in all, Lewes played only two league games between Leek signing and the season being suspended on 13 March.

As the situation developed and it became clear football would not be resuming anytime soon, Leek moved home to Wales with her girlfriend, Martha Thomas, who plays for West Ham United. The shared adversity the pair faced helped them both deal with the situation, and they were perfect training partners as they tried to stay on top of their fitness. However, despite the idyllic countryside location and good company, the situation for Leek was far from ideal with her future at Lewes not completely guaranteed.

'I'd just broken in and then you go into lockdown and you don't know if you're going to get offered a contract next year. There's a lot of anxiety and it's a horrible time of year anyway in the women's game, but also being in lockdown and not being able to showcase yourself just added to that pressure. You're trying to throw a film together so you can send it to Simon [Parker], who was reviewing the side and who he wanted on his team next year. We coped with it as best we could but obviously it was very difficult as well.

'I think because there were so many of us in the same situation, we kind of all just came together and spoke to each other, helped each other through it. I felt lucky that I was working full time so I had something to focus on, and work was going really well for me at the time. I work in recruitment and it's commission-based, I was making deals which kept me motivated. Because I didn't have football, I just channelled my mind to work, and that helped me a lot.'

The further Leek discusses her personal situation, the more you get the sense that the timing of lockdown would have seemed a nightmare at the time. A couple of years earlier she had been playing in France for Le Havre on a professional contract, her first club since playing at university in America. Having met her partner, Martha, out there, the pair moved home to England, but Leek initially struggled with the transition to playing semi-professionally, with another job on the side. A spell at Charlton was an unhappy one, and Leek had taken a break from football before joining Lewes. Lockdown came just as she was starting to fall in love with the game again. Ultimately, though she was only new in the side, the culture of togetherness and team spirit pulled her through.

'I'm someone who's very open about having mental health problems. I suffer really badly with anxiety and I've been in some dark places, but the best way that I've found that I've come out of them is by speaking about it. It's just something I've used as a coping mechanism, which has helped me through the hard times and to deal with it. Also, I feel like because people are so open about it, other people feel like they can confide in people so it does build that team relationship, and makes us a lot stronger. Our team chemistry is so good at Lewes, I feel like I can literally speak to anybody.'

After what ended up being almost a six-month break, the Women's Championship finally resumed on 6 September 2020. Lewes didn't play until the next week, making the long trip up north to lose 3-0 to Durham, but there was a strong element of just being happy to be back. Joining them in the Championship for the 2020/21 season were Liverpool, who had been controversially relegated from the WSL on points per game. The Merseyside club's record had been poor, with just one win in 14 games, but their form was improving and the club criticised the decision in a statement on the official website. At the time of the season suspension, Lewes were in ninth position with a points per game that would move them up the table rather than down. Both Orme and Leek agree that being safe from this cruel method of deciding promotion and relegation helped take the stress away from the side. As it happened, nobody was relegated anyway, with the leagues below the Championship being made null and void, meaning no club could be promoted to replace a relegated side.

Though it was a relief to be returning to play the sport they love, it's fair to say the experience was not the same as before. As with the rest of the country, anyone testing positive for the virus had to self-isolate for 14 days, meaning they couldn't play. Missing one or two players through this was frustrating, but the situation was far more awkward than that for Lewes. With many of the players living together, if one player caught the virus, the chances were the whole household would – and they had to self-isolate in the meantime. All of a sudden, there were four or five players missing, and a game would get postponed. As Orme points out, the constant stress this posed to players created more problems on top of just the practical implications.

'You can't prevent someone catching COVID-19. You can put all the safety measures in place, but you can't eliminate every single risk. So if someone gets symptoms, they get symptoms. It is more about reducing the risk of spreading and a club outbreak. We're very conscious about not creating a blame culture around anyone who tests positive and causing feelings of social isolation on top of the physical isolation required.'

Catching COVID-19 carries the danger of longer-term implications through 'long COVID', where symptoms such as fatigue and shortness of breath persist beyond the usual two-week period. Jamaal Lascelles and Allan Saint-Maximin at Newcastle United were notable sufferers, proving that fit athletes are far from being safe from the problem. The chances of long COVID impacting any given individual are low, but the implications severe, and it was enough to generate even more anxiety at the peak of the pandemic, when levels were already sky-high. On dealing with all these uncertainties, Leek refers back to the 'lockdown learnings' element of the squad's group calls. The team were trying not to think too long term, and were trying to focus on the controllable elements rather than what was out of their hands. Given the circumstances, it's all they could really do.

And then there's the complicated issue of having fans, or rather no fans, in the stadium. Early in the 2020/21 season, the elite-status Lewes played all games behind closed doors. Bizarrely, Lewes' men's team were allowed supporters, though, as they are classed as non-elite. On a normal pre-coronavirus weekend, both teams would attract crowds of a similar size, but now only one was allowed anyone at all. Rules are rules, certainly, but those rules didn't appear to make a lot of sense and were clearly frustrating for those affected. Towards the end of the year, fans were briefly allowed in for the women's team as well, Lewes getting their devoted supporters back for a couple of games. However, as cases rose again, the government's tier system soon put a stop to it. Talking to Leek about the situation, it's obvious how much she loves playing in front of a crowd for the atmosphere it provides, but her concerns go far beyond just that.

'It's always great hearing the crowd roar if you score a goal or do something good. I guess it [the lack of fans] made us as a team feel like we have to be louder and we have to try and encourage our team more because there's not that atmosphere.

'At a club like Lewes where we don't have a men's club with millions behind them backing us, we rely on spectators coming to games, paying for tickets, in order for us to get paid. So, we do worry, I think we all took pay cuts … For me, it was if I can afford to play, then I'll play. I wasn't going to ask for more money or anything like that just because of how fragile women's football is right now. It's scary and sometimes you do think: is it going to last? Are we going to be able to survive it? But I think all of us just keep trying to hope that it's just going to be short term and hopefully we'll have fans back soon and have built a big enough platform where we have people all around the world supporting us financially.'

Understandable concerns have arisen over the future of women's football during the pandemic, particularly as the financial model of clubs like Lewes is based around getting supporters into games. Of the £300m government sports bailout in November 2020, football only received £28m of which just £3m went to women's football. A ground-breaking partnership with Lyle & Scott in December was a huge boost to Lewes, but concerns over women's football remain at many grassroots clubs across the country. With the FA making cuts of £22m a year to grassroots football starting at the height of the pandemic in 2020, there are fears women's football will be disproportionately affected, particularly in disadvantaged communities.

As funding is cut, not just in football but in wider society as well, it is feared that one of the first areas to feel the crunch could be funding for mental health. As of the 2020/21 season, the FA requires every Championship team to have a mental health strategy, but it is possible for clubs to set this up and then largely ignore it if they wish. Orme believes that more funding for mental health is needed in football, but with the FA cuts and the precarious financial situation of the game, she knows such hopes are fanciful. Lewes turned to the community side of their model for backing. One of the club directors works in counselling, and helps the club arrange deals with local counsellors and therapists for when their support is required. A mental health directory is available for players and staff with six pages of cheap and easily accessible resources highlighted. Many of them are based around local charities, so the club looks to support these as much as possible to give back. At a challenging time, when mental health is becoming a national crisis, it is refreshing to see Lewes leading the way in the world of football.

* * *

Whilst the outcome of the 2019/20 season for Lewes was fairly innocuous, not everyone was so lucky. Only the top two divisions of men's football were able to play on to a close during lockdown; every other league in the country opted for either making the season null and void, or deciding the final standings based on a points-per-game method. Whichever option was used, there were bound to be winners and losers, and controversy was never too far away. In League One, Tranmere Rovers were relegated by 0.06 points, with the club bemoaning a deep sense of unfairness and suggesting jobs would be lost there as a result of the decision. Things were even messier in League Two, where initially Stevenage were relegated, but more than two months later a points deduction imposed on crisis club Macclesfield sent them down instead. The Silkmen were then wound up in the High Court a month later, leaving the National League a club short for the 2020/21 season.

Arguably, though, it was non-league football below the National League, in the 'non-elite' category, where the greatest levels of injustice could be found. The season was officially terminated on 26 March, barely a week into lockdown, and immediately declared null and void. This meant there would be no relegation or promotion, with numerous clubs reacting angrily at seeing all their efforts over the previous seven months rendered irrelevant. Two sides from the tenth tier of English football had already mathematically secured promotion, with Jersey Bulls winning all 27 of their Combined Counties League Division One fixtures, but they were told they would have to start the next season in the same division. On 30 March 2020, an open letter calling for the FA to reconsider their decision was sent to the governing body, signed by 66 non-league clubs, with the letter directly addressing the mental health impact of the FA's decision:

> The FA cannot disregard the potential mental health impact on those involved in the running of non-league teams affected by the decision. Football plays a monumental role in the lives of so many people, young and old, and the footballing authorities have rightly started to acknowledge this on a national scale. So we question whether this aspect has been considered when rushing out a decision as important and drastic as this.

Geoff Thompson, chairman of South Shields, was one of the key men behind the campaign. 'There are 1,600 clubs involved in non-league football at those levels [step 3-7]. The clubs at our level have an extremely important role within the community. That was our point, that a lot of fans interact with the club, their whole social life is centred around the football club and the work that the clubs do in the community. We've got our own foundation, for example, where we deliver a whole host of health and wellbeing programmes to members of the community. All of those things, sadly, go slightly unmeasured. It tends to be just first team results that hit the headlines, where you are in the table, as it were. So, our point in that letter was to emphasise the important role that clubs play in those 1,600 communities.

'If you take South Shields as an example, we have tried to be an ambitious club, we have invested not just in the first team but a whole host of things, including our foundation and academies, so we can deliver these programmes in the community. Therefore, decisions like null and void, where all of that effort frankly gets disregarded, clearly have an impact. You've got clubs now who are literally fighting for survival, and a lot of things that I just touched on with their role in the community are under threat.'

The way the club found out about the FA's decision is something that particularly stands out to Thompson as a sign that the FA gives scant consideration to football at that level. The first anyone heard of the decision was over social media.

Feelings ran so strongly that South Shields eventually took legal action against the FA, on behalf of all 66 clubs behind the original letter. An independent tribunal dismissed the case, however, concluding the FA decision was 'taken after due and proper consultation and following careful consideration of the alternative options'. The FA argued the urgency with which they made the decision was so that clubs could have clarity to plan for the future, and they accepted it would not be popular with everyone, for obvious reasons. The hearing did also say it was 'impossible not to feel sympathy for South Shields', but from a legal standpoint, the FA was not in the wrong. To make matters worse, Shields were faced with a £200,000 legal bill after being told to pay the FA's share of legal costs too.

The FA signed the 'Mentally Healthy Football Declaration' in July 2020, committing to make mental health a key priority in the game. Thompson welcomes the intentions of the FA, but feels it is hypocritical given their stance on the null and void decision. He feels clubs and communities below the arbitrary cut-off point of the National League have been left behind, and he certainly isn't the only person to feel this way. Littlehampton Town were another side deeply affected by the decision of the FA. They had won 20 and drawn two of their 22 Southern Combination Division One games, with a goal difference of +76, including a 10-0 victory over Billingshurst in October. After the decision was made, the club released a statement saying they were 'gutted' and that it left a 'bitter taste in the mouth'. Manager Mark Bennett was furious at the decision, and saw the knock-on effect it had on his players.

'I was angry if I'm honest. When you're two-thirds through a season, I think the fairest way of doing it is points per game. I know you're never going to please everybody, but when you've played seven months of a nine-month season, I think who's at the top deserves to be there and who's at the bottom deserves to be there.

'A couple of my players during lockdown actually suffered from mental health. They confided in me and they've come out the other side, which is really nice. A lot of people say, "It's only football." But football, for people with mental health, is a release. This year, we've got more or less the same group of players, and those players are determined to put right what happened last year.'

At South Shields, the implications were significant beyond just the football pitch. The Tyneside club have been invested in heavily by Thompson, who took over when the club was at death's door in 2015. Since then, they have moved back to their home ground, having previously been exiled in Peterlee, won the FA Vase at Wembley, and been promoted three times. Crowds have risen from being barely in double figures to hovering around the 2,000 mark, and the club now also runs a wide-ranging and successful community programme. The ultimate goal for the men's first team is to reach the EFL, and Thompson has continued to invest to try and achieve this. His frustration at being held back by the null and void decision of the FA is clear.

What's more, with South Shields looking virtually assured of the title, their financial model to decide the budget had already assumed promotion. This would have meant crowds even larger still, particularly with a number of local derbies against the likes of Gateshead, Darlington and Spennymoor on the cards. Sponsorship income too would have increased – generally speaking, the rewards would have justified the investment made in not only the playing squad but also the infrastructure and academy. Now, with the club forced to play at least another season in the division below, this was not the case. It even meant the club had to delay their plan of moving towards a fan-owned model and becoming community owned. The club continued to suffer when football restarted with COVID-19-related capacity constraints: they were one of only three clubs in the division where the initial 600 cap was lower than the average attendance of the season before.

Amongst all of these complications, South Shields had to go again. But Thompson, speaking two weeks before the start of the 2020/21 season, was fully aware that it wouldn't be a case of simply turning up and cruising to promotion.

'It's obviously a big challenge. The players were clearly, as we all were, hugely disappointed. They're all fired up, they all want to put what we feel was a wrong decision right, so I think everyone's highly motivated to try and get up again this season and get over the line. We've heard clubs like Buxton and Matlock have got new ownership and are spending money … nothing stands still is the point I'm making.

'I think the supporters will share the frustrations of the players. One thing we did do during lockdown was we had lots of contact with our supporters, not just on social media but we made numerous welfare calls just as a gesture. We didn't make a song and dance about it, but we just made sure we were contacting fans, particularly those who are more elderly. I made a number of them, the manager made some, the chief exec made a few. We all helped out trying to keep contact with fans, and of course we've got the general contact with them via our website and via social media channels. The strength of feeling is strong at the fanbase really. It's one of huge disappointment, a sense of injustice, and the desire to try and put that right.'

In March 2021, the FA announced that non-league's steps 3–6 had been curtailed early once again. South Shields had managed just nine league games, which, if added to last season's tally, would have perfectly made up the 42 required for a full season. Two months later, a series of ninth and tenth-tier sides, including Littlehampton Town and Jersey Bulls, were promoted as the FA looked to restructure the non-league pyramid. Which clubs were selected for this upward movement was based on points-per-game tallies across both the 2019/20 and 2020/21 seasons, giving a delayed reward to the sides that had been regularly competing at the top over the last couple of years. There was no such luck for South Shields, however, who started the 2021/22 season still firmly stuck in the Northern Premier League, 18 months after they looked almost certain of promotion.

* * *

In the EFL, it wasn't until a rescue package worth £250m in loans and grants was agreed with the Premier League that the future of many of its clubs was really secure. The summer of 2020 had been one of significant turmoil and many clubs responded by significantly slashing their budgets for the next season, with many more players than usual let go. Indeed, the PFA reported that, including scholars, 863 of its members were released at the end of the 2019/20 season, creating a market for players vastly more saturated than usual. Downward pressure on wages was exacerbated by the salary cap for League One and Two clubs introduced in August, restricting the number of senior players in a squad to 22, with this number falling to 20 in the following season. For many players, finding a club as a free agent over the summer is already a stressful time without the added implications of a global pandemic.

One of those players forced to search was Paco Craig, a former West Ham youngster who left behind his successful career in the United States to chance his arm at playing in England again. Playing for Louisville City in the USL, Craig won the overall competition, the USL Cup, twice in four years. This included a 1-0 victory over Didier Drogba's Phoenix Rising in 2018 in what turned out to be Drogba's last professional game as a player. The USL season runs on calendar years and so Craig was able to move back to England at the end of 2019. However, within a couple of months, the country was in lockdown.

The timing could not have been much worse for the defender, who had been given a chance at Wycombe Wanderers on a monthly rolling contract. The season being suspended meant Wycombe didn't require Craig's services anymore, and so it was not extended beyond March. He watched on from home as the Buckinghamshire side won promotion to the Championship for the first time in their history when the play-offs were eventually played. Having earlier been turned down by QPR after an extended trial, this double blow was a tough pill for Craig to swallow.

'It [the Wycombe contract] gave me huge confidence and a huge feeling, but it still didn't stop the fact that when they brought me into the office and said that it's not really going to work out, and then the manager starts saying the best thing for me really is to drop low so you can get games straight away and then bounce up: when you get told that stuff, it makes you feel, like, quite sick, to be honest. Because I was 27 at the time and I'm 28 now, if I drop down to the National League it's most likely I'm going to make it to League Two at best. They use every excuse in the book in this industry for a reason for not giving you an opportunity. In my head, I thought that door was just creeping open, and there was an expectation then, but when it slams shut you're like, "For God's sake." It's horrible.

'I understand why they didn't keep me on … but again they just basically dropped me, and from then you just don't hear anything. From there, I'm very much one of hundreds or thousands of footballers just in this country alone who have been sniffing around and not hearing anything. People say they can help you, they can talk here and talk there, and literally nothing has materialised. The amount of times I've heard something and then nothing materialises, it is ridiculous. I've literally asked as many people as I can that I know for help, I've never really done that. It's a tough scenario to be in because you feel like you're begging. You feel like you're going around saying, "Please, someone, help me out, throw me a bone."'

Despite the early sniffs at an opportunity at QPR and Wycombe, Craig remained unable to find a club as time ticked on and football eventually resumed in September. When the country initially went into lockdown he was not too worried, able to find comfort in the fact that nobody was playing football, but Craig found things tougher as the days went by. He believes one of his main issues was the fact his entire senior career had been played 4,000 miles away in a league little known in Europe. Clubs were not keen to take a gamble on a relatively unknown player with hundreds of alternatives with years of experience in the EFL also available. In November 2020, Craig felt his only option was to go back to the US a year after leaving.

There were benefits to being in the UK, though, the main one being his entire family are over here. The financial worries many free agents may have were less acute for Craig, whose father Mikey is the bassist of Culture Club. Whilst many in his position have been forced to turn to part-time work for an income, Craig was able to focus fully on his fitness in the hope of finding a playing opportunity. A self-professed family man, he is grateful for the time he's been able to spend with those closest to him, an opportunity he might not have been afforded had the pandemic not occurred. That's not to say Craig has been without mental struggles.

'I'm quite a grounded and stable guy emotionally for the most part, but even for myself this year, I've been tested, I've been seriously tested,' he said in November 2020. 'I've lost a seriously prime year as a centre-back, 27 to 28, so I feel terrible. There are days when I wake up in the mornings and I have no will to do anything. … I was grumpy or snappy, or just not really good fun to be with sometimes; and you just feel, like, what's going to happen? Honestly, you feel like what is the point of getting up … I can get away with doing nothing for months and nobody would say anything to me, and I hate that, because I'm very big on working and the mentality side of things. I'm not really a depressed-type person, but it comes out in other ways.

'It was a constant flip between feeling good and peaceful, enjoying myself and spending time with people I love, and then waking up and feeling like I have no motivation, I don't want to do anything, I'm wasting my time here, I might as well look for a job or something. So it was a challenge, but I feel like I was able to cope with it a bit better than others perhaps, because of my outlook on life.'

One of the main ways Craig coped was by ensuring he stuck to a strict routine, always staying on top of his fitness and treating it as though he was signed to a club. Drinking and partying were limited, admittedly helped by lockdown restrictions making it virtually impossible anyway, and instead he turned to alternative methods of self-fulfilment. Craig breaks into laughter as he describes the 'spiritual retreat' set up by him and his mum in the back garden, but it's clear he's convinced of the benefits of it. At one point in the summer, he even undertook a four-day fast after extensive research and admits he had an 'incredible experience' with it. With the onset of winter, however, the spiritual retreat in the back garden became somewhat less attractive and Craig made the decision to start training with Hemel Hempstead, a National League South side close to his family home. With a move back to America for a February start to the season on the cards, Craig only signed a short-term deal with them but was grateful for the community feel that being involved in a team again provided.

'My little brother jokes, but we call it the meat market, because you walk in and every week there's a new person, names are changing all the time, people are bouncing all over the place because everyone is trying to find a team … It does actually feel a little bit like there's a little community there, so it has felt nicer than I thought. And you just want to help each other out, you recognise we're all in the same boat, so we share numbers, even if it's just someone I've trained with twice … talking and sharing stories, helps a lot.'

When I ask Craig what the toughest part of his whole situation has been, he responds as I expect many in his situation would. Having been involved in football his whole life, he had built a sense of identity around it. He is 'Paco Craig the footballer', and has been since he was young. Had he not made it as a professional footballer, his back-up plan was to be a drummer in a band instead, the artistic ability of his father clearly rubbing off on him. Watching on as the football world went on without him, it was clear that Craig suffered from something of a loss of identity.

'The thing for me was, when things started kicking back off again, not being involved, missing out. And then the league matches started happening, and then they're on TV and I'm sitting here watching games go on that I know I can be playing in, and not being able to even get anywhere near them, that's when it really was the biggest challenge for me.

'It was my whole life, and it was a success thing, and I pour everything into it when I'm playing. When I'm with a team, I sacrifice everything; I've sacrificed girlfriends many times for football. Football has been my pathway and my number one priority. And then in a year like this where I'm not playing football at all, and then stuff is going on in the world that is far more important and it's going to shape the rest of our society for years to come, I'm supposed to still try and focus on a sport that I've not even been paid to play right now. That has been a tough challenge, to keep the importance of what I love doing at the heart of things when I'm waking up and saying, "What's the point of training when the world is completely fucked up right now?" It's been mad, man.

'I want to keep playing football, it's just sometimes you don't even know who you are anymore because the world is coming down basically.'

On 26 December 2020, rumours started swirling on Twitter suggesting Craig was set to sign for Miami FC in the USL. This was confirmed on 13 January, and despite having to travel to Poland to get his US visa, the defender made it safely across to South Florida for the start of the season. It wasn't the dream return to English football that Craig had yearned for, but after the experience he'd had, simply playing football anywhere was a blessing.

Chapter 9

The Referee

IN FEBRUARY 2005, Swedish referee Anders Frisk took charge of the first leg of what turned out to be a classic Champions League tie between Barcelona and Chelsea. Jose Mourinho's side, who went on to win their first Premier League title that season, took a first-half lead but ended up on the losing side. Perhaps the turning point was a red card shown by Frisk to Didier Drogba, a high challenge on the Spaniard Victor Valdés earning him a second yellow. Chelsea turned the tie around and won the second leg, but for Frisk the damage had been done. A series of death threats in the wake of the first leg left him struggling to sleep. Worried for the safety of his family, and his young children in particular, Frisk decided enough was enough. He retired from refereeing in March 2005.

Anders Frisk is not alone in his experiences. The man who controversially ruled out a Sol Campbell 'goal' in England's defeat to Portugal at Euro 2004, Urs Meier, was advised to go into hiding after his contact details were published in the English press, prompting a campaign of hate against him. Four years later, a controversial penalty awarded against Poland by England's Howard Webb prompted a further series of death threats towards a referee simply doing his job, not helped by the then-Polish-prime minister, Donald Tusk, saying he 'wanted to kill' Webb. Bizarrely, the brunt of the abuse was born by the wrong person, an elderly street lighting and traffic signals engineer for Rotherham Metropolitan Borough Council, with the same name as the man in the middle. Within England's domestic game, Barry Knight was shocked to find one death threat with attached aerial pictures of his house, whilst David Elleray had to have Home Office panic buttons installed in his quarters at Harrow School where he was a housemaster after issuing a controversial red card to Manchester United's Denis Irwin.

It's perhaps a wonder anyone wishes to referee at the top level at all. One thing's for certain: without referees we wouldn't have a game, and perhaps a lot of people are guilty of overlooking the mental health of match officials.

Keith Hackett is one of England's best-known and most successful referees. First picking up the whistle in 1960, he made the full Football League list in 1976 and refereed in and around the top flight of English football until 1994, spending ten of those years on the FIFA list. He's seen both sides of the refereeing fence too, after taking over as general manager of the Professional Game Match Officials Limited (PGMOL) in 2004. The body looks after the Select Group referees, who are in charge of Premier League games, and part of its remit includes considering and supporting the mental health of the referees. Hackett has seen a lot of change regarding attitudes to mental health; indeed, suicide was still illegal in the UK when he took up refereeing, and he is aware that the challenges facing referees have largely shifted over time. For much of his career in the middle, mental health was rarely considered at all.

'I started refereeing in 1960 and I suppose the first time I ever came across anything to do with the mental side of things was sitting at the 1988 Olympics with some of the athletics coaches.' The Yorkshireman recalls watching mesmerised during the 10,000m event, as the Moroccan coach told him the exact times Brahim Boutayeb would run each lap. Sure enough, Boutayeb won the race comfortably, sticking perfectly to these times throughout. The key was visualisation, explained the coach whilst the race was still ongoing; without this psychological preparation, his star athlete might be thrown off by events beyond his control. With his big football semi-final appointment the next day, Hackett considered how using these mental techniques himself could prepare him. As his career progressed, he developed what was originally a sports psychology trick to improve performance, into something that could alleviate stress pre-match, thus benefitting his mental health.

Still, though, Hackett maintains that the biggest challenges for referees in his era came off the pitch. It wasn't until 2001 that referees in England became professional, and the money prior to this was never enough to live off. To put it into perspective, when Hackett took charge of the 1981 FA Cup Final he received just £35 for his troubles. Any ambitions to progress up the refereeing ladder and take charge of the best games were balanced against the basic need to support yourself and your family financially.

'The pressure that came on me was actually about what time I could leave work to referee a football match. If I've been appointed to a game this week, either here or overseas, can I get time off? I might need three days off at short notice. And then you're compensating for that, you're actually saying, "Look, I'm leaving at 4pm but I'll make up for it the following morning." Sometimes I was getting back into the house at 2am, going to sleep and then getting up a couple of hours later to get into work for 7am. People would go, "What the hell are you doing that for?" And I would tell them, "I had a few hours off last night." … That impacted on me greatly at points during my career. Ultimately, the main pressure on me wasn't on the football field, it was from target figures as a salesman that I had to reach. Football didn't pay my mortgage, it was pin money.'

On two particular occasions the conflict between Hackett's work and football really came into focus. An appointment to referee New Zealand vs Australia in a 1986 World Cup qualifier quickly turned into an awkward situation as his permission to take time off from his sales job was rescinded a few days before the match. Hackett went anyway, and lost his job as a result. For three months he was out of work, running down his savings and wondering where the next pay cheque would come from. The Football League didn't compensate for the situation by appointing Hackett to more games, as he would have wished, and his days were filled by looking to stay fit whilst searching for work. Eventually, Hackett landed an impressive new job, but must have had a bad sense of *déjà vu* when at short notice he was summoned to a board meeting the morning after taking charge of a UEFA Cup tie in Stuttgart. This time, he chartered a private aircraft at the cost of £2,000 to ensure he made it back in time, and even then delays nearly meant all the cost and effort was in vain. For other referees, the sacrifices were made in their refereeing careers instead. Perhaps most notably, David Elleray passed up the opportunity to referee at the 1998 World Cup in order to focus on preparing his students for their GCSE and A-Level exams.

As time progressed, the mental health challenges faced by referees shifted dramatically. The birth of the Premier League in 1992 brought global coverage, and cameras appeared to cover the game from every position imaginable. The financial stakes are much higher too, and refereeing errors can have implications that run into millions of pounds for affected clubs. A controversial decision prior to this era might have been shown on *Match of the Day* on a Saturday night, but now refereeing errors can be scrutinised from all angles and provide a significant part of the post-match analysis, or even the post-season analysis. The referee deemed responsible is picked apart by a frenzied media, their embarrassment beamed worldwide.

Graham Poll found this out the hard way in 2006, after his infamous showing of three yellow cards before sending off Croatia's Josip Šimunić in a World Cup group match against Australia. The mistake had no impact on the result – the second of the three yellows was in stoppage time, and Australia progressed at the expense of Croatia anyway – but the mistake clearly had a deep mental impact on Poll. In his autobiography, *Seeing Red*, he talks of falling into a state of deep depression, feeling he had let down his country and every referee in it. In the days following the incident, he thought his career was rendered 'a joke', and says the mistake will haunt him for the rest of his life. The English media had no sympathy, camping outside his family home to pester his wife and young children for an interview, or even just a photo of them looking upset. In the end, Poll spoke to the media whilst still out in Germany to encourage them to disperse.

Poll is not the only top referee to discuss the mental health implications of the job. Former Premier League and international referee Mark Halsey warned in 2013 that levels of mental strain on referees were increasing, and if nothing was done to prepare young referees for this, there would be a refereeing suicide. Two years earlier, German referee Babak Rafati had attempted suicide in a hotel room before he was due to take charge of FC Köln vs FSV Mainz 05 in the Bundesliga, but luckily was found and survived, as his linesmen suspected something was up when he did not turn up to the pre-match briefing on time. Rafati now works as a keynote speaker, helping to raise awareness of mental health issues, and admits that his struggles were in part caused by a growing pressure to perform and avoid mistakes, exacerbated by media coverage of his performances.

Having refereed in the Premier League for its first two seasons before retiring, Hackett has sympathy for those doing the job now in the world of footballing hysteria.

'I think, frankly, a lot of pressure has come in because of the global audience. With Graham Poll making an error of that magnitude through admin rather than an actual refereeing issue, I can understand why he probably felt in a dark place. His confidence would have been affected. It's the pressure of doing something wrong so publicly that affects you. It's not the pressure of what's written in the newspaper, though, because that's fish and chip paper in a couple of days. It's actually the impact it can have on your kids at school. It's the impact on your parents and close family who have witnessed you making a big error and are worried about you.

'To address Mark Halsey's prediction of a referee taking their own life, if that was to happen then somewhere along the line there's been an abject failure of the people who employ that individual. The support mechanisms should be in place to spot and identify those sorts of issues, which I appreciate is not easy. As we all gain more information and knowledge about mental health, it should be almost like going to the dentist. None of us like going to the dentist, and perhaps we don't want to see a psychologist either, but I think that should be the norm within professional referees.'

The introduction of VAR into many of Europe's top leagues is something that should, in theory, reduce the pressure on referees somewhat. The biggest decisions, the ones that could decide titles or relegations, are given something of an insurance policy. Top Scottish referee Willie Collum has been vocal in arguing that VAR is good for a referee's wellbeing as it ensures obvious errors are corrected. Without it, these mistakes would otherwise be talked about for weeks and could weigh on your mind for even longer. Collum's support for VAR is echoed by Mark Clattenburg, who admitted after retirement that he had had nightmares and significant anxiety before big games.

Whether VAR is actually benefitting the mental wellbeing of referees is debatable, though. Hackett argues the technology is not being used properly, and often referees are undermined in their decision-making, as decisions that could go either way are overturned on a second opinion. VAR is meant to be used only for 'clear and obvious' errors, something that a referee might have missed because their view was blocked by a player, for example. With it not being uncommon to see two or three VAR reviews in a Premier League game, it gives the impression that referees are making these glaring errors routinely, which is not the case. The drawing of lines to decide marginal offside calls has a similar effect on the linesmen, and often, the decision made by the technology is more controversial than the original call.

Mental health support for top-flight referees is by and large the responsibility of their employer, the PGMOL. Hackett was general manager of the organisation between 2004 and 2009, and introduced several measures that recognised the significance of mental health. Bringing in sports psychologist Craig Mahoney helped modernise match preparation, as the Australian took the referees through sessions in visualisation, concentration and dealing with stress. Hackett would not intrude on the sessions and would allow the referees to discuss what they wanted with Mahoney. Should any of them require further mental health support this could be arranged, and Hackett wouldn't even need to know which referee had made the request. The move was successful, Graham Poll in particular praising the impact of Mahoney in his autobiography, and the PGMOL have used sports psychologists ever since.

Talking to Hackett, it's clear that having a duty of care is something that he took very seriously during his time in charge at PGMOL. He admits some of his methods, such as using video analysis sessions and demoting poorly performing officials, upped the levels of stress his employees faced, but he took steps to mitigate this. This later reflected in the success of English referees on the world stage, as Howard Webb took charge of both the World Cup Final and Champions League Final in 2010.

'It's important from a management point of view that you're supporting referees psychologically. My view was this: if a referee has a poor performance, there are times when you've got to take that guy away from the spotlight. You're in the public eye massively around the world, you make a massive error, you're likely to compound that the following week by making a big error again.

'It's all about how you prepare the individual. I'll use the example of pilots not starting off in an aircraft. They first get into a flight simulator. I've always talked about a flight simulator for referees. There isn't one yet, but I think we should probably move in that direction. Put them in stressful situations away from the spectators, put them in situations where the engine blows out. How do they deal with it? It's only through experience and dealing with those crises that you can actually handle them efficiently and they don't affect you mentally.'

Exactly what a refereeing 'flight simulator' would entail remains to be seen, but certainly the more that can be done to prepare up-and-coming referees for the furnace of the Premier League, the better. The external pressures that come with money and media coverage aren't going away anytime soon, and the rise of social media means it is easier to abuse a referee than ever before. Support mechanisms should adjust in line to protect the wellbeing of football's unsung heroes.

* * *

Of course, referees in the Premier League are very much only the tip of the iceberg in terms of match officials. With around 1.5 million adults playing football at least twice a month in England, there are currently around 28,000 registered referees in the country to take charge of their games. It's not always the same referees each year, though – according to the Football Association's statistics, 6,700 referees quit the whistle in the 2017/18 season. Although some of these stopped because of age, or because they wanted to focus on making more money in the five-a-side leagues that are springing up around the country, the reality is that many quit because of abuse.

The extent of abuse towards match officials in the English game was quantified by research published in 2020, led by Dr Tom Webb of the University of Portsmouth. Of the football officials they spoke to, 93.7 per cent reported suffering some sort of abuse, compared to just 56.5 per cent of cricket officials and 53.7 per cent of rugby union officials. Indeed, roughly 60 per cent of match officials in football experienced abuse at least once every two games. To make matters even worse, nearly 20 per cent had suffered physical abuse. Despite the FA reporting that abuse has come down in recent years, it's clear the sport still has a massive problem. According to Dr Webb, mental health and abuse are 'intrinsically tied'.

I spoke to the chairman of the Referees' Association (RA), Paul Field, on the matter. The RA is one of the two main organisations designed to support referees throughout their career, the other being the charity Ref Support UK. Founded in Manchester in 1908 as a referees' union, the RA has four key objectives, one being to look after the welfare of its members.

Field says: 'Probably 15 years ago I was threatened and can remember it as if it was yesterday. I would say that out of the 28,000 referees, everyone has faced some type of abuse, whether it is being called a cheat, right through to homophobic or racist remarks, or just being hassled and abused through a whole 90-minute fixture. Everyone's measurement of abuse is different. We all have a different level of mental health resilience, and some have different coping mechanisms to others. But what I can say for sure is that everyone has had an impact mentally through it in some way.'

In the 2019/20 season there were 77 reported assaults towards match officials, of which 15 were then classed as 'not proven'. Field believes the true number is likely to be much higher, with many incidents going unreported as the victim wishes to avoid the often convoluted County FA disciplinary hearing process. Having reported an incident of assault, a referee will often then have to attend the same disciplinary hearing as the aggressor. Failing to do so could bring about a misconduct charge, and will likely mean the guilty players get away with no charge. This is a system that extends right the way down to the country's youngest referees, who are just 14 years old. One notable case saw Ryan Hampson, 19 at the time, given a misconduct charge for 'not acting in the best interests of the game' after emailing a Lancashire FA club when a 15-year-old boy reported being verbally abused by three adult coaches. A barrister-led inquiry found the case against him to be not proven, which Ref Support UK CEO Martin Cassidy said was a 'ground-breaking case' in encouraging others to come forward and report abuse. The 15-year-old in question was scared to give evidence in front of the men who abused him, but was informed he could face a misconduct charge if he did not attend the hearing. Eventually, he was allowed to give evidence by video link instead.

Paul Field and the RA believe these hearings can be one of the main threats a referee faces to their mental health, particularly with young referees. Eager to limit this damage, as well as encourage people to report any abuse they face, they offer a bespoke support system for abused referees. A key part of this, according to Field, is holding the County FAs and specifically their disciplinary processes to account, making sure young people are treated in the best possible way, reflected within the safeguarding best practice. The mental health support available from the RA goes far beyond just this, though. There is a range of information on the website and platforms about mental health resilience, fitness and wellbeing, and the RA also has mental health first aider and welfare teams. In the event of a serious assault, the bespoke support offered extends to handling the local press and legal matters. Extending the focus on young referees in particular, there is a group specialising in supporting parents.

The focus on young referees is particularly key, as there are simply so many of them. Though the number of referees quitting the job is high, they are replaced at a good rate by predominantly children, with roughly four out of five newly qualified refs being under the age of 18. Indeed, FA senior referees officer Farai Hallam recently reported that 90 per cent of the FA's new referees are under 20. At an impressionable age, it is this group that are particularly vulnerable to the mental health impacts of abuse. There are horror stories too: in June 2019, for example, it was reported that a 14-year-old referee in Nottingham suffered a nervous breakdown the day after receiving serious abuse in a junior tournament. It was weeks before the child returned to refereeing, and only after having therapy. Field believes other pressures in today's society also increase the strain on younger referees.

'I think childhood pressures are a lot different to what they were five or ten years ago. I think the desire or pressure from the family for children to succeed in their career, and academia in particular, has increased. So that puts pressure on the child; parents or guardians saying, "Little Tommy, we think he's going to be going to university." Does he really want to go to university? There's that academic pressure, and then there's the pressure of refereeing and fulfilling fixtures, and doing, say, three games on a Sunday because it's more lucrative than a paper round. You put that, and the ambition to achieve Premier League refereeing status in a few years' time in that whole pathway, I think sometimes it's a pressure that children could do without.

'Young people really need the support and help from their parents to help with mental health issues. This is not childminding, dropping your son or daughter off to go and referee a football match and then assuming football will take care of them. If they've got three games on the same pitch, they could be heavily abused in the first game. They've got two more fixtures to fulfil, and who's looking after them? So the parents have got a real role in this.'

It's also worth noting that a lot of abuse directed towards young referees comes from the parents of even younger players. The excellent 2009 'Respect' advert featuring Ray Winstone brought about a lot of conversation on the conduct of parents. It shows a loud-mouthed father (Winstone no.1) hurling a volley of abuse at the referee of a kids' game, and also turning his attentions to doing the same towards his own son. The final scene shows Winstone no.1 shouting at an empty field, before being confronted by the narrator (Winstone no.2), who declares, 'Some of us need to take a long hard look at ourselves.' The message is clear. Lose respect, lose the game.

And though the brunt of this problem is experienced at grassroots level, Field believes it comes from the top.

'Parents expect referees at grassroots level to be as good as those at Premier League level. … It hasn't helped with VAR and Sky and everything else going on with it. If someone makes a mistake on the halfway line, he gives a throw-in the wrong direction in an under-9s game, is that really worthy of abuse? Absolutely not. So, parents and coaches just need to understand, that young person is a child, and that young person would not be abused in a school playground. That's a behavioural thing and a cultural thing, and reflects society.

'Media has a critical role in this whole process. They are about causing a bit of controversy … But it doesn't help referees, and it certainly doesn't help referees at grassroots level, because the players believe what they've heard from the pundits. It's a complete circle or loop.'

It's interesting to note the argument that referees at the top level share some responsibility, and should do more to crack down on dissent to create something of a trickle-down effect in terms of respect. Graham Poll says in his autobiography that when he speaks to referees' societies now, he apologises for not taking tougher action during his time at the top, feeling as though he 'let down' those at grassroots level. Poll does point out that the media reaction to referees producing more red cards for dissent would likely be to accuse the man in the middle of trying to make the game about themselves, and this perception would have to change before we can see any change in refereeing styles in this regard.

There are plenty of other ways to protect your average match official, and some of these have already been explored by the FA. Tougher sanctions for abusing or assaulting referees were introduced in the 2017/18 season, including a minimum five-year ban for striking a match official. A couple of years later, the 'sin bin' was brought in at grassroots level, forcing anyone guilty of dissent into a ten-minute spell off the pitch, leaving their side a player down. The 'purple shirt' initiative came in at the same time, with refs under the age of 18 wearing a different coloured shirt to highlight the fact that they were children. The FA reported that 'threatening behaviour' towards match officials fell by 23 per cent that year.

Still, though, as Field emphasises, there is a lot more that can be done. The County FAs could and should be stricter, but law enforcement itself is not tough enough on offenders, according to the RA chairman. It is not uncommon to see an assault on a referee treated as a 'football matter' for the football authorities, rather than the police, to deal with. This was particularly highlighted in August 2020 when referee Satyam Toki was punched in the face by a Sporting Club de Mundial player in a friendly match, leaving him with a cut above his eye. Toki claimed he was asked not to press charges, as the player who punched him might lose his new job, having just qualified as a teacher. He contacted the Met Police to make a statement anyway, but his attacker was only given a police caution.

Field is frustrated by this lax attitude often shown by the police towards on-field assaults. More than wanting the police to apply the law more appropriately and regularly, though, he also argues match officials should be specifically mentioned in law to afford them extra protections. Furthermore, the Football Banning Order (FBO) system that ensures anyone committing a criminal offence inside a football ground is banned from every ground in the country should extend to grassroots level. Field says his ideas have the support of almost 90 MPs, and, ironically, we have to finish our call slightly early so he can move on to another call on the matter with six of them.

He fears if nothing is done, a referee could soon be killed. This isn't an outlandish claim either. In the Netherlands in December 2012, a volunteer linesman was killed in an assault in a junior game. The public outrage that followed is largely credited for changing attitudes towards referee abuse in the Netherlands, and clearly Field is worried something similar will happen in

England before we reach the same moment of collective realisation.

* * *

Having examined all the pitfalls of refereeing, and the threats to mental health, you could be forgiven for being put off the job entirely. However, 28,000 people still do it every year, so there must clearly be some value to it. Both Keith Hackett and Field describe it as a wonderful experience, and wholeheartedly recommend it. Certainly, one can only imagine the pride Howard Webb would have felt upon receiving his appointment for the World Cup Final in 2010. The World Cup Final in 2030 needs a referee, and those young referees in the early stages of their career today have every chance. Naturally, though, not every young referee can reach this stage, but there are plenty of benefits gleaned by a far greater number.

Field points to some of the life skills developed in refereeing, particularly an ability to act calmly under pressure and assertively when making tough decisions. Not only is this beneficial for an individual's employability, but it will improve their experience of day-to-day life. Having the confidence to back yourself in a tough role is without doubt a transferable skill, with Graham Poll, for example, talking of the significance of receiving praise for his performance from fully grown men, when only a nervous 17-year-old himself. Most referees will also feel similar simple participation benefits to those felt by the players who take to the field on a Sunday morning. I spoke to Surrey County FA referee Harry Yellen to understand why he gives up so much of his time to be a football referee:

'For me, football has always been a chance to get away from the stresses of life and a chance to forget what is going on outside of football, as I fully focus on my game. From the arrival an hour before kick-off until leaving the game, my full attention is on managing the game as well as the preparation that goes on before a match. The constant pressures of a match situation allows me to block the outside world off and have my own 90 minutes where I can push myself and focus fully on the match rather than the thoughts in the back of my head. When 22 players come over and shake your hand and thank you, it really gives off a good feeling inside knowing you've done your job well, and it pushes you on to achieve that feeling again through more strong performances. You always want the next game to come around quickly.

'Refereeing has always helped me cope and keep me motivated in day-to-day life. Knowing I have a game, or games, coming up pushes me to make sure I eat well and I train and condition myself correctly. Without this, I feel I would struggle having any motivation to be active and also have much lower self-confidence. It has helped me build a character and be confident, as this is required in order to assert myself on a pitch. Being a referee has taught me key life skills such as time management and discipline, but above all has helped me build my confidence and improve my people skills. I was always very shy before I started but ever since, I have grown my character to be much more confident and outgoing, translating from the pitch where confidence is essential.

'My aim within refereeing is to go as far as I possibly can. Each day, I think about how to approach games, with this being one of the main focus points in my life. Knowing the opportunities I have available to me due to the work of the Surrey FA and the coaching and support they have given me drives me on to be the best I can whenever I officiate. Being able to referee at the end of each week and even midweek also gives me something to look forward to every day. Refereeing is a great opportunity for any football fan to get involved in the sport and learn new skills in the process. It offers a unique take on the game by being directly involved on the pitch. Any football fan who is struggling mentally should definitely give it a go because it is such a good way to escape the stresses of day-to-day life and has such great opportunities if you want to pursue a potential career as well.'

* * *

It's fair to say that Yellen's refereeing career so far has been promising, and has the potential to open doors for him. Having taken charge of a number of games involving Chelsea's and Fulham's academy sides whilst still a teenager, he was put up for a 'double jump' promotion in 2019, to allow him to referee semi-professional games. Sadly, the impact of coronavirus postponed that, but as the world started to slowly open up again, the young referee had his sights firmly set on reaching the Football League, and perhaps beyond even that in years to come. Wherever he ends up, though, Yellen is sure that engaging in an often underappreciated role will continue to work wonders for his mental health.

As football in general has become more up to date with mental health awareness, so has refereeing. The FA launched a comprehensive *Mental Health Guidance for Referees* document in February 2020. Part of the wider 'Heads Up' mental health campaign, its main purpose is to help referees and those who support them to become more aware of mental health, as well as to know how to spot the signs that somebody is struggling. David Elleray, chairman of the FA referees' committee, introduces the guidance by briefly discussing the pros and cons of refereeing for your mental health, before highlighting the importance of the signposting role everyone can play, even without being a mental health expert.

The guidance document was followed a year later by the Mental Health Champions Scheme, designed to provide support and advice to referees and match officials across the grassroots game. At the time of writing, the scheme is being piloted in 11 County FAs and is due to be expanded nationally. The scheme relies upon volunteers to champion the importance of mental health and wellbeing awareness, as well as acting as a point of contact for any officials experiencing mental health problems. One of the initial champions involved in the roll-out was Lucy Briggs, whose story also featured heavily in the *Guidance for Referees* document. Briggs, now a referee at FA Women's Championship level, struggled greatly with her mental health as a teenager. After surviving a suicide attempt, she took up a refereeing course, something which she instantly fell in love with. Despite discovering this release, Briggs explains that she never really dealt with the source of her initial mental health problems, put off by the stigma around mental health at the time, and she soon fell into a deep depression once more. The Lancashire referee has since come through the worst of her problems and is keen to share her story to promote the mental health awareness that she feels would have been invaluable to her at the time of her first serious spell of mental ill health.

And the work in the field of mental health that Briggs has done has taken her to some pretty amazing places:

'I was spoken to by the head of referees at the FA, and the next thing I knew I was offered the chance to go to a mental health event with Prince William present. I was representing referees as the only referee there. I was just blown away by the experience and being asked to do it was just so amazing. I was playing table football with Tony Adams, Troy Deeney, Fran Kirby and a few others – people who I'd grown up really admiring. The event as a whole has really inspired me to do more and hopefully help others. Since putting my story together and putting that out to all the referees in England, I've had so many people asking me things and coming to me to say "thank you".

'I think sometimes you pinch yourself that people are coming to you and trusting you. The fact that people have said it's helped them, it's a really nice feeling. It makes you feel really good that you've done something to help others. Given the way everything's been over the last year or so with COVID as well, I think mental health has been more of a topic, and we're seeing football making progress in that regard too, with more being said and done. Awareness is moving in the right direction, definitely.'

One of the main things to emerge from both the *Mental Health Guidance* and the Champions Scheme is the sense of community around match officials. Some might consider refereeing a lonely job, given your only 'team-mates' are your fellow officials if you're at a high enough level to have any, but look a bit deeper and this is clearly not the case. Beyond just a match day, a typical referee will interact with a variety of people, from their refereeing mentor right through to referee development officers and their fellow referees. The Referees' Association have regular meetings for officials to socialise as well as develop, and similar events within County FAs also bring referees together. The essence of the signposting system promoted by both the FA *Mental Health Guidance* document and the Champions Scheme revolves around exploiting the wider network that each referee has available to them.

Briggs herself talks of how the referees in the Women's Championship and Women's Super League have their own WhatsApp group which they use more to check in with each other than to necessarily discuss football matters. For her, and countless others, the benefits of little things like this far outweigh any mental health negatives that come from refereeing.

Chapter 10

The LGBTQ+ Community

LIFE WAS tough for the LGBTQ+ community in the early 1990s, and the *Daily Mirror* had no plans to make things any easier for them. Stonewall FC, an all-gay football team set up in 1991 to create a safe space for gay footballers, were planning to join a mainstream 'straight' league. Looking to manage what had the potential to be a controversial situation as best they could, the club consulted with the first 'out' gay team in Europe, Hackney Women FC, for advice on whether they should be open about the nature of their side. As it happened, this decision was effectively taken out of their hands when the *Daily Mirror* ran the headline 'Queens of the South', with the article itself suggesting there was a 'risk of AIDs' from Stonewall FC playing in the league. Founder-member and long-standing player Aslie Pitter recalls the AGM that saw Stonewall FC be officially accepted into the league, in which representatives from every other side sat with a copy of the *Daily Mirror* in clear view. Everyone knew who Stonewall FC were now.

Aslie Pitter MBE, to give him his full title, is a dynamic right-back who wasn't far off playing in the professional game. Spells with south London clubs Sutton United and Carshalton Athletic gave him a taste of the big time but didn't quite prove to be the springboard he needed, and by his 30s he was playing for a local side on Saturdays, whilst starting to turn out for Stonewall on Sundays. After being outed as gay at his Saturday club, Pitter faced a barrage of homophobia and quit the side, focusing his full attention on Stonewall. Homophobia in that era wasn't uncommon. In fact, it was effectively institutionalised by Margaret Thatcher's Conservative government. Section 28 was introduced in 1988, a law making it an offence for local authorities such as schools to 'intentionally promote homosexuality or publish material with the intention of promoting homosexuality'. In practice, it made being gay something that society saw as undesirable and unnatural, creating a whole generation of LGBTQ+ children growing up with internalised shame. The law wasn't repealed until 2003 in England, Wales and Northern Ireland, with the effects lingering long after: a 2014 report by the charity Stonewall (which promotes LGBTQ+ rights) showed that more than a third of primary school teachers didn't know if they could teach on LGBTQ+ issues.

Stonewall FC were treated at best with suspicion and at worst with derision when playing their first few fixtures in straight football. Homophobic abuse was common, arguably reaching its worst point when an opposing team sang the Buju Banton song *Boom Bye Bye*, which glorifies the murder of gay men, outside their dressing room before kick-off. Now regularly facing the sort of abuse he had left his Saturday side to avoid, Pitter was torn. He quit for two weeks before being persuaded to return by his team-mates, who missed both his football ability and his company at training and games. Nonetheless, the simple act of playing football or even just living his life freely as a gay man was not easy for Pitter.

'It was a very, very dark time. We were very good at pretending to be something we weren't because of the climate. It just seemed that everything was going against us. We were accused of being child molesters. The AIDS epidemic, we were blamed for that. All the ills of society seemed to be put on the doorstep of gay men. There was a lot of fear as well. Just going out to our pubs at the time, they had boarded-up windows and were disguised so that the ordinary person wouldn't know it was a gay pub. You'd have to look over your shoulder every time you entered or left. Even what we saw on television was all negative. If we did see any gay people on TV, they were over-the-top camp, loud. If they were in films, they wouldn't last the whole film. Nobody cared if a gay man was beaten up or killed in a film because there was no sympathy there.

'Looking back [on the early days of Stonewall FC], it probably had a negative effect on my mental health. At the time, you just don't think about it. For me, playing my first game was so stressful. The three nights before, once I'd actually committed to going out and playing, I didn't sleep. I didn't eat anything, because I just feared the worst. Everybody knew who we were. I just thought, are we going to be safe? It was quite daunting. I think some of the guys handled it a lot better than others. I was still on the fence about sticking around and almost left the club because of some homophobic abuse on the pitch and outside our dressing room … I just wanted to play football because I enjoyed football. I didn't want to make a statement.'

It's now late in 2022, and Aslie Pitter is approaching his 32nd year with the club. He's retired from working but not from playing football. He captains the Stonewall Spirit of Unity team, a mixed-gender side which plays in the LGBTQ+-friendly London Unity League. The smile on his face when he tells me about his current exploits shows how the Stonewall FC co-founder grew to love a community in which he felt valued, a place where he could talk openly about who he might be dating without fear of judgement. He's travelled as far as Sydney, to take part in LGBTQ+-friendly tournaments such as the Gay Games. He's won a good number of them too, with Stonewall FC now the most successful gay football team ever. Crucially, perceptions have changed – in fact, Pitter admits that when he turned up to his first training session in 1991, he had a 'negative misconception' about gay men in football and didn't think there would be anyone who was any good. Today, he takes great pride in showing the world that stereotypes of gay men only liking sports such as diving or ice-skating simply aren't true.

In February 2011, Pitter collected his MBE from Buckingham Palace after he was recognised for his service both to football and fighting homophobia. When asked about it, he's deeply humble, claiming many other people, such as influential Hackney Women's member Joanie Evans, would have been more deserving of the accolade. Pitter is incredibly proud of his achievement, though, and acknowledges the wider importance of a gay footballer being recognised in such a way. It helped to put gay football on the map, he says, opening the door for anyone to get involved. Certainly, Stonewall FC have continued to go from strength to strength since Pitter's first experience with the club in 1991.

The club's first XI compete in the Middlesex County Premier Division in the 11th tier of English football, just one division below where the semi-professional ranks begin. Home games are played at the London Marathon Community Track in the shadow of the Olympic Stadium, with some matches, particularly against local rivals Clapton Community, attracting crowds of several hundred people. Back in November 2018, Stonewall FC played one of their first XI matches at Wembley Stadium, beating Wilberforce Wanderers 3-1 in a league game that was moved to the national stadium to celebrate the launch of the Rainbow Laces campaign with the FA. The continued success of the club has meant they have been described by commercial experts *Marketing Week* as having 'a growing profile, and potentially a global one'. Adidas acted on this by extending their partnership with the club in 2020, with star striker Jay Lemonius featuring in their 'Change is a Team Sport' campaign. This idea of visibility for the LGBTQ+ community is close to Lemonius's heart, as he explains to me.

'I guess the most challenging that I've found football was when I was starting to come out and started to explore my own sexual orientation. I couldn't see any representation of any other LGBTQ+ people within sport or within football, or even just an LGBTQ+ person who looks like me or comes from the same background as me or has the same experiences as me. So reconciling football with other elements of my identity was quite challenging, particularly when I was 17 or 18 and had so many other things going on. I did question whether it was a space for me.

'There were points when I felt like my sexual orientation was a barrier to me playing football ... or being able to find a home in the game – for sure. I guess if I'd had more examples ... of visible black gay role models in the game, that probably wouldn't have been an issue because I'd have seen positive experiences play out and I probably wouldn't have found it as much of a challenge. So being able to see yourself in this space or any space that you love and care about is really important, particularly if you're beginning to doubt yourself and don't feel like there's a home for you here.'

Lemonius grew up in the 1990s, a decade which started with Justin Fashanu breaking new ground as the first prominent footballer in the men's game to come out as gay. He did so, reportedly, not of his own free will but because the tabloid press were threatening to out him. Despite having been the first black footballer to command a £1m transfer fee earlier in his career, he became an outcast within the game, appearing for the likes of Southall, Toronto Blizzard and Mirimar Rangers of New Zealand. His own team-mates would often maliciously joke about his sexuality and Torquay United reportedly required an HIV test from Fashanu before he signed. Fashanu's own brother, John, wrote in black community newspaper *The Voice* to condemn his brother, who was constantly hounded by the tabloid press when he went out socially. Justin Fashanu took his own life in 1998 after being accused of sexually assaulting a teenager in Maryland, a state in which any homosexual acts were illegal at the time, meaning he had little chance of a fair trial. It was a tragedy that scarred the LGBTQ+ community for years to come, an experience far more likely to put other gay players off coming out than it was to encourage them.

English football took a while to make any progress with regards to attitudes towards homosexuality after the death of Justin Fashanu. Graeme Le Saux was viciously accused of being gay by football supporters of the period, purely because he didn't take part in the laddish activities other players commonly got themselves involved in. Things came to a head when Liverpool's Robbie Fowler goaded Le Saux with a homophobic gesture in a Premier League game in 1999 – less than a year after Fashanu's death. Fowler eventually received a two-game ban for this, which was extremely lenient, given he was handed a four-game ban at the same time for a goal celebration in which he imitated snorting cocaine off the white lines of the pitch. It took until 2014 for Fowler to properly apologise, prompted by Thomas Hitzlsperger coming out as gay. Understandably, the German international had waited until after he'd retired before breaking this news. Graeme Le Saux said he often considered quitting football due to the abuse he continually faced, imagining it would have been overbearing for a player who was actually gay at the time. This abuse has continued to now be predominantly social media-based, with detailed analysis carried out by the PFA in collaboration with Signify Group in August 2021 finding that homophobia was the most common form of abuse aimed at players online.

Robbie Rogers clearly agreed with Le Saux's sentiment when he came out publicly in 2013 weeks after leaving

Leeds United, retiring from football at this time at the age of just 25. In his autobiography, *Coming Out to Play*, Rogers says that throughout his career he felt being gay was not compatible with playing professional football, largely because of the lack of role models. Suppressing his true feelings and having to lie about his sexuality put a huge burden on him, and he talks of feeling down even after impressive on-field achievements, such as winning the MLS Cup with Columbus Crew in 2008. It all became too much for him and he quit the game as a result. Rogers described English football as far more homophobic than in the US, with a macho culture that was much more pronounced. The American did make a comeback to professional football later on in 2013, for LA Galaxy in his home country, but never returned to Europe before retiring for good due to injury problems four years later.

* * *

For all the challenges facing gay players in the men's game, the issue of sexuality in women's football seems to not be an issue at all. Indeed, speaking in BT Sport's *Everybody's Game: Football's Ultimate Goal* documentary, former Everton and England defender Fern Whelan said the dressing room was the place in her life where she most felt like she could be herself. There were reportedly 38 players who were out as gay or bisexual at the 2019 Women's World Cup, and Megan Rapinoe, one of the most decorated players in the history of the game, has joked that there are so many gay players in the typical dressing room that if anyone went to visit a 'friend' on their day off, it would be assumed that they were secretly in a relationship with them. Even so, Rapinoe became one of the first high-profile players to publicly come out in 2011, so it isn't like women's football has always been perfect with regards to visibility of its LGBTQ+ players. Since then, the women's game has seen a huge increase in profile globally, and couples such as Pernille Harder and Magdalena Eriksson are global stars and role models. A picture of the two Chelsea players kissing at the 2019 World Cup went viral, helping to show millions across the globe that same-sex relationships were OK, in fact something to be celebrated. Harder and Eriksson opened up their direct messages on Twitter on Valentine's Day in 2021 to speak to and help anyone who might be struggling to tell family and friends they were gay. Both know the power their relationship has and are keen to use their platform to reach as many people as possible. Certainly, women's football is now leading the way when it comes to visibility.

I was lucky enough to speak to Jahmal Howlett-Mundle of Sheppey United on the morning of Monday, 16 May 2022. At the time, he was the highest-ranking out LGBTQ+ footballer in the men's game, having just won promotion to the eighth tier with his club, as well as winning three cup competitions. It's no coincidence for Howlett-Mundle that his best footballing season to date came after he had come out as bisexual in pre-season, back in July 2021.

'I felt good in myself and didn't want to continue living in a space where I didn't feel comfortable speaking about my sexuality, I didn't feel comfortable living my life. Off the pitch, I'm really mellow, and I used to be really irritable. I'd break out in floods of sweats, for example, because I was so anxious … in my head I was running through scenarios where I might potentially have to speak about something I hadn't felt comfortable speaking about before.

'I've had so much support and acceptance from many different areas, especially the people that are closest to me. I had a perception of them that, "you're not going to like me because of who I am". I do feel like I've gained a lot of respect and likeability just from being me. That's something I never thought would really happen. I thought it would go the opposite way.

'I really did think that this could make or break me. And then I realised that it's not that deep, it's really not that deep. It's just me going out and playing football and thankfully doing well. And then winning the last cup in the last game of the season, it was like, how the hell have I gone from being this boy essentially in a shell to me being super confident and super relaxed and also playing my best football? Because I'd become open about my sexuality.'

It's great to see Howlett-Mundle smiling and enjoying his football so much, given the space he was in back in July 2019. The former Crystal Palace academy player describes his mental health being 'in tatters' to the point where he would often stay in the house, avoiding social situations in which he felt he might accidentally expose his sexuality to the world. He left Hastings United at the end of the 2019/20 season with the plan of giving up football altogether. Though he says there was nothing wrong with the atmosphere at Hastings, Howlett-Mundle was tempted back into the game after speaking to the manager and assistant manager at Sheppey. At Hastings, only the manager had known about his sexuality, and the plan was for things to be the same here. Ultimately, Howlett-

Mundle felt so comfortable around his new team-mates that he accidentally revealed his sexuality to a few of them on a car journey to training, before revealing his truth to the rest of the group a few months down the line.

Things have been good for Howlett-Mundle since coming out, but not perfect. He has faced homophobic comments in matches on two occasions, one a cup final. Howlett-Mundle was reduced to tears on the pitch, but was brought to this reaction by the vocal support of his team-mates rather than the comment itself. The guilty player was sent off and Sheppey United won the cup, the final word belonging very much to Jahmal Howlett-Mundle. As our conversation draws to a close, he acknowledges how hard it was growing up with few gay or bisexual role models in the football world. He talks of hoping to see a 'domino effect' of players coming out, in which the significant media coverage around his own story would play a key role.

A few hours after our conversation, young Blackpool starlet Jake Daniels announced to the world that he was gay, becoming the first professional player in the UK to do so since Justin Fashanu more than 30 years earlier. His action was partly prompted by the inspiration he drew from Adelaide United player Josh Cavallo, who came out in October 2021, making him the world's only out gay player in a male top-flight league at the time. Cavallo was received with love and support from around the world and was able to pass this positive experience on to Daniels. In an interview with Sky Sports, Daniels spoke of wanting to be a role model to any other gay players who feel they need to hide their sexuality. With the Justin Fashanu

Foundation reportedly supporting up to five gay players to help them come out, the hope is that the domino effect Howlett-Mundle refers to is in full swing.

The more professional players come out, the more being gay in football becomes normalised and accepted, even celebrated, as it should be. When I spoke to Jay Lemonius, what struck me was his slightly unexpected answer when I asked about his ambitions for the future: 'I guess if I'm being honest, the ambition is probably for Stonewall FC to not exist. Ultimately, we want every club to feel like Stonewall FC, an inclusive place for everyone, no matter what your gender identity, sexual orientation, or whatever the other elements of your identity are. A space where difference is celebrated and everybody is able to just be themselves. So safe spaces should always exist, but ultimately we want all spaces, all clubs, to be a safe space.'

* * *

Carl Fearn is a lifelong Arsenal fan, but only attended his first live match in 2018. There is more than one reason for this – he lives in Barrow-in-Furness, for example, and his parents were never into football – but perhaps one factor stood above the others until very recently. Carl Fearn is gay. He isn't the only gay football fan to have struggled with the atmosphere of live football matches over the years. Tottenham fan and Proud Lilywhites founder Darryl Telles wrote an entire book about his experiences as a football fan. In it, he admits to having avoided games in the late 1980s due to the prevalent racism and homophobia. He was tempted back by the formation of the Gay Football Supporters Network (GFSN) in 1989, but has still faced incidents that have made him feel isolated and unwelcome, such as the homophobic chants commonly directed at Brighton supporters that may seem like 'banter' to some but are deeply hurtful to the LGBTQ+ community. The stats suggest that Fearn and Telles aren't alone in their fears. A 2017 survey by YouGov for Stonewall found that 43 per cent of LGBTQ+ people didn't think sporting events were a 'welcoming space' for them.

Fearn is part of a relatively older generation of the LGBTQ+ community, one that grew up through intense social stigma around homosexuality. He's seen attitudes in the UK progress significantly but knows there is still a long way to go until true equality is achieved. Now co-chair of the Arsenal's officially recognised LGBTQ+supporters group, Gay Gooners, he is often asked why such groups need to exist. His answer is powerful and clearly reflects his experiences throughout his life, both in and out of football.

'We're often asked, "Why don't we have a straight supporters group?" A straight supporters group doesn't make any sense, because a straight person doesn't look in the mirror on matchday and go, should I wear that, should I do that? It's important for groups like ours to exist because we have the right to go to games as ourselves. We shouldn't have to be something that we're not. Unfortunately, at the moment, in some of society and in a lot of football, we can't … we're identifying as part of a group that historically might have been seen as not welcome here. We get constant abuse, and some people say, "Stop drawing attention to yourselves and stop ramming your agenda down other people's throats." The hostility we get makes us go, "you know what, we're here, we're loud, and we're proud. No amount of your heckling and abuse is going to stop us from being who we are".

'We would rather our groups didn't have to exist and we just all go to football as football fans. Society is not ready for that. There's an element of attracting people like myself that love football but never felt confident or safe enough to go to a game. Groups like ours will make it a better experience. I can't guarantee anybody that there won't be abuse of some kind, but thankfully it's rare. We're not there to make anybody feel uncomfortable; we're certainly not there to ram an agenda. We don't have an agenda. The agenda is Arsenal to win the league!

'Going near a gay person wearing a rainbow scarf at a football match isn't going to miraculously turn you gay. It's pathetic really when you think about it, the fear that people have of seeing a supporter wearing a rainbow scarf. So our group is there, unfortunately, because people in society outside of our group don't want us to exist and don't want us to be seen. No, sorry, we're going to be seen.'

Gay Gooners were set up in February 2013, making them the first club-specific LGBTQ+ fans' group in the UK. Many more have since followed, with a network under the name of Pride in Football bringing the different groups together under one banner. These club-specific groups effectively came in to fill the void in support for LGBTQ+ fans created by GFSN gradually morphing to being more focused on the playing side of things. The network still exists and runs a national 11-a-side league with two divisions and a cup competition. However, there is little mention of match-going fans on the current GFSN website. As we chat about the role Gay Gooners play in helping the LGBTQ+ community feel welcome at games, Fearn proudly reels off some statistics on the group, the largest LGBTQ+ fans' group in the UK. With more than 1,100 members overall, there is presence in all seven continents due to one signed-up member working at an Antarctic research station. Around ten per cent of members are heterosexual but have joined the group as a show of allyship. Fearn acknowledges the particular challenges facing transgender and non-binary supporters, with five per cent of the Gay Gooners' membership base identifying as such.

Paula Griffin is not an Arsenal fan but a regular at Dulwich Hamlet, where she has helped out by volunteering in a number of roles throughout the years. She came out as transgender in January 2021, prompted by surviving cancer and feeling a new lease of life, a second chance in a way. Griffin had experienced gender dysphoria – a mismatch between biological sex and gender identity – throughout her entire life and admits she threw herself into numerous voluntary roles at Dulwich to take her mind off the conflict inside her head. In this sense, football had always been the saviour for Griffin, and so it was vital that her true self was well received by the football world when she did decide to take the big step of coming out. In truth, she couldn't have picked a better club to have supported given the circumstances. With a worldwide reputation for inclusivity, fellow Dulwich Hamlet supporters, players, board members, and even director of football Peter Crouch have showered Griffin with love and support.

Her football experience hasn't always been so positive. Though the non-league game is losing its 'laddish' past, according to Griffin, it wasn't easy to reconcile her identity with being a football fan back in the 1980s and 1990s. She references the Tom Robinson song 'Glad to be Gay', which talks about making 'anti-queer' jokes to avoid detection and persecution. Griffin says she would listen to throwaway comments made by other volunteers whilst working behind the scenes at the club and wonder whether or not she should join in, to ensure nobody would suspect anything. Though the atmosphere around Dulwich Hamlet has changed since then, Griffin has still felt uncomfortable at several away games and received out and out abuse in an FA Trophy tie away to lower-ranked opposition. With discrimination towards the trans community still commonplace in society as a whole, she concedes that she wouldn't feel comfortable attending Wembley to watch the England men's team and would only attend a Premier League game in numbers to ensure her safety.

Coming out as transgender has also allowed Griffin to get involved with something she hadn't done for a long time. At the age of 55, she took up playing football again, in the women's game. There is a lot of debate in the media around whether transgender players should be allowed to participate in women's sport on the basis of fair competition, but the FA have a strict policy to ensure no unfair advantage is gained. Those who have transitioned from male to female must suppress their testosterone levels for at least 12 months before any competition, providing medical evidence of this when requested to do so. This hormone treatment is verified annually. Complying with these regulations, Griffin has once more been able to take up playing the sport she loves, turning out for Peckham

Town Ladies as well as TRUK United and Goal Diggers FC. It's been a liberating experience for the football fanatic.

'On the whole, everybody is incredibly welcoming. It's massively important to me. It puts a smile on my face, I so look forward to it. It's at a stage now where I can get out there and play football and be amongst my peers and other women who just totally accept me. When I first came out, I joined Goal Diggers FC. I'd been with Goal Diggers for probably less than a month and it was trans pride, the first one after lockdown. I thought, OK, I'm going to go. I started chatting to the players and they all came along with me. There were so many players that supported me, it gave me such strength. All these clubs, they've always been very much LGBTQ+-friendly, and the players are all individually supportive. I'm just treated as one of the girls.

'It gives me confidence, not just when I'm out there playing sport but in every walk of life. Even when I get the abuse in social media or real life, to know there's someone there to back me up gives me that strength to fight back against it. To stand up, be myself, not hide and disappear into the shadows. There was an incident where after one of the games one of the players came up and said, "I read an article about you in Sky Sports, it was so educational." She said it was inspirational. To hear the word 'educational' gave me such a good feeling inside – to think that I'd touched one person like that was so good.'

The inaugural TRUK United match, against Dulwich Hamlet Women, was a particularly momentous occasion for Griffin and the whole trans community. TRUK United are the football arm of Trans Radio UK, a 24/7 radio station for the trans community which provides a counselling service as well as a source of entertainment. On 31 March 2022, a team made up entirely of transgender players took to the field against Dulwich Hamlet Women, who play in the fifth tier of the women's game. Watched by a crowd of 410, Dulwich ran out comfortable winners, but the result was secondary. The game, and Dulwich's allyship in hosting it, showed the trans community they were welcome in football. Up in the Premier League, Arsenal too have been a great ally to the trans community, as Fearn explains with an anecdote. At the Gunners' 2-1 home win against Brentford in February 2022, an executive box for 15 people was allocated to fans who didn't feel comfortable coming as themselves to games, specifically trans and non-binary supporters. One transgender teenager went to the game quiet and nervous but returned having 'blossomed' as Fearn puts it, having been able to interact with other supporters similar to himself for the first time. Even small victories like this take football closer to being a place where everyone is welcome, and everyone can feel the mental health benefits as a result.

Finishing on this positive note is problematic, however, given the issues around holding the 2022 World Cup in Qatar, where homosexuality is illegal. As early as 2010, when the World Cup was awarded, Sepp Blatter commented that any gay fans going to Qatar should 'refrain from sexual activity'. Whilst he appeared to be joking, it didn't exactly suggest that FIFA were taking this issue particularly seriously. Closer to the time, further controversy arose when two journalists contacted 69 hotels pretending to be a gay couple and asking if they could stay in that hotel during the tournament. Three hotels allegedly refused, whilst a further 20 asked the fictitious couple to modify their behaviour, one specifically instructing them, 'Don't dress gay'. The tournament itself was marred by FIFA threatening nine of the competing nations with 'sporting sanctions' if they wore the rainbow-coloured 'OneLove' armband to show their support to the LGBTQ+ community during matches.

The Qatar World Cup hasn't been the only talking point with regards to LGBTQ+ rights around football recently, with the Saudi-backed takeover of Newcastle United bringing about similar conversations. The point has been made that pressure from English football fans may be a catalyst for change in parts of the world where social attitudes are currently still highly conservative. Darryl Telles notes as much in his book, recalling a conversation with a Ugandan refugee who said that it is not uncommon for Africans to see their heroes supporting campaigns such as Football vs Homophobia and reconsider their own views as a result. Neither Fearn nor Griffin is convinced by this argument, feeling that the primary concern is money, with any human rights outcomes very much in the back seat. Their view is the dominant one, it would appear, and certainly won't go away anytime soon. As football opens up to investment from outside of its traditional hotspots, it must be careful it does not compromise the good progress that has been made with regards to making everyone feel welcome in the game, regardless of their sexuality.

Chapter 11

The Grassroots Players

A DRONE buzzes over Meadowbank Stadium in Dorking as former Premier League and Great Britain Olympic team footballer Marvin Sordell smiles for a photo with a variety of different cameras pointed at him. The kick-off is delayed slightly, the players only just out to warm up as the clock ticks round to the scheduled 6pm start, but it's no issue for anyone. Pushing kick-off back allows the whole squad to be in attendance, which is the most important thing with Beder FC. The media attention is in response to the club's recent partnership with Pro:Direct, who have supplied the resplendent turquoise shirts worn by Beder. Their home ground, Meadowbank, is an impressive stadium which primarily hosts National League South title challengers Dorking Wanderers as well as acting as home of the Surrey FA. It is another high-profile partnership, with the Surrey FA, that allows Beder to play their fixtures on the pristine artificial pitch. An impressive set-up then; and one founder Razzak Mirjan can take a lot of credit for. Despite this, Beder FC are a football club that Razzak would never have wanted to exist.

Razzak's world was turned upside down in April 2017 when his brother, Beder Mirjan, took his own life. He was just 18 years of age. Just how much he means to people is encapsulated in the number who have turned up both to play and watch the match at Meadowbank on a cold and windy Saturday evening in February. Beder was a hugely popular individual and was due to go to university to study aeronautical engineering before his untimely passing. Though he was having therapy and had periods of feeling down, there were no signs he was planning to take his own life, which made coming to terms with it even harder for Razzak and the rest of the family. Looking to keep his memory alive as well as raise money for a mental health charity, Razzak ran the London Marathon in 2018, but decided he wanted to go further and create a lasting legacy by setting up a charity in Beder's name, with the goal of taking a unique approach to softly raising awareness around mental health and suicide prevention.

'It was impossible losing Beder if I'm being honest … It came out of the blue. He was an incredible individual; quiet but a wonderful, kind, loving kid with a great future ahead of him and a very loving family around him. So when I found out he had taken his own life, it didn't really, and still doesn't to a degree, make too much sense because I never really knew he was struggling. I'd never had my own mental health issues and I think if you've not had it yourself, it's quite hard to see it in others or come to terms with it. We decided to found the charity to do good in Beder's name and keep him with us effectively, but it's much more than a family charity. It's really a chance for us all to play our part in raising awareness.

'We are a very close family and we only became closer. Setting up Beder [the charity] ... has helped me. It's given me purpose, it's given the family purpose, it's given those who knew him, I hope, a sense of purpose as well. It's also allowed us to continue talking about him whether directly or indirectly, because what I found was when you lose someone to suicide, people don't know what to say. Understandably, they try not to talk about it because they're scared of upsetting you.'

Beder, the charity, was set up in November 2019. Partnered with Samaritans and mental health text service Shout 85258, the aim is not to compete with existing charities in the mental health and suicide-prevention space but to supplement them, all the while keeping a personal touch. Beder looks to bring people together through common interests. At first, there were a range of in-person events set up, from painting to cooking, with the highlight being a concert held at Islington's Union Chapel, which attracted more than 700 people. Soon after this, the world went into lockdown and the approach had to be adapted. As Razzak explains, this wasn't necessarily a bad thing, as it forced the charity to broaden its horizons and reach people beyond just London, where the Mirjan family are based. Live cooking sessions held on Instagram proved particularly popular, prompting a cookbook, *From Beder's Kitchen*, to be released. With contributions from a whole host of celebrity chefs sharing their own personal reflections around mental health, it was hugely successful and is sold all over the world.

Gradually, the UK began to open up again and with it came the return of in-person events. Beder FC had been in the pipeline for a while, finally taking to the pitch for the first time in April 2021. With ex-Fulham stars Sean Davis and Barry Hayles playing, alongside Marvin Sordell, perhaps unsurprisingly Beder picked up the win in their inaugural game. The club don't play in a league but arrange friendlies for the first Saturday of each month. Though the ex-pros provide a bit of experience, the team is open to anyone who wants to play, with a player pool of around 45 at the time I speak to Razzak.

A recent FA strategy report claimed that there were 14.1 million people playing some form of football in England, with 101,410 FA affiliated teams. With such vast numbers already interested in the sport, galvanising that comes naturally. On the day I attend the fixture against Virgin Atlantic FC there is a real diverse mix of players – indeed, two of the standout players for Beder are female. A lifelong football fan himself, Razzak knows the power of the sport.

'I think football is an amazing way to bring people together … It doesn't matter where you're from, what you do, what your orientation is. You come together on the pitch. You can be a group of strangers but you play with the simple aim of winning. It allows you to make new friends, meet new people, break down a lot of barriers and potential stigmas. I find football an amazing sport and it's been a big part of my life, so when it came to looking to grow Beder and see what we could do, football was an obvious choice for me, especially in a world where stereotypically men don't talk about their feelings as much and they're a little closed-off about talking about their mental health.

'I've found it incredibly successful so far, from the partnership with the Surrey FA to the partners and sponsors that we've got involved, but most importantly from the players who have signed up and continue to come back and have purchased Beder FC kit and have said to me, "I just came to play a bit of football but I actually found this really powerful, and wasn't expecting to." That's music to my ears and it sometimes comes from people you may not expect to be as open. There's the banter, the louder characters, the quieter ones. I think it is very similar to the typical Sunday League team but I do think because of it being a charity team connected to mental health with the whole approach of us trying to raise awareness, it does have that deeper element to it, which could just allow that conversation to come up in the dressing room if people wanted to talk about it, because it's connected to why people are turning up.'

As Razzak suggests, there can be mental health benefits gleaned from playing any level of football for any side, predominantly through perks associated with exercise, community and a sense of purpose, but Beder goes one step further and provides a safe space and open forum for mental health discussion. The idea of 'mental health football teams' has been growing in recent years, with clubs set up specifically to tackle issues such as social isolation, and fears that an over-competitive environment could actually be to the detriment of an individual's mental health. After all, each person's circumstances and preferences are unique. With Beder, post-match catch-ups are encouraged both within the Beder squad as well as with the opposition, with the players often heading to the impressive new lounge above Meadowbank after matches. Razzak feels this can often be more important than the 90 minutes of football itself, as it allows everyone to catch up with each other and to get any lingering thoughts and feelings off their chest. A WhatsApp group keeps players in touch away from matchdays as well as allowing for signposting to the wide range of other events run by the charity.

Watching the match against Virgin Atlantic, the appeal is clear to see. The game is played in great spirit and is end-to-end right from the start as the visitors take the lead with less than a minute on the clock. For a while, it looks as though Virgin Atlantic might run away with it, but inspired by Razzak's vocal leadership, Beder hit back to equalise midway through the first half and from there it's a blistering game. It may be a friendly but there are delighted celebrations every time a goal is scored, Razzak in particular brimming with pride each time his side register on the scoresheet. Rolling subs allow all 12 men and two women in Beder colours to get a good amount of game time, and everyone wears a broad smile throughout. The biggest cheer is reserved for virtually the last kick of the game – chasing a 5-4 deficit, Sordell breaks free and equalises. The goal looks offside, but nobody is too bothered and the two teams pose for a picture together moments later when the full-time whistle goes.

Just hours before the match, one of Surrey's top sides, Dorking Wanderers, were playing a huge game at the top of the table, beating Maidstone United 1-0 in front of almost 3,000 people. The significance of playing Beder's fixtures on the same ground is something that is not lost on Razzak, who is deeply grateful to the Surrey FA for their partnership. The deal came about after Razzak reached out to them, with the CEO, Sally Lockyer, replying soon after with the admission that Surrey were looking to do more in the mental health space. Realising the power of football to prompt conversation around mental health, the Surrey FA website now has a page dedicated to the subject, and various stakeholders from around the game have been interviewed to build an understanding of what mental health-related issues are present for them. Mental health first aid courses have been offered and bespoke mental health workshops for referees have also been put on.

A YouTube series, called *Team Talk with Beder*, explores various themes around mental health in professional and semi-professional football via behind-the-scenes access at Surrey's top clubs, including the likes of AFC Wimbledon, Sutton United and Woking. As Razzak explains, the idea is that for the loyal supporters of these teams, it is sometimes more relatable hearing their local heroes speak about mental health than it is the likes of Cristiano Ronaldo or Harry Kane. Further attention was brought to Beder and the wider topic of mental health awareness through Marvin Sordell's attempt to break the world record for most penalties taken in an hour, helped by a highly efficient team of ball boys ensuring any loose balls were cleared out of the way. With a total of 577, Sordell smashed the record at Meadowbank back in April 2021. When Razzak speaks about the future of Beder, his commitment and ambition are clear.

'It may sound silly, but I really want to see Beder becoming a charity that can have the impact and reach of one of the leaders like UNICEF, like Cancer Research, but obviously mental health – and suicide presentation-focused. In terms of how we leverage it, I always say we have our own ideas and initiatives in mind but they're never set in stone and because of the size of our charity we can be quite dynamic – it's really a chance for us to do anything. But equally as we grow, I really want it to remain as personal as possible. Of course, that's going to be difficult the bigger we get, but it's of paramount importance to me personally and to us as a charity and us as a family. We set Beder up for incredibly personal reasons, and people's support means the world. So my goal is to keep it as personal as possible.'

It's clear from my experience watching them play, as well as from what comes out in my conversation with Razzak, that Beder FC is a great way of achieving this. All the benefits of playing football at grassroots level are brought out, boosted by the family feel which is encouraged by the very nature of the club and its mental-health-friendly status. Razzak's creation is a fine example of how football can be used to bring people together and create a mental health safe space for anyone, whether they feel they need it or not. Beder FC might not be a worldwide presence yet, but it is certainly an invaluable resource for those who turn up and play, whilst also doing its bit to promote mental health awareness on top of that.

* * *

'I have to say, Ashley Cole was lovely. He was such a really, really nice guy. He came to our offices about one o'clock in the afternoon and he was around till nine o'clock at night. He was really interested. He'd clearly done a bit of research on what mental health was and what he should and shouldn't be saying. He corrected me a few times on some terms. I thought, "all right, mister"!'

The visit of one of England's finest left-backs to the Goodwin Sports Centre in South Yorkshire on a sunny Wednesday afternoon was the latest feather in the cap for Brunsmeer Awareness, a reward for their fine work in bringing mental health awareness and support to the women of Sheffield. Josie Soutar, who set up the Brunsmeer Awareness Ladies team in March 2020, is clearly impressed by the research and preparation Cole had done as part of his ambassadorial work for a project run by suicide prevention charity Campaign Against Living Miserably (CALM) in association with Carling – entitled 'Caring United'. Its website describes the aim as 'to shine a light on the ordinary people doing incredible things', and that's certainly what they've uncovered on the five-a-side pitches at the University of Sheffield.

Brunsmeer Awareness is one arm of local charity Sheffield Flourish's gameplan to support the mental health of the city's residents. Marketed as 'mental health friendly', the hope is that the team can provide a safe space for anyone to turn up and build a sense of community whilst having fun at the same time. Rather than focusing on playing competitive fixtures, sessions are run as more of a kickabout between the players who are signed up; a relaxed environment in which everyone can feel free to express themselves without fear of repercussions should they make a mistake. It is the participation itself rather than any extrinsic achievements which is key here. An established mixed-gender side had been running since 2013, but when Josie took over as managing director of

Sheffield Flourish in February 2018, she spotted a gap in the market, which was soon filled with impressive results.

'There was already an established Brunsmeer team. It was classed as mixed, so they didn't say girls couldn't go, but the reality was only women who had played a lot of football would have the confidence to go and join 20 lads for a kickabout. If I use myself as an example, when I was younger, I got to play hockey and netball, they were my options. I never got offered to play football so short of kicking a ball about with my brothers I never really got into playing it. But I know every rule under the sun and I watch a hell of a lot of football. So, if a pretty confident person like me – I'm a professional, I run a charity – still wouldn't go down and kick a ball about with a load of men, we thought we ought to look at setting something up separately.

'I guess what we wanted to create was somewhere where it doesn't matter if you hear voices and shout out whilst you're playing. It doesn't matter if you suffer from such crippling anxiety you can hardly turn up to practice. So even now we're nearly two years down the line, I would never want someone new to turn up and feel that it's cliquey. We make sure that everyone gets a touch of the ball. We make sure there's little focus on the score, so we don't even keep score, for example. Even if there's someone who literally just stands in the middle and you pass the ball to them and they hoof it out every time, we'll still keep passing the ball to them. To me, that's the idea of mental health friendly. We're not here for competition, but a lot of us are competing with ourselves to try and get better.'

It hasn't always been plain sailing for the ladies' section of Brunsmeer, with COVID-19 plunging the UK into lockdown just weeks after the first session, but there are now around 30 women signed up to play. Josie explains that some of them are on mental health wards, whilst others may not even have a mental health diagnosis and just feel that their confidence needs boosting. Each individual has their own unique story, but they have one thing in common: playing with Brunsmeer Awareness has been of great benefit to their mental health.

Lisa Thompson-Cox, another employee at Sheffield Flourish, is one of those to feel the positive effects of participating. Her passion around the topic of mental health is clear as we talk at length about her own experiences and desire to speak up to encourage others to do the same and access the support they need. The keen goalkeeper acknowledges that she wouldn't have hit the lows she did had the environment around and attitudes towards mental health been more advanced in the 1980s. Childhood trauma suffered at a young age as the victim of sexual abuse at the hands of a friend's father, had been locked away inside Lisa's head for years when she left Sheffield at the age of 18 to move to Canada in search of work. Upon returning to the UK ten years later, she came across her abuser, with just the sound of his voice triggering a breakdown. Things developed to a stage where the self-inflicted cuts on Lisa's arm became so deep that she had to visit her GP, at which point her dad, by now desperate with fear, asked the doctor to section her. What happened next was ultimately the turning point for the massive Sheffield Wednesday supporter.

When recalling her story to me, Lisa makes a point of giving particular credit to the GP who helped her, and it soon becomes clear why. Instead of opting to section her patient in crisis, Lisa's GP instead set up a 20-minute appointment with her every single day to make sure she was all right. If Lisa didn't show up, a receptionist would call to check in on her. Ultimately, these sessions went on in some form for 16 years, with Lisa's GP only ever a phone call away. This helped empower Lisa as she set up her own mental health recovery group, entitled TGI Friday. Lisa makes it clear that living with mental health is about managing the symptoms rather than recovering as such, and turning up to play with Brunsmeer from the inaugural session in March 2020 was another important step in keeping her on the right path, allowing her to tap into some happier memories from her childhood.

Always the tomboy at school, Lisa takes great pride in describing to me how she would not only be the only girl selected to play football on the playground, but would also routinely be one of the first picks. Though predominantly a goalkeeper, she earned the nickname 'Cannonball' for her ability to strike a football. Beaming down the camera at me as we chat over Zoom, she tells the story of making a sprawling save on concrete at the age of 11 and not realising she'd broken her wrist in the process until three weeks later. In the meantime, of course, she had continued in goal despite the pain and the growing size of her hand as the swelling increased. Unfortunately for Lisa, there was no pathway to becoming a professional women's footballer in the 1980s, with the first professional women's side not coming about until

April 2000. By the age of 18, Lisa had moved abroad and football was no longer a part of her life. Her love for the game never disappeared, however, and Josie's brainchild in setting up Brunsmeer Awareness Ladies sparked a long-awaited rekindling of it, helping Lisa through her daily mental health battles in the process.

'I really didn't realise just how much football was in my blood and how much it helped me to realise who I am and just what I enjoy. The minute that very first session started, the minute that the ball came over to me, it was like my childhood just coming back. It was like I belonged on that pitch. The goalkeeper's position became really precious to me. It opened up my whole positive box of memories from back at school where I was playing football, diving around on the concrete. The first person to shoot the ball pelted it quite hard but I saved it and I was like, "yeah, I've still got it!" It's just amazing, I love it. I look forward to every Wednesday night. I have a laugh, we smile, it's just like I'm back on the school playground playing football again, and I actually act like it as well!'

Lisa says the physical act of kicking a ball again after a 25-year break was therapeutic.

'There's so much you can get out of it, whether you're kicking that ball in a net and scoring or just actually passing it … you can get so much release out of kicking that ball. And that's what I learnt, that's what brought me back to my childhood. It is just so much release … I can be having the shittiest day on a Wednesday but then I go to football and leave the pitch at 8pm and I've forgotten what the rest of the day was like because I've just got so much out of me.'

Lisa's passion on the topic of mental health in general carries through to her work as a community engagement officer and volunteer manager with Sheffield Flourish. One of her many tasks involves acting as the secretary of the Sheffield & Hallamshire County FA Flourish League, which provides 11-a-side football in an inclusive environment. The idea of the league, as Josie Soutar explains, is to reduce the stigma around mental health by opening up the league to anyone who wants to get involved as opposed to more typical 'Ability Counts' leagues where a formal diagnosis is required to play. The result is a refreshing mix of those who are struggling more with their mental health and those who simply prefer the atmosphere to one of intense competition. An element of competitiveness is of course maintained by the league format, with three points for a win as in any other league, but the ethos of everyone being welcome remains at the forefront of the Flourish League. At the time I speak to Lisa and Josie, there are seven sides involved, including the Brunsmeer Awareness Men's side, with several more looking to join.

Football is not the only endeavour Sheffield Flourish are involved in. The charity run a blended approach, with half of their work done digitally and half of it done in person. The online centrepiece is the Sheffield Mental Health Guide, a directory where people can search for activities or look for support that is available to them. A feature called 'my toolkit' is provided to help people with their own mental health recovery, including a link to a suicide support and prevention website. The in-person side centres around seven community enterprises, of which Brunsmeer Awareness FC is one. The others offer a variety of activities, from gardening to poetry, with each one helping people learn skills and develop new or existing interests whilst making friends and building a sense of community. Clearly, there is value in each of these activities, but it is the football in particular that appeals to Josie.

'If you've got imposing thoughts happening and you're running about, you haven't really got time to focus on what's going on in your head. You're focusing on stopping a ball, passing it, what your team-mates are doing. I think it's true of most forms of exercise but I guess the nice thing with a team sport is that you haven't got the headspace to be worrying. It's kind of a blocker on those intrusive thoughts that you can get. It's like a bit of time away from it.

'I think with football in particular, that sense of belonging to a team is massive. That sense of team-mates, of "these are my people even though we come from all walks of life and are all ages and have different backgrounds". We rock up and we all feel like we're part of Brunsmeer. I know from the men's Brunsmeer team that there's a guy that has often thought about taking his own life, but he doesn't want to let his team-mates down because he knows they've got practice on Tuesday. There's obviously the fun of playing, there's the fun of learning new skills, but there's also the idea that you're part of a posse, I guess. You're part of a team and that team has each other's backs. And I think when you've been suffering with mental health, finding your place and finding your people is quite tricky because you can always feel like an outsider or feel like your behaviour's going to be odd. Whereas I think with

Brunsmeer, and the link with mental health in particular, it's that idea of, actually, it doesn't matter what's happened or what's going on for me, I can rock up, I can play, and I can have a laugh with the girls.'

This concept of 'football therapy' is becoming more mainstream as the benefits to many people's mental health of playing football become clearer. Characterised by being open to everyone without the intensity of competition you might find in 'regular' football, football therapy runs with the idea of social inclusion at the heart of it. Realistically, the suggestion that playing sport might be a good idea for your mental health is nothing new. It has long been known that exercise releases good endorphins in the brain, as well as reducing levels of the stress hormones adrenaline and cortisol. However, more recent research specifically into football has indicated that the sport is uniquely positioned on a macro level to work as a mental health intervention in society.

For example, a Welsh study conducted in 2020 looked at participants who attended weekly football therapy sessions arranged by Time to Change Wales. The authors noted that a number of prior studies have shown that purely exercise-based mental health interventions have resulted in similar improvements to participants who received therapy-based or medication-based interventions. In their own study, they concluded that individuals who participated in the Time to Change sessions reported clear benefits to their mental health, with key themes being a reduction in stress and anxiety as well as a sense of team spirit that led into a wider sense of purpose. Bettina Friedrich and Oliver J. Mason looked over a series of 16 studies into forms of football therapy to draw inferences on their effectiveness. Their key themes included the suggestion that football, as a sport already enjoyed by so many, is a great way to connect with people who may otherwise be hard to reach. Furthermore, stigma around mental health can be reduced with the presence of teams or tournaments that include people with visible mental health issues – such as the Flourish League run by Sheffield Flourish.

Indeed, the Flourish League is not the only project looking to utilise this idea of football therapy. On Merseyside, Colin Dolan has had particular success in setting up Liverpool Football Therapy, which has over 80 participants, as well as the wider Mental Health Football Association to promote and support initiatives in the area across the whole of the UK. Since lockdown, many more inclusive football therapy clubs have sprung up as the ability to simply get out of the house and stretch your legs is suddenly no longer taken for granted. Predominantly, these initiatives are aimed at men, a demographic stereotypically associated with not talking about mental health but having a strong interest in football, helping to bridge that gap and open up conversation. But, of course, plenty of women love football too, and women are more likely to experience a mental health problem than men – between the ages of 16 and 24, women are around three times more likely than men to suffer from one. A research paper published by UEFA in 2017 runs with the headline that teenage girls who play football feel more confident than girls who do not play sport, and indeed also more confident than girls playing other sports. The primary reasons for this were the enduring friendships made through football, creating a permeating sense of togetherness, along with the ability of the sport to help them deal with pressures elsewhere in life. Speaking to Josie about it, it is clear that the impact that Brunsmeer Awareness has had in Sheffield is a fine case-study to put weight behind UEFA's claim, albeit relevant to women of all ages, as well as the theory of football therapy in general.

'Mental health covers a vast scale and spectrum, the same way physical health does. But there are some things that are commonalities to people, particularly feeling socially isolated. It's massive. If you are stuck at home all the time and occasionally go to see your mental health worker or your doctor or whatever it is, then that might be helping on a very medical model of what's going on for you. But there's no joy in that, is there? There's no pleasure, and an idea of going, "OK, I've got all of this crap going on, but I've got one thing to look forward to every week and that's football practice", is much better.

'It's often an alternative way of people being able to cope with their mental health. That's partly why we're called "Flourish", because it's that idea of, you might have a mental health problem, but how can we make you flourish regardless of what that is? There's obviously a place for medication and therapy, but I think too often that's the immediate thing that people go for when there's a whole host of other ways people can feel human and enjoy life, and I guess spend some time away from the heaviness that can often come from mental health. If all we're offering people is this constant barrage of thinking about your mental health, that is really heavy, you then don't get an escape from it. Whereas if you're able to go and do something else like football where you turn up and people aren't asking about your diagnosis, but equally are conscious there's something going on for you – what a wonderful way of helping people to get over things or even just to have a break from whatever is going on in their heads.'

Brunsmeer Awareness, under the guidance of football fanatic Josie, continues to expand and welcome new members. She jokes that despite being the best kitted-out football team in the country thanks to what was on offer from the Caring United campaign, they are yet to play any competitive games, but this is set to change with a competitive team on the horizon for those players who want to give it a go. The girls will certainly be confident going into any matches with Lisa Thompson-Cox between the sticks, as Ashley Cole found out on his visit to the club. The three-time Premier League winner was challenged to take four penalties by Brunsmeer's number one. He managed to score just one of these, and whilst Lisa is understandably proud of this achievement, I sense she is still somewhat frustrated at not saving the other one too. For the vast majority of the population, saving three penalties from a former England international would be the achievement of a lifetime, but for Lisa an even bigger victory is the smile that adorns her face, brought on largely by the simple joy of kicking a football about every Wednesday afternoon.

* * *

A hundred or so people gather at the otherwise peaceful Lord Halsbury Playing Fields in Northolt on Easter Sunday for a classic top-of-the-table clash in the Middlesex

County Sunday Football League Premier Division. Larkspur Rovers are the home side, but only a handful of the spectators gathered in the sunshine behind the roped-off touchline are backing them. They've not done anything wrong, they're not an unpopular side by any stretch, but it's hard when your opponents are such a special team. The green and white shirts of Grenfell Athletic have the popular backing today, and will do long into the future. Indeed, they have done since the tragic events of the 14 June 2017.

Described by expert psychotherapist Derek O'Neill as 'London's 9/11', the Grenfell Fire was one of the worst tragedies in modern British history. It started in the early hours of the morning, when a faulty fridge freezer caught fire. Residents who were awoken by smoke alarms were advised to stay put – standard policy for high-rise fires where flames should remain confined to the flat in which the fire began. However, flammable cladding installed on the exterior of the building that did not comply with building regulations allowed the fire to spread upwards, quickly engulfing the majority of the tower. At 2.47am, the 'stay put' advice was reversed, but it came too late for many residents. Those towards the top of the tower found their escape route cut off by flames and thick smoke. Only two people on the top two floors survived the blaze, with eyewitness reports stating that some jumped to their deaths, knowing they could not survive. That night, 72 people lost their lives in the worst residential fire in the UK since World War Two.

Rupert Taylor was on holiday that night. Confused by a number of texts asking him if he was OK, he turned on the

TV to find out the tower at the centre of the community he loved so much was on fire. Rupert has spent his entire working life in roles to benefit the community, living just a couple of streets away from Grenfell Tower throughout. A larger-than-life man who oozes charisma, he was the manager of the local youth centre at the time of the fire. As we chat, Rupert takes great pride in telling me about the many vulnerable people he has been able to help over the years. His work, and life beyond that, is defined by helping others, and so his life was absolutely shattered in June 2017. Having booked a flight home from Gibraltar that same afternoon, Rupert was devastated to discover that amongst those who had died were nine children who regularly attended his youth centre.

The weeks that followed saw the community around Grenfell try to pick up the pieces, to make some sense of what had happened. One young resident, wandering around the area in the days following the fire still in a sense of shock, approached Rupert, and the pair discussed how the individual had coped with the loss of his parents a couple of years earlier. The answer, put simply, was football. A lover of football himself, learning his craft on the artificial pitches that sit at the foot of Grenfell Tower, Rupert was inspired by the boy's story and was of the opinion that football could be used to help heal this community as well. Barely a month after the fire, Grenfell Athletic was born, with training sessions advertised in the local community and the side entered into the Middlesex County League for the 2017/18 season. As the tagline of their marketing campaign says, Grenfell Athletic have very much been part of the fabric of the community since. For all the work Rupert has done there throughout his life, it is clear he sees Grenfell Athletic as his most important project.

'Our community was in disarray. The best way to describe it is a modern-day western warzone. And in a warzone, people are vulnerable. People were still in shock and are still facing the trauma that came out of it. The ramifications of the disaster are still to be measured and I'm not sure if we will be able to truly measure it in our lifetimes, to be honest. At the time we started setting it up, we didn't even know how many survivors there were, so we said it would be a community team, not just a team for ex-residents of Grenfell Tower but also the bereaved and lads from the local community. Everybody from this community remembers where they were on 14 June 2017. Everybody. It rocked the nation.'

'If I was going to do it, I knew that I'd have to fully commit and immerse myself into the players' lives and their daily routines … I've been a brother figure, father figure, mentor, an uncle, a punching bag sometimes. I take the whole nine yards. If I didn't set it up as quickly as I did, I believe that potentially there may have been, and it's sad to think about really, a lot more struggles. Not just with the players in the team but also their families and people who Grenfell Athletic has given hope to along the journey. We're not politically driven, so it allows our players to be able to release from their everyday lives. A bit of respite. It's not escapism, as we have faced certain things together, but they deal with Grenfell every single day. If we were politically motivated, they would have to deal with it even when they want a bit of downtime. But because we aren't, they are able to completely release themselves and make me the punching bag.'

Unsurprisingly, the mental health impacts of the disaster in the local community around North Kensington have been devastating. A report prepared for the Royal Borough of Kensington and Chelsea estimated that 67 per cent of those who either escaped the tower on the night of the fire or lost relatives required subsequent treatment for post-traumatic stress disorder (PTSD). Aside from those directly affected, approximately 4,000 local residents witnessed the tragedy in some form, with more than a quarter of these individuals showing signs of PTSD too. Barely a month after the fire had occurred, a local volunteer reported hearing of at least 20 suicide attempts in the North Kensington area. Just as harrowing are the individual stories and eyewitness accounts from those caught up in the blaze that terrible morning. A mother and son who escaped from the 23rd floor appeared on *Channel 4 News* to tell the story of their miracle escape from near the very top of the building. Their husband and father, sadly, did not make it, apparently jumping to his death as the smoke and heat overwhelmed him.

In the interview, which is still available online, the mother describes a recurring nightmare in which she sees her husband one more time and asks him from which floor did he jump. Before she can get a response, he disappears once more. Art therapy sessions put on for children who witnessed the fire gave a devastating glimpse into the mental state of many of those young eyewitnesses. The majority of the drawings showed macabre visions of the fire, some with figures calling for help out of windows, labelled with the name of a friend or relative who perished in the blaze.

Given the scale and impact of the mental health implications arising from the Grenfell Fire, the response from authorities and the community as a whole was essential. The psychologist leading this response, Dr John Green, called it the 'largest of its kind in Europe'. Around 10,000 people were screened for trauma, with 2,000 given some form of treatment. Just as important were the community support groups that sprang up, such as Young Grenfell, a regular meeting in a youth group for children to support each other. Grenfell Athletic was one of these vital enterprises, offering a 'safety net' to the players as Rupert Taylor describes it. Energetic right wing-back, Joseph John, speaks about how the team has enabled him to open up and talk about the effects the fire has had on him in ways he would otherwise be unable to do. John was a resident of Grenfell Tower, escaping from the second floor as the fire took hold. He lost friends who had the misfortune of living higher up in the block, and suffers from PTSD, anxiety and depression as a direct result of the tragic events that unfolded in June 2017. Grenfell Athletic has offered him hope, and as Rupert describes, he is not the only one to have benefitted from getting involved with the club.

'I've had players that have stopped drinking. I've had players that have started working. I've had players that were on suicide watch that have said that without the team they don't know where they'd be. They've got children and they still don't know where they'd be. It's a place for players to be vulnerable. It's OK to take a risk, a calculated risk. It's OK to walk into uncertainty. You won't always land on your feet but … you'll always land in a place where you aren't alone. You do not have to face the trials alone. I've had ex-residents from the tower that have come to me and said that the team lifts them. It drives them, compels them to keep moving forward. So what we're offering the community is something greater than any one of us individually.

'Some of the players need Grenfell Athletic. Some of the players explained that they've got no one, nobody. So this has become their family. It's vital to have those bonds, the connection, the common goal. They've made friends for life and they don't even know it yet. In five and ten years when they start having children or they've got families, or something comes up, they're going to miss each other. If they have a dark day, a moment where they're feeling a bit down, insecure, or vulnerable, they're going to reach out to each other again. What the team offers is a sanctuary.'

All in all, things have been going well on the pitch as well, despite Rupert admitting it was 'heavy on the soul' at the beginning, with the psychological wounds from the disaster still fresh. Since finishing fifth out of 12 teams in their first season down in Division Three, Grenfell Athletic worked their way up to the Premier Division for the 2021/22 season. The game away to Larkspur, which acts almost as a title decider, sadly goes against them, ending in a 2-1 defeat that sends the Northolt-based hosts six points clear at the top with two games to go. Coached by former Reading star Dave Kitson, alongside Rupert Taylor himself, Grenfell eventually battle their way to second place, representing an impressive season despite the disappointment of missing out on the ultimate prize of the title.

Grenfell Athletic's ambitions go far beyond just securing the Premier Division title of the Middlesex County Sunday Football League. Rupert devotes a sizeable proportion of our discussion to telling me all about his detailed long-term plan, which was developed after a series of intense discussions with his other three board members, who each bring different knowledge and experiences to the table. Grenfell Athletic currently play their home games at the King's House Sports Ground in Chiswick, five miles away from Grenfell Tower, but Rupert sees a future in which the club has its own stadium. The community worker saw the best of his local area with everyone coming together in the wake of the fire and envisages a future in which the football club can continue to serve these bonds. He wants classrooms built into the stadium, allowing young people in the area to reach their full potential. The name 'Athletic' was chosen as Rupert wants to expand the club into other sports, providing opportunities for greater numbers of people to get involved and find their calling. As we speak, plans are already afoot for a women's football team to start up in the 2022/23 season. His focus when outlining his vision is broken only when the family cat jumps onto his laptop whilst Rupert is in mid-flow, and even then he's so passionate and engaged with the subject, I'm almost surprised he notices.

You certainly can't accuse Rupert and his board of not taking action towards making this dream a reality. A series of high-profile marketing initiatives started with the club's first official kit launch in 2020, in association with Kitlocker. The campaign asked 72 famous people to wear the shirt and post a picture on social media – a way of remembering the 72 individuals who lost their lives in the fire. The likes of Noel Gallagher, Harry Kane, Hugh Jackman, Sam Smith and many more all got involved, resulting in the campaign reaching 45 million people, with more than 1,000 shirts sold, all within the first couple of weeks of its launch. A second kit launch took place for the following season and the club also partnered with Cadbury in 2021, the famous British chocolate manufacturer releasing a limited-edition Grenfell Athletic chocolate bar with all profits going back into the club.

Despite all this, one of the highlights for Rupert was the culmination of a pre-season tour in the summer of 2021, which culminated in a game against the London Fire Brigade at the home of Corinthian-Casuals in south London. It was an occasion that in many ways was symbolic of the wider purpose of Grenfell Athletic.

'If it gets to Christmas Day and you're in the middle of a war, and you can lay arms down for a football pitch on the ground and say, let's have a game, I don't think I need to say any more about the power of football. Imagine for a moment that some of our players and some of those firemen, the Red Watch that attended Grenfell on the 14th of June 2017, would have had moments crossing each other on the stairs in the smoke. And the first time they were reunited was on the football pitch. It was immense, an absolute moment in history. For our players, they experienced something they had never experienced before. The game meant so much to us all.

'Grenfell Athletic's mission is to be everybody's second favourite team. You could support Liverpool, which I do, you could support Man City, Man United, Arsenal, Chelsea, Spurs, more locally Brentford, QPR, Fulham. You can support any of these clubs, but you will support Grenfell Athletic too. Harry Kane plays for Tottenham but supports Grenfell Athletic. It's incredible. I know that this team will be alive long after I'm gone because of the things that were put in place now to build the solid-rooted foundations, to ensure that Grenfell Athletic will forever keep Grenfell in the hearts and minds of people across the globe.

'The priority is never to forget the 72 lives that were lost.'

Chapter 12

The Loss of Your Football Club

WHAT WOULD you do if the company you worked for suddenly stopped paying you? How would you pay the bills, the mortgage, feed the kids? What if you knew you couldn't find work again for several months due to circumstances beyond your control? For the players at Bury in the 2018/19 season, this nightmare situation became a reality. Facing the toughest challenge to their mental health of their entire careers, the boys representing the Shakers pulled together in remarkable fashion on the pitch. Sadly, the benefits of their efforts were not enough to save the club and its place in the English Football League (EFL).

Bury Football Club had been in trouble before, suffering particularly badly from the collapse of ITV Digital in 2002. The club faced a court order in March of that season which could have spelled the end, but herculean efforts from the supporters to raise money kept it alive. The underlying problem of poor attendances didn't go away, however, and financial troubles meant Bury were placed under transfer embargo in December 2012. The crisis which eventually forced the club into expulsion from the

EFL in August 2019 can be traced back to this point. Bury were taken over by Stewart Day, a property entrepreneur specialising in the building of student accommodation. His ambition was initially met with enthusiasm by supporters, particularly as Day had the support of club legend Neville Neville. Described by several supporters as 'like someone playing Football Manager in real life', Day aimed to bring Bury up through the football pyramid, spending heavily but underwriting losses with the profits made from his other successful business ventures. The club never made it any higher than 16th place in League One, but the real damage came when Day's property empire collapsed. He sold the club to Steve Dale for £1 in December 2018, having overseen staggering losses of £8.3 million during his time at the helm.

Bury were fourth in the League Two table when Steve Dale became the owner, hopeful of an immediate return to League One come the end of the season. Under Stewart Day that season, payments had often been received late, but the players were all paid in full eventually. There was optimism amongst the group when Dale first came in, as he assured the squad that wages would be paid in full and on time going forward. He had paid off an outstanding tax bill to HMRC in February to avoid a winding-up order, but it wasn't long before he claimed the club's financial problems were 'far in excess' of what he had thought when he purchased it. The players soon stopped receiving any money altogether. For midfielder, vice-captain and local lad Nicky Adams, it was a challenging period.

'We're not millionaires. I certainly don't have fortunes where I can say, "All right, I don't need to be paid." It's the real world. We can't go without being paid. Everyone lives to their means. In my situation, me and my partner had just bought a house … and paid for all the stuff to be done on it, then all of a sudden, I wasn't getting paid. I can't go back to the builders and say, "I've got no money, I need my money back." I'm trying to do the best that I can for my family and secure a future for my kids, and the next thing I know I'm not being paid. It did hit me hard, and I don't like borrowing money off people. I think it's more of a pride thing. People can be offering and saying, "It's all right, give it back whenever," but I didn't want to do it. But in the end, I had to.'

Adams said he and his wife were 'panicking' at the thought of losing their home.

'She's a strong woman and she really held it together for the family. But it does affect everyone. She was pregnant at the time as well, that's another thing she had to deal with.'

It wasn't just the players suffering. Midfielder Stephen Dawson told *The Telegraph* how the players chipped in to help the training ground chef buy a birthday present for his six-year-old daughter, after seeing him in tears the week before. Adams describes speaking to staff who had worked at the club for more than 20 years facing the prospect of losing not only their jobs but the club they loved too. Though football is first and foremost Adams's livelihood, he admits he is a big fan himself, often attending games when he isn't playing, and has his own personal connection to Bury Football Club. As we chat, Adams reminisces on the start of his career nearly 20 years ago, when he would catch the 417 bus to Bury Road every day to train at the Centre of Excellence. He made his debut for Bury the day before his 19th birthday, bursting onto the scene by scoring the only goal of the game against Darlington. He left for Leicester City after three successful years at the club, but subsequently returned for a spell in 2014 before signing for the Shakers for a third time in 2018. It was this third spell that was to prove particularly eventful for Adams, with there being an emotional significance in the move from the very start.

In November 2017, with Adams playing for Carlisle United, he suffered an anterior cruciate ligament injury which ruled him out for the season. A tough injury to come back from at any stage of your career, Adams was well aware that at 31 he might find it hard to find a club who would take a punt on him. Bury were his saviours, with manager and close friend Ryan Lowe giving his career a lifeline. He was to repay their faith with some fantastic performances on the pitch as Bury pushed for promotion, but the financial troubles meant it wasn't to be the fairy-tale Adams had hoped for.

As the 2018/19 season reached its penultimate month, the club were in particular turmoil off the pitch but incredibly were sitting in second place in League Two. March's wages hadn't been paid and a winding-up petition was brought against the club on 10 April, three days before a vital 2-0 win against Colchester. The water had been cut off at the training ground, making the pitches unsafe, and the players had to rely on a favour from the fire brigade to water them. Young players even had to borrow money to put petrol in their cars to attend training. With several members of the squad dipping increasingly close to the breadline, particularly on mortgage payments, the players had a tough collective decision to make. Refuse to play in an attempt to bring attention to the situation and get it resolved, or soldier on unpaid to try and help Bury to promotion?

Around the same time, players at Bolton Wanderers in the Championship had also gone for an extended period without being paid. They opted to go on strike, apologising to supporters but noting in a statement that their lack of payment was 'creating mental, emotional and financial burdens for people through no fault of their own'. Bolton's match against Brentford scheduled for 27 April was cancelled, with Brentford awarded a 1-0 win, but Wanderers had already been relegated to League One a week earlier.

The following season, Macclesfield fell into trouble in League Two, with a fixture against Crewe cancelled as players went on strike, citing their 'emotional and mental wellbeing' as being at 'rock bottom'. An FA Cup tie against non-league Kingstonian was fulfilled by youth and loan players, who were beaten 4-0 by the London side.

A players' strike amongst the Bury squad, then, would not have been out of the question, but they decided against it. On the pitch, their decision paid off as remarkably they secured promotion with a game to spare after a 1-1 draw at Tranmere. Looking back now, it is a decision that Nicky Adams does not regret despite the eventual fate of the club.

'We just had the mentality of, "look, all we can do is our thing on the pitch". I take my hat off to every one of my team-mates and everyone who was involved, because we went out there and we got the job done. It wasn't easy to do. It would have been easy for us to say, "We're not playing, we would have got promoted but it didn't happen because we weren't getting paid." We didn't want excuses, we wanted to make history. And no matter what, they can never take that away from us. It's memories for life … obviously what happened was a tragedy, but for those fans, they remember that [the promotion]; they still talk about it and have the memories.

'Mentally, it was a tough time, but as a group of people, all we had was each other. When we went onto the pitch, all those problems went away. We loved each other as team-mates; every time we went over that white line, we were together and we backed each other up. That night … Bury took nearly 3,000 fans and filled the Tranmere away end. You don't forget those nights. And then the last game of the season against Port Vale where it was packed and everyone ran on the pitch and was celebrating – my friends and family were all there. All the tough times go away because everyone's celebrating, everyone's having a good time. But then a couple of days later, reality hits home. You all speak and you know, without saying it to each other, you know that's it. Everyone's going to be going separate ways.'

The hope amongst the players was that promotion to League One would encourage buyers to bid for the club, increasing the chances it would be saved. Failing that, continuing to play would put them in the shop window, as they all faced the prospect of having to find a new club. The season over, things were no closer to being resolved. Wages still hadn't been paid, and though the PFA stepped in to help where they could, the players were all left significantly out of pocket. Furious, Adams released a statement on behalf of the whole Bury squad in May, less than a month after promotion was secured. He spoke about how hard it was for the players, who, instead of relaxing after a hard-earned promotion, were wondering how they were going to fill the gap left by 12 weeks without wages and wondering where they would go next. Adams implored Steve Dale to sell the club, but the owner didn't budge. Reflecting on the decision to put that statement out, Adams says he wasn't afraid of any consequences, as things couldn't have got any worse at Bury anyway. There was no danger of any potential suitors being worried by his comments; in fact, most of the football world was firmly behind the Bury players, and the way Adams saw it, Dale was 'taking food off my kids' plates'. The anger is still clear to see even two years on, when we speak.

The Bury vice-captain had signed a new deal to extend his contract into the 2019/20 season but was later informed by manager Lowe that this contract wasn't valid due to the situation Bury were in off the pitch. To make matters worse, Adams was not insured by the club going into the final few games of the season. If he had suffered any serious injury, he would have had to fund any treatment out of his own pocket. Passionate about Bury Football Club and football in general, Adams decided to play on regardless, but hates to think of what would have happened had he suffered a recurrence of his cruciate ligament injury, for example. The financial impacts, as well as mental health impacts, would have been catastrophic.

As it happened, Nicky Adams's new contract being rendered null and void was a blessing in disguise. He joined Northampton Town on a free transfer in June, ready for the next chapter of his career, one in which he would be paid regularly and on time. The majority of his team-mates also moved on, but a handful stayed behind in the hope that the club would be bought out and would take its place in League One the following season. That hope turned out to be misplaced. Steve Dale had agreed a Company Voluntary Arrangement (CVA) in July to keep the club alive for the time being, but could not provide proof to the EFL of how the conditions of this CVA would be satisfied. Despite having a new manager appointed and numerous players in on trial, Bury's first five games of the season were suspended with their EFL Cup tie against Sheffield Wednesday awarded to the Championship club. Dale was once again implored to sell, but turned down one offer, with a later proposed deal with C&N Sporting Risk falling through close to an EFL deadline to restore financial order. Bury were expelled from the Football League on 27 August 2019 – just three days before the transfer window closed. The likes of Neil Danns, Harry Bunn, Stephen Dawson, Adam Thompson and Tom Miller were left without a club with the season already underway. A good friend of all five, Nicky Adams did not envy them for what they were going through.

'I was speaking to them every other day. Obviously, they were hoping, and they kept getting told, "it's going through, he's going to sell, it's done and dusted". And then literally, as if you could rub any more salt into the wounds, [the club being expelled from the EFL] after the start of the season gave no time for those lads who stayed behind. In hindsight, I would have been one of those players, if my contract hadn't been null and void, I would have been in the same boat. Just bang, gone. I had to speak to those lads. They weren't good phone calls, it was upsetting. The problem the boys had was a lot of clubs had signed all the players they needed or wanted, so there weren't many options for them. It was horrible. It's not nice to see those lads who worked so hard all their lives to be a professional footballer have it taken away from them through no fault of their own. The mental strength that they've got and what they've had to go through, I've got nothing but the utmost respect for all of them.'

Fortunes for those players stuck in limbo were mixed. Centre-back Adam Thompson moved immediately on to Rotherham, where he won promotion to the Championship, but he still found the summer of 2019 a mentally taxing time. Neil Danns too wasn't without a club for long, signing for Tranmere Rovers in mid-September. The others weren't so lucky. Harry Bunn eventually signed for Kilmarnock in the Scottish Premiership, but not until January 2020. Tom Miller didn't find a new club until February, and that required dropping down into non-league football with AFC Fylde. He had rejected offers from two League Two clubs whilst still under contract with Bury in the hope the club would be playing in League One in the 2019/20 season. Perhaps the worst affected player was Stephen Dawson. An experienced player, well into his 30s, there was no concrete interest in him from any Football League clubs, meaning he needed to drop down to local club Radcliffe of the Northern Premier League. Due to unpaid wages at Bury, he was forced to sell his house and borrow around £15,000 from family and friends.

The collateral damage extended far beyond just the men's first team. The successful women's side broke up just months after securing a glorious promotion to the Premier Division of the North West Women's Regional League at Gigg Lane, though the club itself continued with some remaining players after their funding source switched to the still existing Bury FC Foundation. Bury Academy manager Mark Litherland had to inform 140 children as young as eight that they no longer had a club to play for, something he described as 'devastating'. Litherland admits to having tearful conversations with parents concerned for their children's mental health. On a practical level, many faced the same problem as the first-team players left behind at the club, in that youth intakes were already complete at most clubs. But of course, as Nicky Adams alludes to several times during our conversation, the people who suffer the most when a club goes out of business are its supporters.

* * *

In *Star Wars Episode IV*, the destruction of the planet of Alderaan by the evil and narcissistic Empire forces is instantly sensed by Obi-Wan Kenobi, who cries, 'I felt a great disturbance in the Force, as if millions of voices suddenly cried out in terror and were suddenly silenced. I fear something terrible has happened.' Fortunately, nobody is in the habit of vaporising entire planets in the real world, but within the football world, the death of a football club is about as close as it gets. When Bury became the first club since Maidstone United in 1992 to drop out of the English Football League due to their financial situation, those famous words from the iconic film felt very apt. Pictures on the news showed fans in floods of tears outside the ground, simply unable to comprehend that 134 years of history, including two FA Cup wins way back when, had all suddenly been brought to an end. Tributes appeared at the ground not just from Bury fans but from supporters of other teams too, the outpouring of grief from the whole football family perhaps reflecting thoughts of what might have been from fans of other clubs. It's everybody's worst nightmare to see their football club die, and for Bury supporters it was becoming a brutal reality.

The day after Bury were expelled from the Football League, they were due to host Doncaster Rovers in a League One fixture at Gigg Lane. Instead, Bury North MP James Frith addressed a crowd of supporters at the stadium, likening what had happened to a bereavement. Sooner or later, you have to get back up, dust yourself down and go to the shops, he said, making it clear that the next steps to secure the future of football in the town of Bury were now crucial. That comparison to a bereavement wasn't too far-fetched either. In the wake of what happened, Bury fans were offered mental health support on the NHS, with sessions for up to 80 people provided by Bury Healthy Minds. These sessions focused on wellbeing and coping with loss, similar to what would be provided to someone who had just lost a loved one. As I caught up with James Frith over Zoom, it became clear that the pain of what happened is still raw in the town.

'The loss of Bury Football Club ripped the social, economic and cultural capital out of the town. It was an identity, it gave the town momentum or a head of steam, it gave it a sense of propulsion fortnightly, win, lose, or draw. It involved the coming together of people, it involved people coming from outside, it was communal, a reason for seeing other people and speaking to them. To have all of that social infrastructure, economic and cultural capital infrastructure disassembled in an instant was what I called several times on record a "joint enterprise crime", and the victims of that crime are the people of Bury.

'When you go to a football match you're not being sold a ticket for an emotional connection, but you know full well it is going to involve that … It is a huge part of people's identity. Match days are far more important than simply the 90 minutes. It's the ritual, it's the apprehension, the hope, the joy, the celebration. It's sharing in victory or defeat. To have that taken from us against our will caused great anxiety and in fact it also removed those touch points for people to check in on each other. Of course, blokes in particular aren't particularly good at that.'

In order to get a sense of the magnitude of the feelings of loss resulting from Bury's expulsion from the Football League, I travelled up to visit the town in August 2021. Visiting the stadium, Gigg Lane, was an eerie and sombre experience. Tributes I recognised from watching the news on the day the club were expelled from the Football League two years ago almost to the day still hung on the fence around the ground, weathered in their appearance but not in their emotional significance. Reading each note left behind captured an individual story of heartbreak, really bringing home the human impact of what happened. One note, which judging by its condition had been there a while, spoke of the heartbreak of somebody's two young children not being able to go to the football at the weekend anymore. Another, more fresh and recently placed, mourned the loss of a lifelong Bury fan just three days earlier. Amongst the sadness, there was an undercurrent of anger – 'He died without his football club', it read.

With every anecdote I read, each a harrowing insight into someone else's torment over the last couple of years, I became drawn into a trance which was only broken when the silence itself was shattered by two kids running through the car park. Disappearing as quickly as they arrived past the Banksy-style graffiti that depicts a child painting the words 'Save Us' on the brick wall of Gigg Lane, the atmosphere outside the stadium returned to being markedly similar to that of the graveyard adjacent to the ground. I can't help but ask myself how I would deal with such a situation were it to happen to the club I support? I don't have the answers.

When Gigg Lane went silent on Saturday afternoons, the pubs and cafés around the ground faced a similar bleak outcome. The local Labour councillor for the nearby Unsworth Ward, Nathan Boroda, showed me round to introduce me to the people who have lived with the situation since August 2019. It's Sunday on a bank holiday weekend, usually a night of revelry, but when we walk into the Swan and Cemetery pub opposite the ground at just past 10pm, we're the only two people in there. The Staff of Life, another typical match-day pub, seems livelier, with the jukebox cranked up to full volume, but there are still just a handful of people inside to go with the two small dogs yapping away. The solitary woman behind the bar explains that Saturday afternoons when Bury were at home would be a guaranteed payday for the pub as well as herself – but her shifts have been reduced since the club were expelled from the EFL, personally costing her at least £50 a week in lost income. Happy to chat, she points me in the direction of a gentleman sat in the corner to tell me more, but he looks pained and tells me he'd rather 'have a day off from it'. The look on his face tells me more about what the collapse of Bury Football Club meant to him than any conversation would.

Amidst all the sadness is a powerful sense of anger, still tangible despite the time that has elapsed since it was at its most acute. Steve Dale's intentions when purchasing the club are unknown, but he certainly had the opportunity to allow the club to continue playing in the Football League. The week before the deadline set by the EFL, Dale rejected an offer to buy the club, perhaps holding out for a better one. Unsurprisingly, given the debts the club had at the time, a better offer never came. In a now infamous interview with BBC Radio 5 Live, Dale told presenter Tony Livesey that not only had he never been to Bury before, but he hadn't even known there was a football club there before he took it over. I asked James Frith if he thought Dale was aware of the mental health impact of his actions on the town, and of the strength of the persisting sense of anger. Interestingly, his response showed that the anger was not aimed exclusively at Steve Dale.

'He [Steve Dale] is oblivious to all of that. I would like to think there will be a moment where that comes back to him. But if I'm honest, it was a very transactional, crude relationship he was expecting from his time owning Bury FC. But at no point, and this is why I talk about it being a joint enterprise, at no point did he expect the EFL to finally actually hold clubs accountable for what they're supposed to be doing. The issue I have with the EFL ... is that it was a completely unjust act to expel Bury. I believe that they deserved discretion and a second chance. I mean, just rekindling the conversation now and making the same arguments I made to ministers at the time, it boils the blood. I'm not a card-carrying member of Bury FC. I used to go to Gigg Lane with my son and watch matches, but for some it was their life and religion, and that was ripped out.'

Frith was frustrated that the EFL would not further extend the final deadline given to Bury prior to their expulsion, particularly as they had been tied into a condition of exclusivity with one potential bidder that they did not want, meaning that once this had collapsed, any further potential bidders were left out in the cold. Even after expulsion from the EFL, Frith campaigned for Bury to be reinstated in League Two for the 2020/21 season, but this proposal was rejected by the remaining 71 EFL clubs. It is clear that Frith believes there were a number of opportunities to prevent the ultimate fate of Bury being removed from the football league and the mental health impacts that came with that.

On the day of his speech at Gigg Lane, the anger amongst fans was apparent, with anti-EFL chants breaking out spontaneously in the audience on several occasions. The Bury North MP made it clear that this anger needed to be channelled into productive action. It hasn't been easy, the road to a future for football in Bury is a forked one with many hazards along the way, but the formation of phoenix club Bury AFC in December 2019 was no doubt a significant step. I went along to their home match against Daisy Hill on the bank holiday Monday of my weekend in Bury to find out more about this new club and what it means to the supporters who have got behind it.

To do so required a short tram journey down to Radcliffe, home to Radcliffe FC's Stainton Park, where Bury AFC play their home games. Three miles down the road from Gigg Lane, it is still in the borough of Bury, the closest ground to the spiritual home of Bury that can meet the demand of supporters on a match day. Radcliffe itself feels like an archetypal football town, the walk from the station to the ground taking you past rows and rows of terraced houses that could easily be straight from the backdrop of L.S. Lowry's *Going to the Match*. Pride of place on Ulundi Street is a goal painted on the wall of the end house, facing out towards a car park with only one car in it. To the local kids, it's a nearly full-size football pitch with only one car in the way.

I stopped off at the Victoria Hotel on the way to Stainton Park, happy to benefit from paying £2 a pint away from London. It was past midday, but the only football supporters in there were those of Radcliffe, about to set off to an away game at another well-known fan-owned club: FC United of Manchester. Their only real reaction to Bury AFC moving in to share their ground was contention at the fact that it has prompted the board to raise the price of drinks by 90p in the club bar to try and cash in. It seemed to be a good strategy when I did eventually arrive, a good number of Bury fans congregating ahead of the match. One supporter explained to me with a poignant anecdote just what it meant when Bury FC were expelled from the EFL.

'The football itself is obviously a massive part of why you follow football, but for me a big part of it is also that family feel. It's about seeing the same people and building those bonds. For example, before we got kicked out of the Football League, my season ticket was sat next to an older couple. We got talking and they were really lovely, they were well into their 80s. Her husband passed away during the season and she didn't come for a few weeks. You kind of got a bit worried about them but I obviously didn't know at the time that the husband had passed away. She came back and told me. It was very sad and you feel very sorry for her. But she made sure she came to every game after that, it's kind of like carrying on a tradition. To be honest, I think that kept her going.

'But now we've been kicked out the league, I've not seen that lady since. Now we're at a different stadium, I don't know if she can make it. I still have that little bit in me that thinks I hope she's OK and I'd love to speak to her and see her again, but I probably never will. For me, I think that's what makes me really sad. At the time [Bury were expelled from the EFL], it absolutely destroyed me. It was the toughest time of my life by far.'

The formation of Bury AFC was vital for some people to replace that vital sense of community. It wasn't an easy process, particularly with the COVID-19 pandemic halting all non-league football just months after the club were formed, but the project now appears to be a resounding success. Despite being placed in the North West Counties League First Division North, the tenth tier of English football, there were 1,464 people in attendance for the game against Daisy Hill. The ground felt busy, with an announcement midway through the second half instructing those behind the goal who had spilt over to sit on the pitch-side wall to move for health and safety reasons. The feeling that Bury are a big fish in a small pond was emphasised when Daisy Hill opened the scoring to the sound of almost complete silence, but the home faithful soon fired up their voices once more, and Bury AFC came back to win 2-1.

At the time of writing, they are playing at the next level up – the NWCL Premier Division – and as they attract bigger crowds than their rivals, the funding available for the playing squad should enable them to keep moving up, despite the club having no external funding. Bury AFC are entirely fan-owned, with supporters having the opportunity to become a member for the fee of £5 a month. Each member gets the right to elect members to the board, as well as voting on any decisions considered pivotal to the future of the club, such as a hypothetical decision to try and purchase Gigg Lane, for example. As chairperson Marcel de Matas explains, the model enables people to feel a sense of ownership, engagement and involvement. Though his aim is to climb the football pyramid as far as possible to try and eventually return to the EFL, he recognises the limitations of the model. A couple of tiers higher, you will start to come across rival clubs with strong external financial backing, as well as those with crowds not too dissimilar to what Bury AFC are getting. It certainly won't be a cruise back to the promised land, though the success of AFC Wimbledon acts as a good model to follow.

Though Bury AFC has been set up to try and get as many Bury supporters as possible on board, not everyone has been convinced. The main reason for that is the continued existence of the original Bury FC, albeit in a dormant state with no players or staff and no league to play in. Steve Dale put the club into administration in November 2020, and just a couple of days before I travelled up to Bury, it was reported that a supporters' working group entitled Est. 1885 had tabled a bid for Bury Football Club and Gigg Lane, with the backing of a benefactor and Forever Bury, the supporters' group set up following the crisis in 2002. Throughout my conversations with various supporters on the day of Bury AFC's fixture against Daisy Hill, I learnt that using the term 'phoenix club' was considered contentious by some due to the continued existence of the original Bury Football Club. To try and get a balanced view, I spoke to long-term Bury supporter and writer James Bentley.

Bentley has written two books on Bury, describing his second (*Things Can Only Get Better*) as a '370-page love letter'. It tells the story of Bentley's teenage idols, the Bury side of the mid-1990s who won successive promotions under Stan Ternent to reach the second tier of English football. This piece of work followed *The Forgotten Fifteen: How Bury Triumphed in British Football's Worst Year*, which covered the Bury side who won Division Four in 1984/85 using just 15 players all season. Understandably, it was a hammer blow to Bentley when Bury were expelled from the EFL in August 2019.

'I was like a rudderless boat. I was just going round in circles. The thing that always defined my life was next Saturday. It was the focal point of the week. It's what you look forward to more than anything else and all of a sudden that's taken from you ... and it's incredibly hard to deal with, because you've not done anything wrong.

'It batters your head, it absolutely batters it … I don't think I've ever really given it the thought it deserves, because if I did, I'd just go absolutely crazy.

'I thought what Bury AFC did from the start was fantastic. I thought the way they set up, the way they were all about inclusion, the way they were all about a community, I thought it was brilliant, but I couldn't get behind it, because I thought Bury Football Club were still alive. I think it was all about stages of grief. I was still grieving for the club, whereas they'd moved on to the next stage. They were able to do something productive.

'I went to the first league game down here against Steeton and when I walked through the turnstile I saw familiar faces. For me, that was when it felt like something I could get behind, because I don't believe the spirit of Bury Football Club lies in the bricks and mortar of Gigg Lane or getting behind a team called Bury Football Club. I think it's the people. I've always said that when I went to my first game in 1988, I felt welcomed into a secret society. I think AFC has that same welcoming spirit to it. You know everybody when you walk in, you recognise them. It was that spirit where I felt I was able to get behind the club … I'll be the first to admit I wasn't an evangelist straight from the start. It took me a while to get behind the concept and idea, but here we are and I absolutely love it.'

Every other person I speak to has their own individual story of how they came to get behind Bury AFC. For some it was very natural, for others like James it was a longer process. A couple of supporters I speak to are attending a Bury AFC fixture for the first time. There's no doubting the mental health impact on the supporters of Bury from the club's troubles are huge, but it seems things have been exacerbated further in many cases by the continued uncertainty that lies around the original club. There have been arguments between those who have got behind the 'phoenix club' and those who think such an act has decreased the chances of the original Bury Football Club surviving and playing at Gigg Lane. The split in the fanbase is an unavoidable topic, to the point where several people I speak to raise it before I get the chance to do so myself. That sense of community, so important for supporters of the club, appears to have been fractured.

Throughout 2021, hopes grew that Bury's spiritual home of Gigg Lane could be salvaged and saved from being turned into housing. Est. 1885 and benefactor Peter Alexander entered into an exclusivity deal to buy the ground in October, whilst two days before Christmas a government-run community ownership fund pledged £1 million towards the purchase. However, Alexander spoke of his funding being on the condition that there was an attempt at reconciliation with Bury AFC. It is interesting to note the language used in the *Bury Times* article, which describes Bury FC and Bury AFC as 'rival clubs', whilst Alexander himself describes 'bad blood' between them. The comments section, far from being on board with the wishes of their saviour, sees one fan describe those who watch Bury AFC as 'turncoats', whilst another says he simply cannot forgive those who went to watch AFC. In an earlier report, Ryan Hampson of supporters' group Forever Bury said his only issue with Bury AFC was that it was set up too early, weakening the force behind saving the original Bury Football Club. Steve Dale himself appeared to wade into the debate in September 2020 when a bizarre statement appeared on Bury FC's website, blasting Bury AFC as 'fakes' looking to imitate the original club.

It's been made clear by several representatives of Bury AFC that it is not an attempt at a protest club and they will stand down should Bury FC be saved. A volunteer on the day I attended the Daisy Hill fixture told me they aren't trying to 'steal' the history of Bury FC and are something new, designed to give supporters something to engage in at the weekend. With regards to the timing of the formation of Bury AFC, the argument around supporters collectively prioritising their own and indeed each other's mental health is key. It would be tough for some supporters, each in their own unique grieving process, to sit and do nothing with no prospect or hope of returning to support their local team, see familiar faces, feel proud of something. It was vital for them to do something proactive with concrete results – a game of football to see on a Saturday afternoon. The large attendance figures since lockdown restrictions have eased indicate that these supporters are by no means insignificant in number. Concerns of a 'lost generation' of young Bury fans too seemed to play a role in the setting-up of Bury AFC in December 2019. History shows that the longer you leave it to set up a new club after the loss of a previous incarnation, the lower support will generally tend to be. People find other things to do at the weekend, perhaps new teams to support, and are less likely to regard the new club as a continuation of the old. If nothing else, some of the heart-wrenching notes left at the gates of the vacant Gigg Lane show that having to tell their kids there is no Bury team to watch was the toughest part for some supporters and wasn't a problem they wanted to have for any longer than they needed to.

Even if Peter Alexander's desired reconciliation is achieved and football returns to Gigg Lane with a united front between the two currently existing teams in the town, the damage from the fallout may have already made its mark, as one supporter explained to me after Bury AFC's victory over Daisy Hill:

'Now you've got a fanbase that is split massively, it's probably 70/30 with the 30 per cent that believe Bury FC will come back. Fair play to them, we all want Bury FC back, but I think what has happened is you have a very small minority of fans in that 30 per cent who abuse others, who have been vindictive, malicious – they're horrible. To them, anyone who watches AFC is known as a 'rat', which is unreal, because you've got genuine Bury supporters who are only here to watch AFC to watch football in Bury.

'I'm sure if Bury FC came back they'd go back to it, depending on what the circumstances are. So all you're doing is alienating your fanbase further. Why aren't you concentrating your attacks on the people who put us in this situation in the first place? … You need to be prepared that a lot of people might not want to come back and stand on the terraces with people who have attacked them continuously over the last couple of years.'

Clearly, it's a tough situation, with the fracture lines running deep and no easy solution to fix them. However, the 1,400 or so smiling faces gathered at Stainton Park on a bank holiday in August indicate progress, the renewal of hope and the resurrection of a community that could have been lost forever.

Eventually, almost two years after my visit to Stainton Park, the saga had a happy ending. Supporters group Est.1885 confirmed the acquisition of the club's trading name, history and memorabilia in February 2022. However, the company Bury FC had been representing, The Bury Football Club Company Ltd, remained in administration under Steve Dale's ownership. A proposed merger between Bury AFC and the club that now had the Bury FC name was rejected by a vote of Bury FC Supporters' Society members in October 2022, but a second vote in May 2023 passed by a convincing margin. The town of Bury was unified once more, with one club representing the town and ready to begin the long and winding journey back to the EFL from the ninth tier. It won't be easy, and certainly isn't something anyone would have yearned for during the club's glory days, but regardless of the league Bury FC are playing in the bigger victory for the supporters is simply having a team, and a close-knit community, to get behind at the weekend.

Chapter 13

The Supporters

DURING 2020, a total of 4,912 people took their own lives in England – more than 13 every day. For the fifth time in the last ten years, the suicide rate was higher in the north-east than any other region across England and Wales. Tyne and Wear in particular saw figures that were the highest recorded going back 20 years, with 122 deaths. The sheer size of these figures means it is easy to be almost numb to them, but each death represents an unimaginable tragedy for the family and friends of the individual who has passed away. Looking deeper into the mental health landscape, it is thought that roughly one in four people in the UK will experience a mental health problem at some stage in any given year. Of these, only one in eight adults with a mental health problem is actively receiving treatment for it.

Newcastle United's St James' Park is one of the iconic landmarks of the north-east. When sold out, over 50,000 people can create a cacophony of noise to roar their heroes on to victory. The Geordie supporters are known as some of the most passionate in English football, despite having been starved of success in recent years, with a major trophy not having been won since the 1960s. It was this vision of the stadium packed to the rafters that got Ashley Lowe and her colleagues at the Newcastle United Foundation thinking. Using that one-in-four statistic, they deduced that on a sold-out matchday there are 12,989 fans on average attending the game who are currently experiencing a mental health problem. It's enough to fill the entire East Stand. Using this shocking fact as something of a focal point, the Be a Game Changer campaign was launched in 2019.

At its simplest, the aim of the campaign is to improve mental health across the city of Newcastle. Holistic and wide-ranging, it encompasses a variety of different programmes aimed at different target audiences, ensuring nobody is left wanting. Perhaps the centrepiece is the 12th Man programme, a 12-week, healthy lifestyles course aimed at men aged between 30 and 65. Developed meticulously by a PhD student working for the Foundation, it introduces participants to a range of different sports to help them find something they enjoy, as well as teaching best practice for important components of good mental health, including sleep, diet and coping strategies for anger and stress. Older Newcastle supporters can get involved in walking football to keep fit and increase their social circles, whilst those who just want to open up about their mental health can utilise the weekly talking support group facilitated by the charity Andy's Man Club, which started off at St James' Park and has since moved to Northumbria University to accommodate the large numbers attending. All in all, more than 800 people are currently engaged with the Be a Game Changer campaign, with around 3,500 members currently on its Facebook group.

Speaking to Ashley Lowe, health and wellbeing manager at the Newcastle United Foundation, it is clear that she's very proud of the set-up where she works, with a talented and dedicated team able to bring real change to her home city. Despite having all the essentials in place, however, the main factor behind the success of Be a Game Changer is arguably its link to one of England's biggest football clubs, as Lowe explains.

'The crucial part of the campaign is that we start it off at St James' Park, so people feel part of the club. We're in a very unique position that we can engage men in our programmes incredibly easily. It's not difficult for us to get men to join up to health and wellbeing intervention, which is really rare. We've got that USP, so we should use it. The draw of the stadium and the club can't be underestimated.

'The football fans that we spoke to wouldn't pay attention to a campaign from Mind or from their local GP because they didn't think it was for them, and there was quite a lot of misconceptions over the term 'mental health'. People thought it just meant something really negative, and I quote one guy that said to me, "I've not got mental health." We went on to have a conversation about how he was quite stressed and had sleep issues and things like that. So, we wanted to change those perceptions, which helps to reduce stigma. The slogan we use is "Be a Game Changer – let's talk about mental health". We ummed and ahhed about whether we should use the phrase "mental health" because we knew that can be a big turn-off for the people engaging, but then we realised the stigmas around the terminology would never be removed if we didn't use them. So we wanted to stick with that and it's been really successful. Ultimately, the main aim of the campaign is to encourage football fans to talk openly about mental health, to look out for their friends and to seek help if they need it. We hope that it will reduce stigma and ultimately suicides as well.'

Football clubs, of course, are often at the centre of the community, and the power of the sport to be a mental health force for good is widely recognised within the football world. The majority of funding for the Be a Game Changer campaign comes from the Premier League charity fund, which distributes in the region of £35m a year to its partners, including charities such as the Newcastle United Foundation. The result is each Premier League club having some sort of community provision, with the majority incorporating a focus on mental health as they look to give back to the areas which support them. Aside from the work the Newcastle United Foundation do, Everton in the Community are particularly acclaimed for their mental health provision, with a new dedicated facility currently being built next to the People's Hub, a community centre close to Goodison Park. Burnley too have received much praise for the work of their community arm's Schools' Mental Wellbeing Project, which involves placing a mental health worker across 11 different schools.

North of the border, Motherwell are arguably leading the way in terms of mental health focus. The local area has struggled with high suicide rates, linked to economic decline in the town after the closing of the Ravenscraig Steelworks in 1992. The relationship between economic factors and mental health is well documented – those living in households in the lowest 20 per cent income bracket in Great Britain are more than twice as likely to develop mental health problems as those living in the highest. Mental health problems are also statistically more likely to occur amongst the unemployed and those who are economically inactive than those in work. Fan-owned since 2016, the club, and chief executive Alan Burrows in particular, are perfectly placed to be aware of the issues facing the town. The logo of the local council's Suicide Prevention North Lanarkshire campaign has been displayed on the first team shirt since 2016, with mental health helpline information displayed around the club's Fir Park stadium on matchdays. Fundraising in aid of mental health charities is common, with the beneficiaries often including Chris's House, a crisis centre in nearby Wishaw set up by Anne Rowan after her son took his own life in 2011.

In a BBC documentary on the topic back in 2019, Burrows said that he was aware of at least 24 of the club's supporters taking their own lives in the previous two years. This number would surely have been a lot higher had it not been for the work of the football club and the continuing drive to tackle the suicide rate in the local area. Even more recently, this approach was adapted to suit the environment created by the pandemic, which was a huge shock to the local economy, with many supporters finding themselves out of work and struggling to afford to attend matches once football stadiums reopened. Motherwell's response was to launch the 'Well In' scheme, which asked supporters to donate to provide season tickets to those who were unemployed or from low-income families. The club matched whatever was donated to further subsidise these tickets, providing a community for a number of people who may otherwise have found themselves cut off due to their financial situation. By July 2021, almost £60,000 had been raised.

Despite all the amazing work in the mental health space by the likes of Newcastle United and Motherwell, however, Gavin Green still feels that the strongest sense of community is felt at clubs in the lower leagues. A lifelong Crawley Town fan, Green has been a regular attendee at matches since 1977, when his dad took early retirement from a job at ITN to become the club's press officer. As well as following the team home and away, Green also volunteered to record first team matches for the manager as the idea of video analysis began to enter the world of non-league football. I ask Green how he would explain why he is a football fan to someone who doesn't follow the sport, and without hesitation his response is, 'the camaraderie'. So many of his connections, both socially and professionally, have been made through the football club – something that was to ultimately save his life.

A hiatus hernia issue meant he had to leave his job, enduring a nightmarish search for work that saw him submit over 4,000 applications across a period of five years without any luck. On 29 October 2019, he snapped. At his wits' end after a series of rejections, Green posted of his intention to take his own life on his Twitter account, before going to bed for what he thought would be the last time. But having spent his life supporting his beloved local team, it was time for the club and the people who make it what it is to repay him.

'I came down the next morning and was writing my suicide notes. But what had happened was that there were certain people that I followed on Twitter who were involved in the club, including the former owner, Paul Hayward. He had phoned my dad, because my dad knew him, so he had rushed back to the house and was downstairs. I'm looking for paper for notes and he's there saying, "What's going on? Paul Hayward's contacted me. You're going to kill yourself?" And then the police turned up to see if I was OK.

'There was another guy called Ewan Dunlop, who was the commercial manager of the club. Together with Paul Hayward, they came up with this thing where the club were offering me a job. Instantly, the weight was lifted from my shoulders. It gave me a purpose in life, it gave me a meaning. I was there for just short of two years and got involved in all sorts of stuff, from tickets to marketing, to commercial stuff, hospitality, etcetera. Depression never completely goes away, but I think what the club did was to take it mostly away from me, and if I got into that situation again early on, I now know where I could go for help.'

During my conversation with Green, we come back to the concept of community on several occasions. It was the close-knit sense of brotherhood at the League Two club that caused him to be besotted with the club in the first place – the fact you can go into the bar and chat with the players after the game, drop the chairman a message on Facebook, and in Green's case, even get a discount with the local taxi company because you often chat all things football with the owner over a pint in the Redz Bar. Understandably, given how powerful the ultimate results of this have been for him, Green feels that advising someone to get involved with a local football club is a fantastic way for them to alleviate their struggles. As he notes, with a football club like Crawley, you get a whole variety of people who can provide you with support and help you through whatever it is you might be facing.

It is a sense of community too for big Newcastle United supporter Josh Banyard that has resulted in him falling so in love with football. I meet with the Be a Game Changer campaign ambassador outside St James' Park ahead of a Premier League fixture against Aston Villa in February 2022. The rain comes teeming down, but still Banyard stands outside the Milburn Stand and hands out business cards that contain details of the campaign's text support service in association with Shout 85258. It's a big day, with the match itself sponsored by the Foundation. The players warm up with Be a Game Changer t-shirts on, and banners in the stadium spread the message further. Everyone has mental health, it's good to talk about it, and support is available for you should you need it. Shivering in a waterproof jacket that seems to be about as effective as a chocolate fireguard, you might be forgiven for thinking the father of two would be feeling as though he had drawn the short straw. His smile shines through the whole time we speak, however, and it's clear Banyard is delighted at the opportunity to give back to the club and community he holds so close to his heart.

'We came up with this campaign to use the club and the badge as a beacon of help. A bit like the Batman beam if you put it that way. It's something we use to guide people, support people, and tell them the club supports them as much as they support the club. It's a massive push to make people realise this. It's been really successful so far and the way people have embraced it and the support we get is amazing. Do you know what? We're Newcastle United and it's called United for a reason. So, "United as One" is a mantra we use around the club and the city. And it really is … it's like a big family. Once you know people and you're surrounded by friends and family at the club, it's just a different feeling. You walk in, there's 52,000 people here, and everybody will say hello to you.

'Coming here … it's the cathedral on the hill, isn't it? You walk in and you can see the whole city … you're there for 90 minutes and it just feels like home, and I think that feeling makes you feel so much better about yourself. The whole club is a community project. You come, you forget all your problems, and this has always been my mental health release since I was a teenager. You fall in love, and once you fall in love with a club, that's it.'

I'm not the only person to stop and chat with Banyard before we both head inside for the game. He's something of a local celebrity, in part because he's actually from south-east London, winding up a Newcastle supporter after attending a fixture they played at Selhurst Park and being amazed by how vocal the supporters were. For years, he travelled up to virtually every single game before finally moving to the north-east in 2016. In more recent years, though, Banyard has become better known for his openness in speaking about his own mental health. A big part of the Be a Game Changer campaign is the supporter testimonies featured on the website. Ashley Lowe explains to me it is vital to include these personal stories, as it makes the work of the Foundation relatable for the average fan in the stadium. The thought process she wants this to spark is along the lines of: 'If Johnny the builder that comes to the match has said, "I'm depressed but I sought help and I feel better," then maybe I can seek help and get better as well.'

Josh Banyard knows how it feels to be at rock bottom. Having struggled with his mental health since his teenage years, the larger-than-life character admits he didn't know how to deal with it, acting the 'typical alpha male' to his mates to mask his true feelings. When he moved north to Newcastle in 2016, Banyard was in a particularly dark place and put his faith in the move to restore him to good mental health. It didn't work. Despite being a hugely popular figure with a loving family around him, Banyard took himself to a railway bridge and was ready to jump. By chance, a call from his five-year-old son interrupted him and brought him back to his senses. Knowing he needed to do something, Banyard opened up to his family upon returning home and has been on the road to recovery ever since.

The Newcastle United Foundation were the superfan's next step. Having only just moved to the city, Banyard admits that other than his family, all he knew in the local area was the football club, and so he enrolled on to the 12th Man programme. Having completed the course, making friends for life along the way, a member of staff asked Banyard if he would feel comfortable sharing his mental health story. Despite being unsure at first, the prospect of being able to offer help to others in their own journeys was enough for Banyard to agree. He can't put his finger on exactly why it happened, but acknowledges that of all the personal stories shared with the Foundation, it was his that took off and reached the widest audience. There's no knowing just how many people have been helped, or even saved, by his bravery in opening up, but Banyard has been recognised by the club for his part in tackling high suicide rates in the north-east. The United as One dinner in November 2021 saw Banyard presented with the United as One award – the centrepiece of an illustrious evening.

It hasn't all been plain sailing, though. A season-ticket holder and someone who admits he uses the match at the weekend as a vital mechanism to unwind, Banyard struggled during lockdown as football went on temporary hold. Ashley Lowe and her team at the Newcastle United Foundation knew he wouldn't be the only one. With this in mind, it was crucial that the Foundation responded, as Lowe explains.

'Often, the match at the weekend is the only chance people may have to go and see their friends. They may not socialise other than going to the match, so it can reduce the risk of social isolation. We see football in a way as an act of mindfulness, because you go to the match and you just forget about everything else. You spend 90 minutes concentrating on the pitch in front of you, even if you lose. It can sometimes be the only highlight of someone's life if they're going through a lot of things … so lockdown was a huge concern.'

The Foundation and the football club itself committed to calling each and every season-ticket holder to check in on them, making sure they were coping with the travails of being stuck inside all day. The Foundation's walking footballers were identified as being more at risk of social isolation, and so a WhatsApp group was set up for them to all stay in touch with each other. When the rules allowed for it, walking meet-ups were arranged, with Zoom 'football talks' sessions running throughout, allowing those who usually participated in face-to-face sessions with the Foundation to alleviate any sense of social isolation. In addition to this, the response from Newcastle United Foundation to the COVID-19 pandemic saw 200 people directly provided with mental health support. Crucial in this was the Shout 85258 text helpline, which was launched in September 2021.

Having come through this major challenge with flying colours, Lowe and her team are looking to the future, and things look bright. Everything centres around the new community hub, NUCASTLE, which was officially opened by Newcastle United Foundation trustee and club legend Shola Ameobi in March 2022. Situated just a five-minute walk from St James' Park, NUCASTLE is expected to attract more than 100,000 visitors annually for sessions from career skills to walking football on the rooftop 4G pitch. There is even a specialist science, technology, engineering and mathematics (STEM) room to provide educational facilities of the highest quality to the people of Newcastle. With the infrastructure in place, Lowe is now able to look forward to achieving the strategic goals of the Foundation – which ultimately will all result in as many people as possible receiving the best mental health care possible. She is aware of the danger of trying to do too much too soon, and so every mental health-related programme is developed off the back of rigorous research, ensuring the right messages are delivered with outcomes monitored and evaluated appropriately. One area of growth will be a youth mental wellbeing programme, with funding recently received from the National Lottery to set it up. Ensuring Be a Game Changer becomes more diverse is a must for Lowe. Initially, the campaign was aimed predominantly at middle-aged men but has since broadened its horizons, and focus groups have been held with different populations, including female fans, disabled fans and the club's LGBTQ+ group, United with Pride. Lowe confesses she was not a football fan herself before taking up the role with the Foundation, but now she has seen its worth, she is driven to use the beautiful game to change the lives of as many people as possible.

'I think it's huge. If you think about the reach of football, it's the most popular sport in the country. Everyone, even if you don't like football, probably has to watch it at some point if their partner's got it on. It's got such a huge voice. The players as individuals have a huge voice, but the sport itself can reach millions upon millions of people. So the more the sport can do, I think, the better. It can definitely drive change.'

* * *

I've been a Sutton United season-ticket holder for 12 years now. Between September 2015 and November 2022, I didn't miss a single away game (that fans were allowed into), a streak broken only by heading off to Qatar to watch England's World Cup campaign. We've had an incredibly successful time on the whole with an unexpected promotion to League Two, a Wembley appearance, and a surreal last-16 FA Cup tie against Arsenal whilst still a non-league club ourselves.

Despite all these successes, the reality is that we still win less than half of the time. In other words, I'm more likely to come away from a weekend at least slightly more disappointed than I am satisfied. There are many people who are as dedicated as me but follow a side who are on what seems like an interminable downward slide. I can't imagine what it must have been like to have been a Luton Town fan between 2006 and 2010, for example, as the club slid from the Championship to non-league football via financial crisis and hefty points deductions. Yet still there would have been people who barely missed a game, if at all, during this time. Why do people have such an undying commitment towards their football club? A fair chunk of the answer to that question can be found in and around the concept of mental health.

Paul Brown's excellent book, *Savage Enthusiasm, A History of Football Fans*, shows that this dedicated form of fandom is nothing new. Even prior to the 20th century, football supporters felt a local pride in their clubs. The trend of wearing club colours and demonstrating love of a team more publicly arose after the Second World War, whilst communal singing on the terraces came to prominence around the 1960s. Attendances declined somewhat around the height of hooliganism in the late 1970s and 1980s, but even at the lowest point in 1984, an average of 18,834 people would attend one of the 11 First Division fixtures on any given weekend. Clearly then, there is some consistent worth in the simple act of attending a football match. Perhaps the best-placed man to put his finger on exactly where this value may lie is Mansfield Town and Scotland supporter Alan Pringle.

Pringle's background is as a mental health nurse who has long had an interest in football as a means of mental health promotion. He completed his PhD in 2008, which looked at how supporting a football team could affect mental health. Having lived in Mansfield since 1987, holding a season ticket at Mansfield Town for the majority of these years, it was his local club he honed in on. The research process consisted of two stages – the first asked supporters to keep diaries based around matchdays, with the second comprising interviews with Pringle, based on the themes identified in that first stage. The participants were not specifically people with mental health problems but the general public who had replied to adverts from the club and in the local press. Amongst the 29 fans who completed diaries and 29 fans who were interviewed (only three people featured in both stages), Pringle, who jokingly attributes his strong mental health resilience to his own experiences as a football supporter, was somewhat surprised to find the results were overwhelmingly positive with regards to mental health.

So, what specifically makes being a football supporter good for you? I spent more than two hours in fascinating conversation with Pringle as he took time off from marking his students' assignments at the University of Nottingham, where he works. One of the key ideas we came back to time and time again was catharsis.

'Interestingly, I spoke to solicitors and police officers who said that in this confine the rules are different. They essentially said, "All week, I deal with scumbags and it really gets to me. I don't want to go home and shout at my wife and kids so I come here and take off my uniform or my suit and I put on my shirt. These fans can't reach me, I can't reach them, fucking come on." If people saw me, they'd be going, "good grief".

'We can suffer anything if we think there's a redemption at the end, whether that's "I can suffer a life because I think there's heaven at the end" or "I can suffer this shitty job because at least I'm getting a decent wage for it", or whatever. We have to have something in the future that we can aspire towards to keep us going through the really bleak stuff. I think what football does, is it means that no matter how bad things are, there is a time where you are not faced with your problems. If your job is rubbish, your job isn't with you at the football game. If you're having problems at home, these problems are left at home whilst you're at the football game. You step out of your real life … and OK, at the end of the final whistle you're going to have to go back to that real life again, but you've had that period where you've been able to step out and focus just on what's happening on the pitch.'

As Pringle explains, going to the football at the weekend is probably the most prominent communal form of catharsis since the Renaissance period carnival explored by Russian philosopher Mikhail Bakhtin. Bakhtin suggested that in the Middle Ages, people would effectively live two separate and distinct lives. The dominant one would be their strait-laced, official, day-to-day existence, but during a time of carnival they would take on an entirely different persona, often literally covering their faces and dressing up to encourage this new identity. Carnival broke down social boundaries and allowed behaviours that would not be acceptable in normal life. Centuries on, the mechanisms are broadly similar. You can swear at the referee and opposition supporters on a Saturday with no questions asked, so long as you don't replicate this in the street. The knowledge that you have this designated period to get everything off your chest stops you breaking social boundaries in the period leading up to this sacred afternoon.

The scientific theory on whether or not catharsis is actually beneficial to someone's mental health, however, is mixed. The internalisation of stress and frustrations is often cited as a factor in poor mental health and self-harm in particular, with catharsis offering an opportunity to release this, like letting air out of a balloon to stop it bursting. Nevertheless, research does not tend to support catharsis as a technique in mental health provision, and it hasn't been used as a mainstream form of treatment since the 1920s. Pringle agrees that catharsis isn't a long-term solution or substitute for other mental health treatment, but can be very effective in the short term. There may even be uses for catharsis in dealing with grief, captured by Irish musician David Balfe in his debut solo album, *For Those I Love*. Balfe lost a close friend to suicide and took to watching the team that friend supported, Shelbourne FC from Dumcondra in Dublin, as a way of feeling connected to him. It provided a release he couldn't find from talking to his grief counsellor.

Perhaps the main benefit of catharsis, though, is the anticipation of it rather than the effect itself, linked to the fundamental concept of hope. Pringle makes it very clear that hope, the notion that things will change for the better, is key to all mental health care. Football gives people a reason to hope, because there is always a next game, always a next season, and unbelievable things do happen – remember Greece winning Euro 2004 and Leicester City securing the Premier League title in 2016? No doubt the remarkable recent rise of my own side, Sutton United, has inspired the belief in the supporters of a plethora of non-league clubs that they could do the same. It has certainly instilled a deep sense of optimism across the broader spectrum of life within myself.

Another club to have had a hope-inspiring ascent through the English league system in recent years is AFC Bournemouth. Lifelong supporter Simon Kay has relished the journey and is adamant a film should be made about it, such was the contrast with the Premier League from the start of the 2008/09 League Two season, when the club were at serious risk of going out of business and started the season on -17 points as a result of those financial issues. Despite their scarcely believable success since then, Kay is aware that the importance of the football club goes far beyond just results on the pitch and has made his own significant contribution towards the mental health of supporters in setting up the Talking Cherries group in 2019.

Talking Cherries is a fan-run mental health initiative born out of tragedy after Kay's fellow Bournemouth supporter, Peter Humphrey, took his own life after a long struggle with his mental health. The outpouring of grief from the AFC Bournemouth community was harnessed by Kay to create a legacy for Peter and make a difference to the next person who might be facing their own mental health battle. The COVID-19 pandemic meant the group was set up at a difficult but crucial time, with fortnightly catch-up calls on Zoom providing a vital means for fans to stay in touch throughout lockdown. The Zoom calls still take place, but Talking Cherries, in partnership with Bournemouth University and AFC Bournemouth Community Sports Trust, have other big ideas. With the ultimate goal of creating an informal way for Bournemouth fans to feel comfortable with speaking about their feelings, the group currently have seven trained mental health first aiders who can signpost people to professional services as and when required. Looking forward, Kay's ambition for Talking Cherries is to help build a network of football-loving counsellors for football fans who need mental health support.

When Kay and I sit down to discuss why Talking Cherries has been so successful, he gives an answer that you would be unlikely to see delivered in the mainstream media. Tribalism in football has long been maligned as the cause of division and violence in particular. It has connotations of insularity, even racism, and has been used as a stick to beat football fans, painting them as simple-minded and out of control. This image is almost always created by those who aren't football fans themselves, whether it be politicians looking to play the blame game or journalists looking to sell copy, and Kay agrees with me that the criticism of tribalism is overblown. Racism and violence should, of course, be condemned, but they are more the products of society itself than some football-specific phenomenon. Indeed, the positives of what you might term as tribalism can be harnessed to the benefit of the mental health of supporters, as Kay explains.

'Going to a football match is an incredibly tribal moment and an environment where you feel free from everything else that's going on in your world. For a lot of people, it's an escape, a chance to sing your heart out, have a common objective. You're all there for the single same reason that you want your team to win. Because you have that emotive power of being there and you're all in it together, there are often conversations you have sitting next to somebody or while you share a beer before or during a game, where asking somebody if they're OK takes on a whole different perspective because you're in a very comfortable environment on the whole. There are many people who have said, "Sometimes I open up more at a football match than I would to my mum or dad." You're relaxed, you're focused, you're just all there for the same reason and you end up talking about all manner of things … That's quite powerful.

'I think tribalism is overused as a negative purely because you have connotations of tribes and how they used to fight each other. I think perhaps a better word might be comradeship … you are all comrades together with a common objective. You want your team to win; you don't want your team to lose. You want to see an amazing performance. I think that element is what brings it to the fore and allows a conversation to start.'

When I speak to Alan Pringle on the topic of tribalism, he is wary. His concern is that tribalism refers more to a defensive mindset than one of community first. However, one of the main motivations for his research was the negative media depiction of football fans that Pringle feels has put many people off the sport and the associated mental health benefits over the years. This he refers to as the 'folk devils' concept – the portrayal of a group as separate from the rest of 'normal' society and a threat to its rules and ideals. The hooliganism that engulfed the game amidst the economic hardship of the 1970s allowed the media to sensationalise events and produce an image of football fans that has endured right through to the present day to some extent. Things have changed now, with violence at matches the exception rather than the norm, and Pringle notes that the perception of fans in the media is changing too. His hope is that the positives, rather than the negatives, of the sport's tribal nature will become more prominent and encourage more people to attend games, providing a gateway to the mental health benefits that come with that.

On these positives, Pringle acknowledges that 'tribalism is the cousin of social inclusion'. Social inclusion feeds into the level of social support an individual can call upon, which is a significant factor in anyone's mental health. Using his knowledge of the field, Pringle explains that most hospital trusts now prioritise a 'recovery model' ahead of the previous 'medical model' when it comes to mental health. This approach treats mental health as an experience someone is going through rather than something which can be immediately cured with the prescription of medication, with social support vital to most people's experiences in that regard. In many cases, poor mental health is associated with feelings of resentment and isolation that come from being socially excluded, and so being welcomed into the fanbase of a club is a great way to dispel this. There is a unique power in the sport to bring people together, creating a tight-knit community of many faces that can otherwise be hard to find in the modern day.

'If you join a dance group, you need to be able to dance. If you join a band, you need to be able to play. But for football supporters, you don't need a great set of skills, so it's open to everybody. There's also the sense that it offers a vehicle for different parts of extended families to connect. Mansfield is a mining town. Most teenagers don't want to hear their grandad talk about what it was like down the pit and certainly most grandads wouldn't have a clue about the latest computer games. But if you're just talking about the match or the team, the language of it cuts across. So, 70-year-old fans and 20-year-old fans use the same terms, they use the same clichés. Linguistically, it binds generations and opens doors to connect generations in a way that talking about Sonic the Hedgehog or talking about the pit just won't do.'

Both Kay and Pringle agree that a greater sense of community is often found at football's smaller clubs, where there are fewer fans and lower expectations of success. There are suggestions from those interviewed in Pringle's research paper that you feel a greater component of a team if there are fewer of you to support it. What's more, a club like Mansfield in a former mining area has more defining characteristics to help create a sense of identity for its supporters than a giant like Manchester United. There is no stereotypical Manchester United supporter, as they draw support in the tens of millions from all over the globe. Mansfield Town, by contrast, are unlikely to have too many supporters from outside Nottinghamshire. Related to tribalism, this gives fans a sense of belonging and pride in the local area that can be confidence-boosting, particularly when the side are doing well.

Football can create a sense of community on a more macro scale as well, namely during major international tournaments such as the World Cup and the European Championships. This effect is perhaps best captured in the iconic book that combines statistics and football: *Soccernomics*, by Simon Kuper and Stefan Szymanski. The authors, working alongside Greek statistician Nick Dessypris, studied suicide rates in the month of June across different years for 12 countries and found that in ten of these countries the rate fell during that month when that country was involved in a major tournament. The most clearly visible example is Norway, where there were 55 suicides on average in the seven months of June in which Norway were not involved in a tournament. In June 1994, when Norway finished bottom of their World Cup group in the US, there were just 36 suicides. There was no compensating rise in suicides across the ten countries after their teams had been knocked out either, showing this wasn't a short-term mental health effect linked to the performance of the national team. Rather, this effect seemed to show that common interest and a rise in national unity was powerful in boosting social cohesion and therefore mental health outcomes as a result. Kuper and Szymanski also showed that the average self-reported happiness of a country's population rose just after that country had hosted a major tournament.

So, football does seem to have a positive effect on people's mental health. The next question is, so what? How can this be harnessed to promote positive mental health amongst the UK's football-loving population? Talking Cherries are a fine example of how a shared love for a football club can be utilised to help people with their mental health, but Simon Kay does not see it as a replacement for professional mental health services. He talks of an 80:20 model with the people that come to Talking Cherries – 80 per cent of people can be helped just by the group being there for them, providing that crucial social support and creating an environment in which they feel comfortable in discussing whatever it is they want to talk about. The other 20 per cent of people, however, will need to be referred on, as Talking Cherries can only facilitate a section of their journey, rather than the whole thing. Kay acknowledges the group aren't in a position to take referrals from a GP perspective and is aware they only really reach current supporters of AFC Bournemouth. He is concerned about the long waiting times for counselling and other mental health support with the NHS, which is a major driver behind Talking Cherries' plan of rolling out the network of football-loving counsellors that Kay talks about. He sees a future in which the football family, can come together and fill that 20 per cent gap as best it can.

Alan Pringle agrees that football cannot replace formal mental health care, but he sees a use for the sport in helping certain people, and perhaps not necessarily people who are existing fans of a club.

'I think for some people [attending football matches] is a step forward. Funnily enough, when my study was running, the local newspaper had a cartoon in it with a doctor's reception and the receptionist shouting over, "Another prescription for a ticket to Mansfield Town."

I think we're moving in that direction – if somebody is overweight, they can get a prescription from the doctor that gives them six free sessions at the gym. I think there are certain mental health conditions where being allowed free access for seven or eight games would help people take those first tentative steps. If I'm coming back from a depressive illness and I don't want to talk to people, this means for eight consecutive games I can disappear and blend in. There's a fair chance that if I like it, I'll start going, so it's good for the clubs too because it will introduce people to the clubs who might not otherwise go.

'I think what could happen could be local GP surgeries and local clubs setting this up ... I don't see any major reasons why not. When I did a PhD in mental health in football, starting in 2004, it was quirky. It's now so mainstream.'

Writing this chapter has been a real eye-opener for me, as I've been able to relate to so much of what has been said without ever having explicitly considered it before. When I was struggling with my mental health in my teen years, I always knew I could make it through the week because I had a Sutton game to go to at the end of it. When it was the summer break, well, there would be a whole new season to look forward to in the next few weeks. On each Saturday afternoon from August to May, I would scream myself hoarse at the players, the referee, the opposition fans, feeling drained but satisfied at the end of it. It wasn't all good, don't get me wrong. For a while, I would allow my mood for the week to be dictated by the result at the weekend, something I only really got out of in my late teens after a 2014/15 season in which I had to quickly adapt or face almost permanent misery, given the way we were playing. In many ways, that season was a blessing in disguise, forcing me to adopt more mental-health-friendly practices but never cutting off the support group I had – not to mention we won the league the following season.

When I did feel the time was right to open up about my mental health, who did I speak to first? You guessed it, my fellow supporters at Sutton United whom I'd been going to games home and away with for years. I felt we had a special bond, more than I had with any of my other friends, bound by our love of an otherwise unfancied and unremarkable football club from our home town. As I've grown older and the team have gotten stronger, I've invited mates along who have been captivated by the community feel of the club. Several have since bought season tickets. Having experienced first-hand just how powerful football can be in helping me look after my own mental health, I'm keen to share that with the world.

If you're reading this and you're having a hard time with your mental health, try your local football club out. Whether that's a top-flight side or a semi-professional one attracting crowds of 50 people, there will be something out there for you. If you're reading this book, there's a good chance you've given a lot to football throughout your life, whether that be in terms of time, money, or whatever. Allow yourself to take something back from it. Football can help you with your mental health.

Bibliography

Foreword

1. https://www.youngminds.org.uk/about-us/media-centre/mental-health-statistics/

Chapter 1 – The Player

1. Richardson, John: *Gary Speed. Unspoken: The Family's Untold Story*. (Trinity Mirror Sport Media, 2018)
2. https://en.wikipedia.org/wiki/Gary_Speed
3. Reng, Ronald: *A Life Too Short: The Tragedy of Robert Enke.* (Yellow Jersey, 2012)
4. https://thesefootballtimes.co/2020/04/17/the-troubling-career-of-sebastian-deisler-one-of-germanys-great-natural-talents/
5. Elliot, Richard: *The man who would be worth billions: Vincent Pericard, migration and mental illness*. European Journal for Sport and Society, 2018
6. https://www.portsmouth.co.uk/sport/football/portsmouth-fc/a-career-unfulfilled-ex-juventus-portsmouth-and-stoke-striker-vincent-pericard-on-prison-depression-injury-and-suicidal-thoughts-2614739
7. https://www.swindonadvertiser.co.uk/sport/11132033.former-swindon-town-striker-vincent-pericard-talks-about-his-struggle-with-depression/
8. *A Royal Team Talk – Tackling Mental Health*, 2019: https://www.youtube.com/watch?v=Yn_shQZz5tw
9. Bellamy, Craig: *Craig Bellamy: GoodFella: My Autobiography.* (Trinity Mirror Sport Media, 2013)
10. https://theathletic.co.uk/1813743/2020/05/15/luke-chadwick-manchester-united-stoke-bbc/

11. https://theathletic.co.uk/1884118/2020/06/24/stephen-ireland-onuoha-manchester-city-play-again-anelka-messi/
12. https://theathletic.com/3285672/2022/05/08/special-report-john-yems-crawley-town-and-the-racism-allegations-that-saw-him-lose-his-job/?redirected=1
13. Collymore, Stan: *Stan: Tackling My Demons*. (Willow, 2015)
14. https://theathletic.com/3219587/2022/03/31/theres-help-out-there-whether-you-are-a-footballer-or-not-the-tragic-deaths-of-lee-collins-and-chris-barker/
15. Anon (The Secret Footballer): *I Am the Secret Footballer: Lifting the Lid on the Beautiful Game.* (Guardian Faber Publishing, 2013)
16. Anon (The Secret Footballer): *Tales from the Secret Footballer.* (Guardian Faber Publishing, 2014)
17. Anon (The Secret Footballer): *The Secret Footballer: Access All Areas.* (Guardian Faber Publishing, 2016)
18. https://www.bbc.co.uk/sport/football/59866029
19. https://www.dailystar.co.uk/sport/football/footballers-fell-out-love-propper-25859154
20. https://www.thisisoneighty.com/
21. https://www.dailymail.co.uk/sport/football/article-10793279/2-500-players-ask-help-mental-health-young-stars-reach-PFAs-support.html
22. Michael Bennett: *Understanding the lived experience of mental health within English Professional football.* University of East Anglia, 2020
23. *Rooney*, 2022: https://www.amazon.co.uk/Rooney-Matt-Smith/dp/B09Q1QR3V1/ref=sr_1_1?crid=3RPAYP9V06ACQ&keywords=rooney&qid=1657465449&s=instant-video&sprefix=roone%2Cinstant-video%2C313&sr=1-1
24. https://www.bbc.co.uk/sport/football/60311100
25. https://www.sundaypost.com/sport/sporting-memories-jimmy-greaves-breaks-the-british-transfer-record/
26. https://www.bbc.co.uk/sport/football/60296727
27. https://theathletic.co.uk/1903978/2020/07/07/michael-johnson-where-is-he-now-manchester-city/
28. Matthews, Stanley: *The Way It Was*. (Headline, 2001)
29. https://theathletic.com/2275875/2020/12/29/how-to-look-after-a-premier-league-footballer/
30. https://www.eveningnews24.co.uk/news/brandon-williams-abuse-by-norwich-city-fans-claim-8951906

31. https://www.theguardian.com/football/2018/jun/06/danny-rose-tells-family-not-travel-world-cup-player-racism-fears-abuse-england-football-team
32. https://www.skysports.com/football/news/11095/12118038/ben-chilwell-chelsea-defender-sought-help-with-every-day-issues
33. https://www.bbc.co.uk/sport/football/61559088
34. https://inews.co.uk/sport/football/ashley-cole-mental-health-chelsea-arsenal-england-coach-1263550
35. https://www.bbc.co.uk/sport/football/60843380

Chapter 2 – The Manager

1. https://theathletic.com/2657319/2021/06/28/how-gareth-southgate-works-pre-mortems-his-bad-cop-empowering-players-and-being-nice-but-not-fluffy/
2. Carson, Mike: *The Manager: Inside the Minds of Football's Leaders*. (Bloomsbury Paperbacks, 2014)
3. Allardyce. Sam: *Big Sam: My Autobiography*. Headline, 2015
4. Ferguson, Alex & Hayward, Paul: *Alex Ferguson: My Autobiography: The autobiography of the legendary Manchester United manager*. (Hodder & Stoughton, 2013)
5. Clough, Brian: *Clough The Autobiography*. (Corgi, 1995)
6. https://www.scotsman.com/sport/football/interview-kenny-burns-father-figure-clough-2474547
7. https://www.bbc.co.uk/news/uk-england-lancashire-17012978
8. https://www.bbc.co.uk/sport/football/15780061
9. https://www.bbc.co.uk/sport/football/53339102
10. https://www.wigantoday.net/sport/football/paul-cook-i-feel-physically-sickwe-feel-weve-let-wigan-athletic-supporters-downbut-we-did-everything-we-could-2921537
11. https://www.bbc.co.uk/sport/football/34665949
12. https://www.bbc.co.uk/sport/av/football/42968278
13. https://theathletic.com/2807089/2021/09/05/billy-kee-the-striker-who-swapped-league-one-for-bricklaying-professional-football-took-its-toll/
14. Calvin.,Michael: *Living on the Volcano: The Secrets of Surviving as a Football Manager*. (Century, 2015)
15. https://theathletic.com/2881697/2021/10/20/steve-bruces-newcastle-reign-strained-uncomfortable-mutinous-and-finally-over/

16. https://talksport.com/football/833378/steve-bruce-son-alex-bruce-brutal-online-abuse-newcastle-manager/
17. https://www.telegraph.co.uk/football/2021/10/20/steve-bruce-sacked-newcastle-reveals-hard-called-inept-cabbage/
18. https://www.bbc.co.uk/sport/football/59108785
19. Warnock, Neil: *The Gaffer: The Trials and Tribulations of a Football Manager.* Headline, 2014
20. Redknapp, Harry: *Always Managing: My Autobiography.* (Ebury Press, 2014)
21. Wenger. Arsene: *My Life in Red and White: The Sunday Times Number One Bestselling Autobiography.* (Weidenfeld & Nicolson, 2020)
22. Fry.,Barry: *Big Fry: Barry Fry: The Autobiography.* (Willow, 2001)
23. https://www.bbc.co.uk/sport/football/56406648
24. https://theathletic.com/3120079/2022/02/10/carla-ward-you-have-to-make-a-lot-of-sacrifices-in-football-management-there-are-some-days-where-i-feel-horrendous/
25. http://filipinofootball.blogspot.com/2010/08/simon-mcmenemy-new-philippines-nt-coach.html
26. https://en.wikipedia.org/wiki/Simon_McMenemy
27. Venables, Terry: *Born to Manage: The Autobiography.* (Simon & Schuster UK, 2014)
28. Toshack. John: *Toshack's Way: My Journey Through Football: My Journey in Football.* (deCoubertin Books, 2018)
29. https://en.wikipedia.org/wiki/Bhayangkara_F.C.#First_National_Trophy

Chapter 3 – Injury

1. https://www.telegraph.co.uk/football/2019/08/15/exclusive-football-clubsdeficient-neglectful-treating-mental/
2. https://www.ccfc.co.uk/news/2020/june/news-coventry-city-confirmed-as-league-one-champions-and-promoted-to-the-championship/
3. Misia Gervis, Helen Pickford, Thomas Hau & Meghan Fruth: (2020) *A review of the psychological support mechanisms available for long-term injured footballers in the UK throughout their rehabilitation*, Science and Medicine in Football, 2020, 4(1): 22-29

4. Wilson, J: *Brian Clough: Nobody Ever Says Thank You: The Biography*. (Orion, 2012)
5. https://www.bbc.co.uk/sport/football/54094886
6. https://www.coventrytelegraph.net/sport/football/football-news/teigan-coventry-city-jodi-jones-19458684
7. https://www.mirror.co.uk/sport/football/news/david-busst-opens-up-career-20811232
8. http://www.ccfpa.co.uk/?p=54763
9. https://www.ccfc.co.uk/community/about-sky-blues-in-the-community/
10. https://theathletic.com/1745196/2020/04/15/aoife-mannion-acl-injury-recovery-inside-story/
11. https://www.theguardian.com/football/2020/jan/23/female-footballers-suffering-acl-injuries-more-susceptible-solution
12. https://theathletic.com/3369076/2022/06/17/aoife-mannion-acl-manchester-united/
13. https://www.skysports.com/football/news/11095/12114927/francis-duku-the-attitude-in-football-is-that-if-a-player-gets-injured-its-on-them
14. https://www.theguardian.com/football/2016/feb/17/mandatory-insurance-amateur-footballers-fa-grassroots-ngis
15. https://www.isthmian.co.uk/acl-injury-rules-top-scorer-out-of-season-21814
16. https://twitter.com/charlesy10/status/1182404054053457920

Chapter 4 – Retirement

1. https://theathletic.com/1636737/2020/03/03/marcus-bent-interview/
2. Serena van Ramele, Haruhito Aoki, Gino M.M.J. Kerkhoffs, Vincent Gouttebarge: *Mental health in retired professional football players: 12-month incidence, adverse life events and support*, Psychology of Sport and Exercise, Volume 28, 2017, Pages 85-90
3. Gernon, Alan: *Retired: What Happens to Footballers When the Game's Up*. (Pitch Publishing Ltd, 2016)
4. GS Fernandes, SM Parekh, J Moses, et al: *Depressive symptoms and the general health of retired professional footballers compared with the general population in the UK: a case–control study*. BMJ Open, 2019

5. https://www.getsurrey.co.uk/news/surrey-news/footballer-marcus-bent-charged-cocaine-11507771
6. https://www.bbc.co.uk/sport/football/28950665
7. https://www.dailyrecord.co.uk/sport/football/football-news/angus-beith-opens-up-heartbreaking-14304897
8. https://www.open.ac.uk/about/main/
9. https://www.open.ac. uk/courses/fees-and-funding
10. https://www.bbc.co.uk/sport/football/55177696
11. https://www.firstpost.com/health/coronavirus-outbreak-manchester-united-doctor-sends-players-meditation-videos-mental-health-blogs-to-help-tide-through-lockdown-8296431.html
12. https://www.bbc.co.uk/sport/football/38396290
13. https://www.thescottishsun.co.uk/sport/football/397585/im-giving-up-on-my-scotland-dream-to-become-an-accountant-says-under-21-keeper-james-bransgrove/
14. https://www.lfe.org.uk/the-pfa/
15. https://www.thescottishsun.co.uk/sport/football/4451346/angus-beith-john-robertson-hearts-inverness-benefit-match-indebted/
16. https://www.laps.careers/features/
17. https://www.laps.careers/about/
18. https://www.bbc.co.uk/sport/42871491

Chapter 5 – Addiction

1. Roberts, Benjamin: *Bottled: English Football's Boozy Story.* (Pitch Publishing Ltd, 2019)
2. https://www.irishtimes.com/news/george-best-showing-no-signs-of-recovery-1.1185107
3. Adams, Tony & Ridley. Ian: *Addicted.* (Willow, 1999)
4. Merson, Paul: *How Not to Be a Professional Footballer.* HarperSport, 2012
5. Sansom, Kenny: *To Cap It All.* (John Blake Publishing Ltd, 2008)
6. https://www.youtube.com/watch?v=sfPd96g89-A
7. https://www.dailymail.co.uk/news/article-4675166/Kenny-Sansom-stumbling-street-downing-wine.html
8. McGrath.,Paul: *Back from the Brink: The Autobiography.* (Arrow, 2007)
9. https://www.spbespoke.com/
10. https://theathletic.com/2380337/2021/02/13/inspired-by-you-footballers-gambling/?source=emp_shared_article

11. https://www.sportingchanceclinic.com/gate-gambling
12. https://www.sportingchanceclinic.com/post/open-letter-from-our-ceo-the-relationship-between-sport-and-gambling
13. Gillespie, Keith & McDonnell, Daniel: *How Not to be a Football Millionaire Keith Gillespie My Autobiography.* (Trinity Mirror Sport Media, 2013)
14. Hartson. John: *The Autobiography.* Orion, 2006
15. https://www.ft.com/content/e993ec51-5f8c-33e7-a7af-63927a962709
16. Twaddle, Kevin: *Life On The Line: How to Lose a Million and So Much More.* (Black and White Publishing, 2012)
17. https://theathletic.com/2640942/2021/06/10/hidden-scale-gambling-addiction-among-women-uk/
18. https://www.mirror.co.uk/sport/football/news/huddersfield-charged-fa-over-paddy-18875603
19. https://www.ft.com/content/e46afb14-c36a-11e9-a8e9-296ca66511c9
20. https://www.theguardian.com/society/2017/aug/31/uk-gambling-industry-takes-14bn-year-punters
21. https://www.theguardian.com/society/2018/nov/24/rise-in-gambling-ad-spend-fuels-fears-over-impact-on-children
22. https://www.begambleaware.org/news/gambleaware-publishes-donations-2020-2021
23. A. Karlsson, A. Hakansson:. *Gambling disorder, increased mortality, suicidality, and associated comorbidity: A longitudinal nationwide register study.* J Behav Addict. 2018 Dec 1;7(4):1091-1099
24. https://www.gamblingwithlives.org/key-gambling-stats/
25. https://www.begambleaware.org/media/1628/gambleaware-annual-review-2016-17.pdf
26. https://www.theguardian.com/football/2021/jun/10/norwich-axe-bk8-sponsorship-deal-over-sexualised-marketing
27. https://theathletic.co.uk/2361984/2021/02/03/gambling-premier-league-shirt-sponsors-investigation/
28. https://www.bbc.co.uk/sport/football/53261364
29. https://www.theguardian.com/society/2023/apr/27/uk-to-tighten-rules-on-online-gambling-after-long-awaited-review
30. https://www.fgr.co.uk/news/fgr-back-campaign-to-end-gambling-ads

31. https://www.skysports.com/football/news/11095/12856367/premier-league-clubs-agree-to-withdraw-gambling-sponsorships-on-front-of-shirts

Chapter 6 – Social Media

1. *The Social Dilemma*, 2020: https://www.netflix.com/gb/title/81254224
2. https://talksport.com/football/713395/instagram-top-earning-athletes-cristiano-ronaldo-lionel-messi-neymar-paul-pogba/
3. https://www.echo-news.co.uk/sport/18406856.ex-southend-united-goalkeeper-ted-smith-opts-retire-playing-24/
4. https://www.sportbible.com/football/news-reactions-community-a-league-player-josh-hope-retires-from-football-aged-22-20201106
5. Leonardo S. Fortes, Dalton De Lima-Junior, Lenamar Fiorese, José R. A. Nascimento-Júnior, Arnaldo L. Mortatti & Maria E. C. Ferreira: *The effect of smartphones and playing video games on decision-making in soccer players: A crossover and randomised study*, Journal of Sports Sciences, 2020, 38(5): 552-558
6. https://www.thepfa.com/players/social-media
7. https://theathletic.co.uk/2244047/2020/12/08/neco-williams-liverpool-social-media/
8. https://theathletic.com/2259822/2020/12/14/el-ghazi-twitter-mings/
9. https://www.eurosport.co.uk/football/premier-league/2021-2022/its-a-little-scary-arsenals-martin-odegaard-warns-of-social-media-dangers-after-deleting-twitter-acc_sto8624378/story.shtml
10. https://www.skysports.com/football/news/11095/12219811/bernd-leno-arsenal-goalkeeper-says-he-stopped-reading-social-media-after-robert-enke-abuse
11. https://www.instagram.com/p/CG0v9BQp99Q/?hl=en
12. https://inews.co.uk/sport/football/homophobia-most-common-abuse-footballers-online-new-pfa-report-1135870

13. https://edition.cnn.com/2020/07/29/football/wilfried-zaha-instagram-racist-abuse-premier-league-spt-intl/index.html
14. https://www.skysports.com/watch/video/12442858/someone-will-take-their-own-life-if-we-dont-act
15. *Football, Racism, and Social Media*, 2021: https://www.bbc.co.uk/programmes/m000w9mq
16. Onuora, Emy. *Pitch Black: The Story of Black British Footballers*. (Biteback Publishing, 2015)
17. https://www.skysports.com/football/news/11667/12218327/anthony-martial-man-utd-forward-receives-racist-abuse-online-after-west-brom-draw
18. https://www.skysports.com/football/news/11661/12383739/racism-in-football-most-fans-worried-about-witnessing-players-receive-abuse-according-to-yougov-survey-for-sky-sports-news
19. https://theathletic.co.uk/2361495/2021/02/02/social-media-firms-must-do-more-to-combat-racist-abuse-but-what/
20. https://www.bbc.co.uk/sport/football/56007601
21. https://www.ppf.org.uk/news/pfa-calls-for-social-media-interventions/
22. https://www.thefa.com/news/2021/may/12/update-on-social-media-boycott-20210512
23. https://www.bbc.co.uk/sport/football/58497685
24. https://www.gov.uk/government/news/government-sets-out-action-to-stop-online-racist-abuse-in-football
25. https://www.bbc.co.uk/sport/football/58489648
26. https://www.bbc.co.uk/sport/football/58497685
27. https://www.bbc.co.uk/news/uk-england-birmingham-58738771
28. https://www.bbc.co.uk/news/uk-england-sussex-57326901
29. https://www.smartinsights.com/social-media-marketing/social-media-strategy/new-global-social-media-research/
30. https://www.dailymail.co.uk/sport/football/article-9610905/Jordan-Henderson-opens-joined-BTs-Hope-United-squad-tackle-online-abuse.html
31. Southall, Neville: *Mind Games: The Ups and Downs of Life and Football*. (HarperCollins, 2020)
32. https://www.newsshopper.co.uk/news/19438681.opon-new-social-media-app-designed-ban-faceless-trolls/

33. https://www.liverpoolfc.com/news/features/329977-yapa-app-launch-chris-kirkland
34. Hae Yeon Lee, Jeremy Jamieson, Harry Reis, Christopher Beevers, Robert Josephs, Michael Mullarkey, Joseph O'Brien & David Yeager: *Getting Fewer "Likes" Than Others on Social Media Elicits Emotional Distress Among Victimized Adolescents*. Child development, 2020
35. https://www.bbc.co.uk/news/newsbeat-57721080
36. https://www.theguardian.com/technology/2021/sep/14/facebook-aware-instagram-harmful-effect-teenage-girls-leak-reveals
37. https://www.theguardian.com/society/2017/apr/09/social-networks--children-chat-feel-less-happy-facebook-instagram-whatsapp

Chapter 7 – Academy Football and Those Who Don't Make It

1. https://inews.co.uk/sport/football/david-bernstein-football-association-academy-players-released-max-noble-fulham-931989
2. https://www.theguardian.com/football/2017/oct/06/football-biggest-issue-boys-rejected-academies
3. https://theathletic.com/2482551/2021/04/02/jeremy-wistens-tragedy-through-the-eyes-of-his-best-friends-we-go-to-the-grave-then-it-hits-you-and-you-just-start-crying-again/
4. Calvin, Michael: *No Hunger In Paradise: The Players. The Journey. The Dream.* (Century, 2017)
5. https://www.sussexexpress.co.uk/news/young-footballers-life-crushed-after-spurs-dream-was-dashed-2318246
6. https://theathletic.com/2755972/2021/08/08/the-story-of-per-weihrauch-the-poster-boy-plunged-into-darkness/
7. https://theathletic.co.uk/2409062/2021/02/27/doping-ban-for-15-year-old-pl-academy-player-raises-truly-worrying-questions/
8. https://inews.co.uk/sport/football/max-noble-fulham-fc-academy-bullying-racism-interview-certified-sports-845000?ico=in-line_link
9. David Blakelock, Mark Chen & Tim Prescott: *Psychological Distress in Elite Adolescent Soccer Players Following*

Deselection. Journal of Clinical Sport Psychology. 2016, 10: 59-77

10. https://theathletic.com/2188095/2020/11/24/ben-marlow-matt-carter-released-west-ham/
11. David Blakelock, Mark Chen & Tim Prescott: (2019). *Coping and psychological distress in elite adolescent soccer players following professional academy deselection*. J. Sport Behav. 2019, 42: 3–28
12. https://theathletic.com/news/premier-league-overseas-tv-rights-will-top-domestic-rights-for-first-time-in-next-cycle/PCVIj5mN8OBk/
13. https://www.telegraph.co.uk/football/2016/10/12/liverpool-introduce-youth-wage-cap-to-halt-too-much-too-young-cu/
14. https://www.vice.com/en/article/8gka8v/ex-footballer-drug-dealer-394
15. https://mtagfootball.com/2020/06/05/interview-ellis-myles/
16. https://trainingground.guru/articles/manchester-city-under-5s-elite-squad-described-as-absolute-madness
17. Green, Chris: *Every Boy's Dream: England's Football Future on the Line: Britain's Footballing Future*. (A & C Black Publishers Ltd, 2009)
18. http://news.bbc.co.uk/sport1/hi/football/teams/g/gillingham/9628629.stm
19. https://en.wikipedia.org/wiki/Elite_Player_Performance_Plan
20. Susan Jone: *How well are the Elite Players Performance Plan (EPPP) supporting young players with psychological welfare?* Journal of Psychology & Clinical Psychiatry, 2018
21. https://www.theguardian.com/football/2017/oct/10/howard-wilkinson-review-academy-system
22. https://theathletic.com/2599415/2021/07/21/fa-investigating-racist-abuse-at-cardiff-city-after-child-allegedly-had-bananas-rubbed-into-kit-by-team-mates/
23. https://www.joe.co.uk/sport/premier-league-prospect-youth-football-players-net-269963?utm_source=twitter&utm_medium=FootballJOE&utm_campaign=feed
24. https://inews.co.uk/sport/football/mental-health-football-academy-depression-anxiety-suicide-safeguarding-1036371

25. https://inews.co.uk/sport/football/tottenham-hotspur-academy-mental-health-job-1168175
26. https://www.liverpoolfc.com/news/academy/395334-the-alumni-project-how-the-academy-looks-after-former-players
27. https://www.bbc.co.uk/news/uk-58600845
28. https://theathletic.com/2861397/2021/10/02/agents-survey-minors-being-exploited-window-should-be-scrapped-and-why-many-dont-have-women-clients/
29. https://theathletic.com/2854169/2021/10/06/agents-clubs-or-parents-who-is-to-blame-for-exploiting-young-players/
30. https://www.skysports.com/football/news/11669/10826282/liverpool-banned-from-signing-academy-players-over-rule-breaches
31. Pike, Sonny: *My Story: The Greatest Footballer That Never Was*. (Reach Sport, 2021)
32. https://www.youtube.com/watch?v=vnVH3fjQAAU

Chapter 8 – The Coronavirus Pandemic

1. https://www.bbc.co.uk/sport/51605235
2. https://www.theguardian.com/sport/2021/oct/15/liverpool-v-atletico-placed-fans-in-danger-will-anyone-be-held-to-account
3. https://www.gov.uk/government/statistics/coronavirus-job-retention-scheme-statistics-16-december-2021/coronavirus-job-retention-scheme-statistics-16-december-2021
4. https://www.theguardian.com/society/2020/jun/30/uks-mental-health-has-deteriorated-during-lockdown-says-mind
5. https://www.centreformentalhealth.org.uk/news/least-half-million-more-people-uk-may-experience-mental-ill-health-result-covid-19-says-first-forecast-centre-mental-health
6. https://www.forbes.com/sites/jessicagold/2020/08/06/covid-19-might-lead-to-a-mental-health-pandemic/#25423588706f
7. https://www.bbc.co.uk/sport/football/52356272
8. https://lewesfc.com/football-for-good/equality-fc/
9. http://www.thefa.com/news/2020/jun/05/fa-womens-super-league-and-womens-championship-2019-20-seasons-decided-on-ppg-basis-050620

10. https://www.skysports.com/football/news/11678/12169435/newcastle-duo-jamaal-lascelles-and-allan-saint-maximin-suffering-long-term-effects-from-covid-19
11. https://thefsa.org.uk/news/how-we-brought-fans-back-at-lewes-fc/
12. https://www.gov.uk/government/news/government-announces-300-million-sport-winter-survival-package-to-help-spectator-sports-in-england
13. https://www.womeninfootball.co.uk/news/2020/12/15/lewes-fc-announce-ground-breaking-partnership-deal-with-lyle-and-scott/
14. https://www.theguardian.com/football/2020/sep/22/fa-cuts-to-hit-grassroots-football-and-futsal-hard-leaked-documents-show
15. https://www.theguardian.com/football/2020/jun/15/tranmere-ready-to-challenge-relegation-in-the-courts-says-owner-mark-palios
16. https://www.skysports.com/football/news/36067/12073238/macclesfield-town-wound-up-in-high-court-over-debts-exceeding-500-000
17. https://www.lancashiretelegraph.co.uk/sport/18371482.fa-confirm-decision-declare-non-league-seasons-null-void/
18. https://www.itv.com/news/channel/2020-06-22/jersey-bulls-to-play-in-same-league-next-season-as-promotion-hopes-dashed/
19. https://twitter.com/vauxhallmotorfc/status/1244672657943035904
20. https://www.soundhealthandlastingwealth.com/covid-19/huge-fa-legal-bill-hits-south-shields-who-fronted-appeal-against-expunging-of-non-league-divisions/
21. https://www.thefa.com/news/2020/jul/27/mentally-healthy-football-declaration-270720
22. https://www.pitchero.com/clubs/littlehamptontown/news/201920-season-declared-null-and-void-2525762.html
23. https://scefl.com/fa-ratifies-curtailed-2020-21-season
24. https://www.bbc.co.uk/sport/football/57161687
25. http://hassocksfc.net/2021/05/three-new-clubs-in-southern-combination-premier-division-for-2021-22/

26. https://www.theguardian.com/football/2020/dec/03/premier-league-agrees-bailout-with-efl-to-help-struggling-clubs
27. https://theathletic.com/2101632/2020/09/30/free-agents-efl-bolton-port-vale-northampton-town/
28. https://www.efl.com/news/2020/august/squad-salary-caps-introduced-in-league-one-and-league-two/
29. https://www.goal.com/en-bn/news/drogbas-phoenix-rising-lose-usl-cup-final-to-louisville-city/sytgxc5jrgsj1ea4dip401itj/match/clfrjyrcdbrsy8xg1g30j3f56
30. https://twitter.com/TheMiamiFC/status/1349378495990951942

Chapter 9 – The Referee

1. https://www.theguardian.com/uk/2005/mar/13/football.deniscampbell
2. https://www.theguardian.com/media/2004/jun/30/pressandpublishing.football
3. https://www.thetimes.co.uk/article/polish-fans-target-wrong-howard-webb-with-euro-2008-penalty-hate-mail-fqnn2f2ppfh
4. Poll, Graham: *Seeing Red.* (HarperSport, 2008)
5. Elleray. David: *The Man In The Middle.* Time Warner, 2004
6. https://en.wikipedia.org/wiki/Keith_Hackett
7. https://www.bbc.co.uk/news/magazine-14374296
8. http://news.bbc.co.uk/sport1/hi/football/1386841.stm
9. Halsey, Mark & Ridley, Ian: *Added Time: Surviving Cancer, Death Threats and the Premier League.* (Floodlit Dreams Ltd, 2013)
10. https://www.bbc.co.uk/sport/football/15890525
11. https://www.youtube.com/watch?v=6ThYTNcn1A0
12. https://www.bbc.co.uk/sport/football/55468896
13. https://www.statista.com/statistics/934866/football-participation-uk/
14. https://www.thefa.com/news/2020/feb/05/referee-mental-health-guidance-notes-lucy-briggs-account-060220
15. https://swappingshirts.com/why-the-standard-of-refereeing-is-so-poor-in-the-premier-league/
16. https://www.theguardian.com/football/video/2019/may/14/blood-sweat-and-fears-special-report-on-abuse-towards-grassroots-football-referees-video

17. T. Webb, M. Dicks, R. Thelwell, J. van der Kamp & G. Rix-Lievre: *An analysis of soccer referee experiences in France and the Netherlands: abuse, conflict, and level of support.* Sport Management Review, 2020, 23(1): 52-65.
18. https://www.the-ra.org/about
19. https://www.skysports.com/football/news/11095/12221014/football-association-considers-lifetime-bans-for-referee-assaults-in-bid-to-maintain-high-recruitment-numbers
20. https://www.bbc.co.uk/news/uk-england-lancashire-43209949
21. https://www.bbc.co.uk/sport/football/43823501
22. https://www.the-ra.org/why-join
23. https://www.youtube.com/watch?v=njYwTsBIyo4
24. https://www.bbc.co.uk/news/uk-england-nottinghamshire-48573592
25. https://www.youtube.com/watch?v=AZj_Hb3NVfY
26. https://www.telegraph.co.uk/football/2017/07/25/players-grassroots-levels-will-receive-five-year-bans-assault/
27. https://www.bbc.co.uk/sport/football/54838892
28. https://www.bbc.co.uk/sport/football/54220555
29. https://en.wikipedia.org/wiki/Death_of_Richard_Nieuwenhuizen
30. https://www.thefa.com/news/2021/feb/03/mental-health-champions-grassroots-referees-20210203

Chapter 10 – The LGBTQ+ Community

1. https://www.skysports.com/football/news/11095/12222420/football-in-the-time-of-its-a-sin-aslie-pitter-and-joanie-evans-share-memories-in-lgbt-history-month
2. https://en.wikipedia.org/wiki/Section_28
3. https://tribunemag.co.uk/2021/05/the-long-shadow-of-section-28
4. https://www.planetfootball.com/in-depth/stonewall-fc-lgbt-football-club-non-league-world-cup-gay-games-london/
5. https://web.archive.org/web/20110303201006/http:/www.thisislondon.co.uk/lifestyle/article-23917950-black-gay-bullied-a-footballers-journey-to-honours-at-the-palace.do

6. https://www.claptoncfc.co.uk/event/stonewall-fc-vs-clapton-cfc-3/
7. https://www.bbc.co.uk/sport/av/football/46483780
8. https://www.marketingweek.com/adidas-and-stonewall-fc-partnership/
9. https://en.wikipedia.org/wiki/Justin_Fashanu
10. https://roadsandkingdoms.com/2014/the-life-and-death-of-justin-fashanu/
11. https://theathletic.com/2382097/2021/02/14/we-know-justin-fashanu-died-now-let-us-hear-how-he-lived/
12. Le Saux, Graham: *Left Field: A Footballer Apart*. (HarperSport, 2007)
13. https://www.youtube.com/watch?v=QTtqfavkXu0
14. https://inews.co.uk/sport/football/homophobia-most-common-abuse-footballers-online-new-pfa-report-1135870
15. Rogers, Robbie: *Coming Out to Play*. (The Robson Press, 2014)
16. https://www.youtube.com/watch?v=cL2YIbHgw6A
17. https://www.outsports.com/2019/6/11/18660301/out-gay-lesbian-bi-2019-women-world-cup-soccer
18. Rapinoe,Megan: *One Life*. (Penguin Press, 2020)
19. https://theathletic.com/2693960/2021/07/09/magdalena-eriksson-some-people-say-footballers-shouldnt-talk-about-big-issues-theyre-wrong/
20. https://jahmalhm.co.uk/
21. https://www.kentonline.co.uk/sheerness/sport/sheppey-defender-claims-homophobic-abuse-in-trophy-win-265368/
22. https://www.kentlive.news/news/kent-news/footballer-convicted-hate-crime-against-7250458
23. https://www.skysports.com/football/news/11095/12614531/jake-daniels-blackpool-forward-becomes-uks-first-active-male-professional-footballer-to-come-out-publicly-as-gay
24. https://theathletic.com/2982951/2021/12/03/i-got-really-good-at-lying-im-trying-to-undo-that-its-hard-to-live-a-double-life-josh-cavallo-on-being-an-lgbt-footballer/
25. Telles, Darryl: *We're Queer And We Should Be Here: The perils and pleasures of being a gay football fan*. (Mereo Books, 2017)
26. https://theathletic.com/2991105/2021/12/03/how-to-be-an-ally-for-lgbt-community-in-football/

27. https://www.bbc.co.uk/news/health-57739132
28. https://www.stonewall.org.uk/lgbt-britain-health
29. https://www.arsenal.com/fanzone/gay-gooners
30. Beasley, Neil & Burkett,Seth: *Football's Coming Out: Life as a Gay Fan and Player*. (Floodlit Dreams Ltd, 2016)
31. https://www.thefa.com/-/media/cfa/suffolkfa/files/the-fa-policy-on-trans-people-in-football.ashx
32. https://www.transradiouk.com/truk-united-fc/
33. https://trukunitedfc.com/historic-night-at-dulwich-hamlet
34. http://news.bbc.co.uk/sport1/hi/football/9284186.stm
35. https://www.queerty.com/journalists-pose-gay-couple-try-book-hotel-qatar-ahead-world-cup-20220513
36. https://www.scotsman.com/sport/football/international-football/onelove-armband-what-is-the-onelove-armband-and-why-wont-it-be-worn-during-qatar-2022-3925346
37. https://www.bbc.co.uk/sport/football/59378193

Chapter 11 – The Grassroots Players

1. https://beder.org.uk/
2. https://www.skysports.com/watch/video/sports/football/12291025/beder-fc
3. https://www.thefa.com/about-football-association/what-we-do/strategy#group-STATS-OF-THE-GAME-1t70DkOEGb
4. https://www.kentonline.co.uk/maidstone/sport/report-stones-v-dorking-263123/
5. https://www.surreyfa.com/news/2021/aug/24/mental-health-in-sport
6. https://www.surreyfa.com/news/2021/dec/15/mental-health-first-aid-course
7. https://www.youtube.com/watch?v=A9p53BAcAcE&list=PLeqOl7jjvYeH6hVu45Lr5OA6ouYWFPAgz
8. https://www.skysports.com/watch/video/sports/football/12428756/marvin-sordell-world-record-attempt
9. https://www.thecalmzone.net/more-than-a-game
10. https://theathletic.com/3028983/2021/12/27/pioneers-film-premieres-and-unrivalled-dominance-when-al-fayed-turned-fulham-women-professional/
11. https://www.sheffieldfa.com/news/2018/sep/04/flourish-league-launched

12. https://www.sheffieldmentalhealth.co.uk/
13. https://sheffieldflourish.co.uk/our-enterprises/
14. https://www.mentalhealthunited.co.uk/football-therapy/
15. Mark Llewellyn, Alecia L. Cousins & Philip John Tyson: *'When you have the adrenalin pumping, it kind of flushes out any negative emotions': a qualitative exploration of the benefits of playing football for people with mental health difficulties,* Journal of Mental Health, 2022, 31:2, 172-179
16. B. Friedrich, O.J.Mason: (2017) *"What is the score?" A review of football-based public mental health interventions.* J Public Ment Health, 2017, 16(4):144-158
17. https://merseysportlive.co.uk/2021/04/23/liverpool-football-therapy-merseyside/
18. https://www.mentalhealth.org.uk/explore-mental-health/statistics/men-women-statistics
19. https://www.uefa.com/MultimediaFiles/Download/EuroExperience/Women/General/02/47/04/27/2470427_DOWNLOAD.pdf
20. https://www.youtube.com/watch?v=YGDnk0KHbPw
21. https://en.wikipedia.org/wiki/Grenfell_Tower_fire
22. https://www.campaignlive.co.uk/article/nike-grenfell-athletic-fc-fabric-community-brothers-sisters/1720949
23. https://www.theguardian.com/uk-news/2018/jul/24/most-grenfell-tower-survivors-suffering-from-ptsd-finds-report
24. https://www.independent.co.uk/news/uk/home-news/20-suicide-attempts-grenfell-tower-fire-kensington-council-meeting-a7862096.html
25. https://www.youtube.com/watch?v=LoAwto7HJ38
26. https://www.youtube.com/watch?v=meSnU5sLz84
27. https://www.youtube.com/watch?v=ictMsyd0KP8
28. https://www.standard.co.uk/news/london/ grenfell-youth-group-first-to-get-ps45k-from-standard- s-young-people-s-fund-a4022441.html
29. https://www.bbc.co.uk/sport/av/football/56449058
30. https://football.mitoo.co.uk/LeagueTab.cfm?TblName=Matches&DivisionID=348&LeagueCode= MDXS2021
31. https://www.prweek.com/article/1702419/fabric-community-grenfell-kit-launch-backed-72-stars
32. https://www.voice-online.co.uk/sport/football/2021/08/09/cadbury-support-grenfell-athletic-fc-with-grenfell-athletic-dairy-milk-bars/

Chapter 12 – The Loss of Your Football Club

1. https://www.foreverbury.org/?page_id=2
2. https://www.mancunianmatters.co.uk/sport/10122012-its-just-a-cash-flow-problem-bury-fc-explain-football-league-transfer- embargo-after-pfa-emergency-loan/
3. https://www.bbc.co.uk/sport/football/25105961
4. https://d3d4football.com/stewart-days-financial-mishaps-revealed/
5. https://www.thesun.co.uk/sport/football/9783813/steve-dale-bury-owner-net-worth-companies/
6. https://www.theguardian.com/football/2019/jul/11/bury-takeover-without-full-football-league-approval-transfer-embargo-efl
7. https://www.bbc.co.uk/sport/football/47150388
8. https://www.bbc.co.uk/sport/football/48058322
9. https://www.telegraph.co.uk/football/2019/09/27/human-cost-burys-demise-laid-bare-former-captain-stephen-dawson/
10. https://www.carlisleunited.co.uk/news/2017/november/adamsinterviewpartone27nov17/
11. https://www.bbc.co.uk/sport/football/47792110
12. https://www.thegazette.co.uk/notice/3246387
13. https://www.fourfourtwo.com/features/bury-fc-liquidation-winding-up-high-court-hmrc-neil-danns-inside-story-gigg-lane
14. https://www.bbc.co.uk/sport/football/48151016
15. https://www.theguardian.com/football/2019/dec/05/macclesfield-preparing-boycott-of-league-two-match-with-crewe
16. https://www.bbc.co.uk/sport/football/48091074
17. https://twitter.com/nickyadams10/status/1131244386208092161
18. https://www.bbc.co.uk/sport/football/49133556
19. https://www.bbc.co.uk/sport/football/49410172
20. https://www.bbc.co.uk/sport/football/49451896
21. https://www.theguardian.com/football/2019/aug/28/bury-harry-bunn-players-struggling-stressed-life-at-club-expelled-football-league
22. https://www.newsandstar.co.uk/sport/17991745.interview-former-carlisle-utd-defender-tom-miller-left-football-limbo-burys-demise/

23. https://www.bbc.co.uk/sport/football/54028474
24. https://www.bbc.co.uk/sounds/brand/p08q9nr2
25. https://www.bbc.co.uk/sport/football/49514852
26. https://www.theguardian.com/football/2019/aug/27/bury-takeover-cn-sporting-risk-collapses-hours-before-football-league-deadline
27. https://www.youtube.com/watch?v=aty_d4Alvpg
28. https://www.theguardian.com/football/2019/sep/04/distressed-bury-fans-get-mental-health-support-from-nhs
29. https://www.facebook.com/watch/?v=741717519611572
30. https://www.bbc.co.uk/sport/football/49841324
31. https://en.wikipedia.org/wiki/Bury_A.F.C.
32. https://buryafc.uk/match/25329-bury-afc-v-daisy-hill/
33. https://buryafc.uk/donations/become-a-member-2-2/
34. https://www.est1885.co.uk/latest-news/statement
35. https://www.burytimes.co.uk/news/19674929.new-benefactor-shakers-wants-reconcile-rival-bury-clubs/
36. https://www.joe.co.uk/sport/bury-revisited-272626
37. https://fanbanter.co.uk/bury-chairman-steve-dale-launches-astonishing-attack-at-bury-afc/
38. https://www.thebusinessdesk.com/northwest/news/2093579-bury-fcs-gigg-lane-ground-sold-to-fans-group
39. https://buryafc.uk/2022/10/majority-in-favour-but-amalgamation-blocked-by-bury-fc-supporters-society-minority/
40. https://www.bbc.co.uk/sport/football/65484165

Chapter 13 – The Supporters

1. https://www.samaritans.org/about-samaritans/research-policy/suicide-facts-and-figures/latest-suicide-data/
2. https://www.chroniclelive.co.uk/news/north-east-news/north-east-suicide-capital-england-21510701
3. https://en.wikipedia.org/wiki/St_James'_Park
4. https://nufoundation.org.uk/beagamechanger/
5. https://www.nufoundation.org.uk/what-we-do/be-a-game-changer
6. https://www.premierleague.com/communities/plcf
7. https://nufoundation.org.uk/newcastle-united-foundation-welcome-newcastle-hospitals-as-be-a-game-changer-champions/

8. https://www.evertoninthecommunity.org/projects/health/mentalhealthprovision/
9. https://www.burnleyfccommunity.org/community-welfare-inclusion/health__trashed/schools-mental-wellbeing-project/
10. https://www.mentalhealth.org.uk/explore-mental-health/statistics/poverty-statistics
11. https://www.dailyrecord.co.uk/sport/local-sport/motherwell-hailed-proactive-mental-health-25175762
12. https://www.glasgowworld.com/news/motherwell-fc-supports-launch-of-suicide-prevention-campaign-2139478
13. https://www.glasgowworld.com/sport/football/motherwell-football-club-pitches-in-with-access-for-all-scheme-3313997
14. https://www.bbc.co.uk/news/uk-scotland-50081909
15. https://www.chroniclelive.co.uk/news/north-east-news/international-mens-day-josh-baynard-22207756
16. https://www.nufoundation.org.uk/news/newcastle-united-foundation-officially-open-8m-community-hub-nucastle
17. Brown, Paul: *Savage Enthusiasm: A History of Football Fans.* (Goal Post, 2017)
18. https://www.european-football-statistics.co.uk/attn/nav/attnengleague.htm
19. A. Pringle: *Can watching football be a component of developing a state of mental health for men?* Journal of the Royal Society for the Promotion of Health. 2004, 124(3): 122-128.
20. https://theathletic.com/2434827/2021/03/11/feeling-alive-again-how-football-and-music-helped-david-balfe-after-friends-death/
21. https://www.talkingcherries.org.uk/main/about.php
22. https://www.dorset.live/sport/football/football-news/meet-talking-cherries-football-led-6438358
23. Kuper, Simon & Szymanski, Stefan: *Soccernomics.* (HarperSport, 2012)